EXPLORING PAST LIVES

Also By Mary Lee LaBay

Past Life Regression: A Guide for Practitioners
Hypnotherapy: A Client-Centered Approach
Through the Open Door: Secrets of Self-Hypnosis (with K. Hogan)
Irresistible Attraction: Secrets of Personal Magnetism (with K. Hogan)

EXPLORING PAST LIVES

YOUR SOUL'S QUEST FOR CONSCIOUSNESS

Self-discovery and Awareness through Past Life Regression

MARY LEE LABAY, PH.D.

Order this book online at www.trafford.com
or email orders@trafford.com

Most Trafford titles are also available at major online book retailers.

Print information available on the last page.

ISBN: 978-1-4251-7616-7 (sc)
ISBN: 978-1-4269-2630-3 (e)

Edited by Carol Costello.
Cover and Book Design—Think2a
www.maryleelabay.com

Trafford rev. 02/10/2020

www.trafford.com

North America & international
toll-free: 1 888 232 4444 (USA & Canada)
fax: 812 355 4082

To Scott,

my playmate in many lifetimes

ACKNOWLEDGEMENTS

It has taken twenty years of experience and research to acquire the information, knowledge, and stories in this book. It would be almost impossible to credit everyone's contribution adequately. However, many people have had a direct impact on this book, and it is with deep gratitude and pleasure that I acknowledge them here.

First, I want to recognize all the participants at Boot Camp, where I began these studies in earnest. Those experiences were life-altering. Special thanks go to Robin, Nancy, Ernie, Katie, Joel, Patrick, JD, Catharine, Kellie, Donnalynn, Lorraine, Amy, Jeff, Aimee, and the rest. You know who you are.

I appreciate the additional support, encouragement, and participation from Lori Shen, Jann Finley, and Winnie Mann for being students, friends, and supporters in so many ways, over so many years. To Giavonne Mitchell for her intuitive hits, loyal friendship, quirky Aquarian creativity, and synchronistic words of wisdom. To Lauren Archer and Charles Finkelstein who are spearheading Positive Central, bringing leading thinkers and talent into an intimate setting to share cutting edge experience and setting a sophisticated standard for events.

My special appreciation to Keith Livingston for being a great sounding board, for offering grounded suggestions and technical support, for being ready with the camera and the microphone, and for quick wit at the other end of the phone line. Many thanks also to Katie Evans for her fearless marketing suggestions and high energy, to Mary Lee McRoberts for bringing the elegant Gathering to the Northwest, to Wendi Friesen for awesome support for all in the world of hypnosis as well as for friendship and laughter, to Ayhan Yavuz for spiritual vision and earthly support, and to Don Parks for his steady friendship and his willingness to share his vast network of connections.

Sincere appreciation goes to Patti McCormick of the Ohio Academy of Holistic Health for the superb education she is providing in the alternative healing fields. And special gratitude to KC Miller and Linda Bennett of the Southwest Institute of Healing Arts for the exceptional educational opportunities offered there.

I wish to acknowledge all the venues that have contributed so much to my career – Discover U, Learning Exchange, Open U, Knowledge Shop, Bellevue Community College, Stargazers, Stonehouse, Kirkland Holistic Center, East West Books, and Evergreen Hospital. Thanks, too, to the organizations that have offered support: International Association for Research and Regression Therapy, National Guild of Hypnotists, and the American Board of Hypnotherapy.

Grateful appreciation to Lee and Steve Ater, principals of Think2a, who have offered business development, branding, web development, book and product design, and much more...including deep and lasting friendship sharing many wonderful dinners, fine wine, and travel adventures. Life is good!

The delicate yet effective influence of my editor, Carol Costello, has been highly valued. You are a special light in my life, being both imaginatively ethereal while richly grounded.

I have been blessed to have Sher Emerick of Satori Seven Productions lend support in so many ways, including detailed proofing of this book. I have deep gratitude for your presence in my life both in our work together and in our friendship.

My loving appreciation also goes to my brother, James LaBay, for his lifelong love and friendship, as well as for his support, creativity, and brilliance. You are such a bright light!

Special thanks to Scott Wetstone, my life partner and husband. You are so easy to love and appreciate for all that you do—including giving me the support, environment, space, and time to concentrate on this work. You have allowed me to bring my dreams (including this book) into reality. And oh yes, the travel adventures, laughter, good wine, and home cooked meals when I'm working late. Thank you, my love!

I extend special acknowledgement and gratitude to my clients and fellow students. Over the years and through every regression, you have brought me memories, experiences, and perceptions that have built my understanding and skills. Many of your memories are included in this work, and I am grateful that you agreed to share your stories with the world. Through our work together, we have all had the opportunity to grow while we contribute to the collective knowledge about past life regression.

My love and gratitude encircle my mother, Margery LaBay, and my children, Quincy and London Miller. Your loving energy warms my heart. To Dad: Thank you for your support throughout our time together during this Earth walk. You taught me so much on many levels—and your experiences at the end of your life, and beyond, further contributed to my body of knowledge on this subject.

My loving appreciation [illegible] goes to my brother, James, [illegible] years of long love and friendship, as well as for his support, creativity, [illegible] knowledge [illegible] such a bright light [illegible].

Special thanks to [illegible] Weintraub, [illegible] the p[illegible]er and husband [illegible] love and appreciate [illegible] that [illegible] support, encouragement, space, and time to concentrate on this work. [illegible] to being [illegible] home cooked meals when I was working [illegible] encouragement [illegible] permission you have given me [illegible] stories [illegible] experiences that have [illegible] understanding and skill [illegible] moments [illegible] share your [illegible] with [illegible] possible permission.

My [illegible] [illegible] grace and [illegible] energy [illegible] for your [illegible] this [illegible] work. You [illegible] and [illegible] [illegible].

TABLE OF CONTENTS

INTRODUCTION

It has been my privilege to study, research, and explore past life regression for more than twenty years—and my honor to share what I have learned with others as author, group leader, and individual facilitator. I am grateful to my clients for all that they have taught me, and for allowing me to include their stories in this book. Their names, and some of their circumstances, have been changed to protect their privacy.

My personal journey into past lives has been a source of enormous spiritual riches. It has brought healing, learning, wholeness, and an understanding of my strengths and purpose. It has enhanced my relationships, taught me to trust myself and my direction, and deepened my capacity to embrace and enjoy all of life.

I consider the exploration and discovery of our past lives a hero's journey. This book's purpose is to share with you all that I have learned about reincarnation and past life regression so that you can reap the richest rewards from this quest. The understanding and illumination we receive by embarking on this journey can be practical and matter of fact—or suffused with the mysteries at work behind our physical existence and set to the music of the spheres...

Imagine stillness everywhere, bathed in neither light nor darkness. A vast yawning, yet nothing. No awareness, no thing of which to be aware. No consciousness. No existence.

Out of nowhere, and of nothing, a movement. A ripple in the still pool. A nudge—infinitesimal, and at the same time infinite. A gentle rhythm develops. Force and resistance. Friction. Reaction. A vortex. Swirling masses. A storm.

Out of the storm bursts forth the conscious awareness of existence. Reflection and wonder. Thirst for knowledge. Hunger for experience.

And with the dawning of self-awareness, the birth of separation. Awareness of self conjures the recognition of other. Curiosity. The lust for survival. Competition.

Knowledge, and the wisdom of its use, provides the fundamental means of survival. Self-awareness becomes the instrument for a soul's furthering of its existence.

In this primal quest for survival, the spirit seeks a hero. It requires a courageous servant who will plunge to the depths single-mindedly in search of its personal brass ring—life-extending experience and knowledge. Our soul is that champion of the spirit. As our soul descends into the dense medium of a physical incarnation, it embarks on a hero's adventure. It crosses the threshold, leaving the gates of the eternal community. It accepts the challenge of seeking out truth, morality, virtue, growth, and ultimate survival through the experiences of physical incarnation.

At death, the soul returns to the spirit, bearing gifts of memories, character, and change. Those pieces of the character find places in the spirit's architecture. The alterations in its structure demonstrate movement—the expansion and contraction of the spirit, as if it is taking a breath. Memories are all that remain of the sensual physical experiences, relationships, and adventures that give color to the spirit's perceptions and imagination.

Awaken to the reality that you are the hero of your own tale. You are the greatest hope that your spirit has of ultimate survival. Although there are infinite aspects of you existing throughout history, marked by your numerous incarnations, the present aspect of you is the culmination of all the others. You are the result of all your experiences. You, in this moment, represent all the expansive growth, minus all the contractive movement, that you have ever experienced. You are the full, and singular, representative of your spirit.

Be the hero. Plunge deeply and seize your brass ring!

Part One

Reincarnation: How It Works, and Why We Do it

Part One is an overview of reincarnation and past lives. We discuss how it works, the benefits and the purpose, as well as how to make good choices and get the maximum rewards.

1

PAST LIFE REGRESSION: THE HERO'S JOURNEY

"Not everyone has a destiny...only the hero who has plunged to touch it, and has come up again with a ring."
—Joseph Campbell

You are about to embark on a hero's journey. This adventure takes faith, imagination, and courage—and rewards you with gifts that illumine your path, enrich your soul, and make each day a unique treasure.

As you explore your past lives, you will discover the many facets of who you are and expand your perception of the world. You will understand why you may have forgotten these parts of you, and learn how to begin remembering them. You will start to reap the benefits of expanding self-awareness, and master tools to help you achieve that goal. For many of you, this adventure will become a way of life.

My Journey

Past life regression is a topic close to my heart. I have studied it, researched it, explored my own past lives, and supported others in exploring theirs for more than twenty years. For me, it has always been a given that we lived before. I knew it as a child; I assumed it as an adult. There was never a doubt in my mind.

When I began to experience my own past lives, I was excited to share the fascinating news with anyone who would listen. I quickly learned that not everyone had made up their minds about past lives and reincarnation. Many people were enthusiastic. Some were intrigued, but had questions. Others were downright skeptical. From the skeptics, I received a wonderful gift. Their questions forced me to go even deeper with my own thinking and experience, and to discover new information and levels of awareness that brought clarity and expanded possibilities. If you have not yet made up your mind about reincarnation and past lives, I invite you to keep reading.

Over the years, working with hundreds of people, I have seen that investigating our past lives is like exploring the facets of a diamond. Each aspect contains its own perfection and its own flaws. Each shines brilliantly as its own unique expression of the light that passes through it. And each facet is part of the whole. So it is with us.

What Is Past Life Regression?

Past life regression is the deliberate, conscious retrieval of memories and experiences that occurred in other lifetimes. We look beyond the veil of separation into the subconscious mind to gather knowledge and understanding of the deeper aspects of our personality and character. This wisdom often brings healing, change, and expansion. The larger objective is the pursuit of completion and wholeness.

Imagine that you had amnesia, and could not remember anything that happened before you were twenty-one years old. How much would you know about yourself? Chances are, you would have gaping holes in your understanding of:

- Your relationships with other people
- Your personality traits and patterns of behavior
- Health issues
- The origins and meaning of your occupation
- The source of your knowledge and wisdom

Without any knowledge of our past lives, we have these same kinds of holes in our memory and understanding. Exploring our past lives fills in the blanks. It gives us access to all the experience, wisdom and growth that we have accumulated through the millennia, and lets us bring that information and illumination to bear on our lives today. It also gives us a broader understanding of the flow of all life—and the true purpose of our existence.

Understanding our past lives also dramatically increases our power to change and improve our current lives. Each of us is already successful. We are exactly where we need to be. At any given moment, we are demonstrating the sum total of all the choices we have ever made. Each choice has led us to precisely where we are today, and we can embrace that reality.

But if we want to *change* the conditions of our lives, the questions we must ask are, "What must I do differently? What different kinds of choices must I make now?" Accessing our past lives can give us the wisdom and strength to make choices that help us achieve our goals, enjoy greater spiritual growth, and experience "heaven on Earth" and beyond.

How Does Reincarnation Work?

Let's begin by looking at the difference between "spirit" and "soul." These words are used in many different ways. Here is how we define them in this work.

Spirit and Soul

I believe that each of us has one spirit—and that this spirit exists eternally. I have come to this belief through a combination of Eastern and Western philosophies, as well as through ideas from new physics and religion, and my own experience and clients' discoveries during past life regressions.

The soul is an aspect, or subset, of our spirit—that portion of the spirit that enters a physical body. A spirit may have many parts, or aspects, that can achieve physical incarnation. They do so in order to gather the information, experience, knowledge, and wisdom that are the spirit's nourishment. Our focus is the soul that is in our body at this particular time.

The best metaphor for the relationship between spirit and soul is a hand with five fingers. The fingers stretch out to sense the physical world, and then relay messages back to the hand and, from there, to the central nervous system. Each finger may operate independently and have the illusion that it is separate from the others. However, the brain understands the connection between them, and benefits from the input that each provides.

Our spirit contains all the information and experiences garnered by all of its aspects over its entire existence.

The Spirit's One Life

Our spirit's life is like a book. Its epic story is divided into chapters, or episodes. From the human perspective, these divisions are called lifetimes. In each lifetime, the soul enters a physical existence in order to bring back experiences and wisdom to the spirit. These chapters begin when we cross the threshold from being aware of the spiritual realm (in the astral plane), to being aware of the physical realm (in a body). They end when we cross back again into the spiritual realm. There, we begin preparing for the next crossing.

We can illustrate the movement back and forth between the astral plane and the physical plane like this:

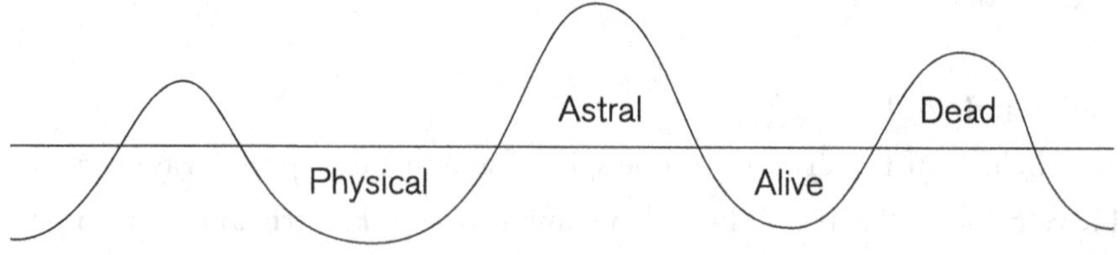

The wavy line indicates our travel between what we call "being alive" and "being dead" as it oscillates between the physical and astral realms. As you can see from the uneven progress of the wavy line, the length of time we spend in the astral plane, or in the physical plane, can vary. We may die young, or live to a ripe old age in the physical plane. We may spend a short time, or a long time, in the astral before returning to a physical body. These periods of time are not preordained.

And it is only from our human perspective that we are "dead" or "alive." From the perspective of the astral, people actually "die" when they are born into a physical body. They "die" to the astral. Their conscious awareness is separated from the astral and from those who reside there. They are missed there, just as we miss people whom we know here when they die.

We will discuss reincarnation more fully in the coming chapters. Right now, let's look briefly at some of the benefits we can expect from exploring past lives.

Gift Of The Journey: The Benefits Of Past Life Regression

Why would we undertake this journey? Past life regression gives us gifts that further the spirit's quest for consciousness, existence, self-discovery, and enlightenment. It also yields rewards that make life richer and happier in the short term, in this particular incarnation.

Chapter 2 explores in detail what we stand to gain through exploring our past lives. Here is a short list:

- *Richer, more fulfilling relationships.* We gain information and wisdom about our relationships with family, friends, and mates. Understanding the lives we may have shared with these people can give us insight into our purpose together, what lessons we can learn with them, and how we may support them. It can even explain "recognizing" people we have not met before, and having an immediate positive or negative response to them.
- *Wisdom about choices we have made.* Past life regression yields a wealth

of information about birth and death, and why we choose the gender, body, and situations we do.

- *Personal growth.* The ability to view our patterns of behavior over lifetimes, not just decades, gives us greater clarity about our character and a more honest, objective assessment of ourselves. It helps us see what we want to change, and what we want to nurture in ourselves.
- *Healing.* We gain understanding of both physical and emotional diseases, and how to heal them. Phobias, unexplained pains and syndromes, chronic pain and illness, birthmarks, and other health-related phenomenon frequently have their roots in other lifetimes.
- *Help with challenges, blocks, and fears.* Seeing the roots of challenges in our past lives can help us work through them in this life.
- *Knowing our Spirit Purpose.* This is the overriding intention for which our spirit was created by the nature of its energy and direction.
- *Seeing and embracing our Life Purpose.* Our Life Purpose is the primary mission our soul wants to accomplish in any given lifetime. Memories of past lives may reveal why we have a natural penchant for music or the arts, or for science, or healing. They may yield clues to our purpose in this life, as well as guidance for occupations, hobbies, and sports.
- *Access to the powerful subconscious mind.* We learn to work with the subconscious, where the wisdom of many lifetimes and the power to realize intentions resides.
- *Understanding the bigger picture.* We not only gain greater understanding of our own spirit's journey, but also expand how we see the universe. We acquire a broader and often awe-inspiring perspective, and a greater sense of our position in the larger scheme of life.
- *The power to change.* As we gain greater access to our past lives, we discover the power to alter not just our present, but our future—and even our past!
- *Seeing the divine in all life.* We begin to realize that all of us are part of one another, and connected in a significant way.

Is Reincarnation Real?

How do we know whether or not reincarnation is real? In our society, we have been taught that everything "real" must be measured and proved by the scientific method. Sometimes the facts and experience of our past lives cannot be measured or proved in this way, and so we are told not to trust them. Many people start out as skeptics, even those who later come to consider past life regression a fundamental part of their spiritual life and emotional wellbeing.

Let's take a closer look at this notion of "reality."

Beyond the Scientific Method

The scientific method can only measure and detect phenomena that are designed to be measured and detected. That is its limitation.

In the West, what cannot be detected or measured numerically is often considered unreal or irrational. This excludes many important aspects of our own world, not to mention realities that exist in other planes. Do we really want to exclude "independence," for example, simply because no numbers can describe or measure it?

Perhaps one day we will find a way to measure the mystical, so that these spiritual experiences will be deemed "real." Until that day, we can focus on allowing ourselves to experience the extraordinary, make sense of the magical, and integrate the infinite possibilities into our reality.

To do this requires imagination and belief.

Imagination

Imagination is the capacity to visualize or intuitively "know" something that is not physically present. It is one of the most powerful tools for discovering your past lives. Some people "see" people, events, or circumstances. Others "hear" them in their imagination. Still others have a kinesthetic sense of what is happening. We will explore all these modes of experience and imagination in the next chapter.

People sometimes say that they don't have any imagination. While it is true that some individuals' imagination may be more highly developed than others', we all have imagination. Without it, we would not be able to communicate at all. In fact, we are using our imagination all the time. You are using yours as you read this book. It is such second nature for us that we often don't even realize we are using it.

For example, suppose your dinner companion says, "Pass the ketchup, please." You reach out, grab the ketchup, and hand it to the person. That may not sound very imaginative—but in fact, your imagination was working during the entire process. Your mind heard the request, and immediately called up from its memory banks a mental picture of "ketchup." You looked around the table and found an image that duplicated your mental picture, or that matched closely enough to be identifiable. Then your mind imagined the act of picking up the bottle and handing it over to your friend. Finally, your body executed the action.

Of course, the mind and body go through even more minute steps in the process of fulfilling your friend's request, but they are beyond the scope of this book. The point is that we are using our imaginations almost all the time, and certainly on a daily basis.

Belief

To believe in something does not mean that you suspend reason, or that you lose touch with reality. Nor does it mean subscribing to ideas that are at odds with what you know.

Rather, belief is a final leap of faith beyond reasoning, facts, and substantiated evidence. When all the information you have collected points to a probability, even when it cannot be proved, belief is the next reasonable step.

Belief is at the core of most scientific discovery and invention. There is, and has always been, more to the universe than is known or perceived at any given time. There was a time when the idea that Earth was round was beyond the beliefs of most people. At that time, we had no proof that the world was round—but a few daring souls were willing to take the leap of faith.

Not long ago, the common belief was that man would never fly, let alone reach the moon. Today, we send probes into deep space, far out into our solar system, as a matter of course. Only a few decades ago, we believed that the atom was the smallest physical entity. We now have instruments that reveal electrons, quarks, and particles—and those who embrace "string theory" postulate that there are even smaller phenomena.

It takes curiosity, imagination, and belief to advance our understanding of reality.

This is not to suggest that we should believe everything we hear. That would simply be gullible and foolish. But it makes sense to stay open to possibilities that have not yet been proved or measured—possibilities that are outside our current experience.

This is especially true when such exploration is reasonable and harmless, as it is with reincarnation. Our job is to study all the information available and listen to the experiences of others—and then be open to the possibility of having a similar experience.

Even when we don't actually *believe* in something, we may still have an *experience* of it—but that experience may be altered by our beliefs and mental filters. In other words, Experience A happens to us, but we interpret it as Experience B because Experience B is all that our beliefs and prejudices will allow into our "reality." For instance, a person who does not believe in UFO's may see a flash of light and lose two hours from his memory. He may interpret the flash of light and memory loss as the symptoms of having suffered a stroke, or eaten something that didn't agree with him. He may completely discount the possibility of a UFO being involved. An experience has occurred, but the interpretation is dictated by his filters.

Suspending Disbelief

Suspending disbelief is just that. We refrain from rejecting an idea. We don't rule it out. We may not entirely embrace it, but we stay open to the possibility.

The capacity to suspend disbelief until we can gather more information and experience is an invaluable tool for expanding our ideas about reality. It keeps us open to new input and new possibilities, and is often a crucial first step before we can actually believe in something.

To suspend disbelief during a past life regression, simply give yourself permission to experience whatever thoughts, visions, experiences, or ideas come your way, without judgment or criticism. You may receive some information that is useful, and other information that is not credible. But until you have all that data available to you, you won't have anything to work with. You won't be in a position to choose what to keep, and what to discard. Once you have let all the information in, you will have plenty of time to go back over it and analyze how much of it is valuable.

Belief is important to the experience of past lives, because what we believe filters our experience of reality. If we don't allow ourselves to believe in past lives, or at least to suspend our disbelief in them, then we can't get the value that is waiting for us.

If we expand our range of beliefs, we get access to much more information—and that, in turn, helps us expand our beliefs even further.

Reincarnation—Yes or No?

There are only two sides to the question of whether or not reincarnation occurs. Either it does, or it doesn't. If you have not yet decided that you have lived before, you may want to consider the following proposition.

If reincarnation does not occur, then the question doesn't even matter. When we die, we simply cease to exist. There is nothing left of us. We will have no regrets, no longing, no exultation, no joy, and no karma. There will be nothing at all—and we will not even be there to observe the nothingness. There will be no awareness or consciousness of anything.

If there is no afterlife, there is no need to worry about lessons, purpose, or even fears. Why not just go wild, and do anything we want? Why limit ourselves in any way, if this is our one and only chance to experience anything at all? On the other hand, it doesn't even matter if we do experience anything, because there will be no memory of it after death. Why bother to do anything? In the end, it will make no difference at all.

However, if we believe that there is nothing beyond this one physical life, it makes sense to ask this question: How did the combination of sperm and egg create consciousness, if there was no consciousness before conception?

Science has determined how the physical body is formed through cell division and specialization. It has not come up with definitive answers concerning the creation of that spark of life, that force that initiates conscious awareness, and it has not pinpointed the spatial location of that consciousness in the mind.

A possible answer, one that favors reincarnation, is that consciousness continues beyond the existence of the particular body which we inhabit right now—and that this consciousness can choose if and when to enter another body.

Throughout most of human history, people have believed in some sort of afterlife. If a person believes in ghosts, poltergeist, angels, spirit guides, or the visiting energy of their deceased loved ones, they believe in life beyond the grave. Believing in a savior who will come back to Earth also indicates belief in an afterlife—as do beliefs in Bardos, nirvana, or heaven and hell as places where souls reside after death.

Making a Decision: Parts Therapy

Whenever we are choosing between two contradictory ideas—whether or not to put our faith in reincarnation, for instance—there is a simple and effective tool that can help us make the decision. It is commonly called Parts Therapy.

To discover your own stance on the issue of reincarnation, do this Parts Therapy exercise:

When we are divided on an issue, we often say, "A part of me sees the issue one way, and another part of me sees it differently." In this case, you might say that a part of you believes that reincarnation exists, and another part of you believes that it doesn't.

If this is the case, imagine separating those two parts of you so that the part that believes in reincarnation rests completely on one of your hands, and the part that does not believe in reincarnation rests completely on the other hand.

When you have done that, so that the two parts in no way intersect, go into the perspective of one of the sides. Allow it to fully express its opinions and the reasons that substantiate them. When that side is done, go into the perspective of the other side and allow it to express its opinions and substantiating reasons. Without allowing either side to interrupt the other, continue to go from one hand to the other, granting each part permission to express its views fully.

After moving from one perspective to the other several times, you will likely find that one hand begins to concede to the other. Continue until both hands are in complete agreement on the issue. When this is achieved, imagine integrating the energies of both hands, reuniting them now at this new level of agreement.

You can use Parts Therapy to address any conflict or decision that arises in your life. This technique is discussed more thoroughly in my book *Hypnotherapy: A Client Centered Approach* (Pelican Publishing, 2003).

The Enlivening Choice

If there is life beyond this body, then some part of our consciousness has figured out not only how to leave once that body's term is over, but also how to attach itself to a new physical body and animate it throughout a lifetime. If this is the case, then the idea of multiple lifetimes is not so confounding. If we can do it once, it is easy to imagine that we can do it again—and again.

Belief in reincarnation carries with it the acceptance of a spirit that encompasses more than the physical body. This implies there is a component of our consciousness that is more aware, and more capable, than we presently recognize. It also suggests that there is a location outside our tangible realm where our spirit can reside—and that in all likelihood, other beings reside there as well.

Finally, belief in reincarnation begs the question: *Why?* We may not have a complete answer to this question, but we do know that we gain more experience of existence, and greater depth of consciousness, through our various lifetimes. So minimally, we are here to experience as much as possible, to be aware of what we are experiencing and learning, and to grow and develop a wider and wider perspective. Certainly, that is a more enlivening option than simply being extinguished.

Now What?

If reincarnation does occur, then it seems wise to know as much as possible about it—especially if its purpose is to learn lessons that enrich our existence and consciousness. What can we learn? How can we grow? What opportunity can we find to deepen our spirit's understanding, experience, and wisdom?

If reincarnation does *not* occur and we simply cease to exist after death, then it won't matter if we have invested time and energy in learning these things—but it will do no harm. But if reincarnation *does* exist and we have squandered the opportunity, then we will have missed out.

Obviously, the smart money is on believing in reincarnation. If we don't let ourselves believe in reincarnation, then we risk a loss. If we do allow ourselves to believe in and explore reincarnation, we can't lose anything and we may gain enormous riches.

THE HERO'S JOURNEY

Noted mythologist and author Joseph Campbell says that, at some point in his journey, the classic hero must trust his instincts and make a leap of faith into a new reality. Luke Skywalker did this in *Star Wars* when he closed up his radar and electronics, and trusted "The Force" to guide his release of weapons into Darth Vader's Death Star. When the hero is willing to make this leap, he wins the prize, discovers fire, slays the dragon, saves the maiden, or gains whatever it is that fulfills his quest.

Discovering your past lives is a hero's journey. It is more than simply finding out who you were in another lifetime; it is a quest for enriched existence and deeper consciousness that honors and feeds your spirit. It expands your reality and your capacity to move through the universe. You let go of old baggage that has been holding you back, work through karma and patterns, expand your awareness, and begin to make choices that enhance life.

Best of all, you gain a larger perspective that makes every day of this life something to treasure. Imagine being in the future, and regressing back to this life. What do you see? What have you accomplished and contributed? How have you grown and expanded while here in the physical plane? Will you be proud of your adventures, or be filled with remorse or regret? Are you, in fact, paying attention to your life?

When you treat life as a hero's journey, the spirit's quest for self-discovery and enlightenment become a driving force underlying all of your behaviors, actions, reactions, emotions, and pursuits. It is the most delightful and fascinating journey you will ever take.

Be the hero of your own saga. Meet the challenge. Plunge to the depths of this physical experience to bring home your personal holy grail, your own true self.

How To Use This Book

This book is a guide for you to begin experiencing your own past lives. Part 1 covers how reincarnation works, the value we receive from it, life's true purpose, and how reincarnation supports that purpose. You will discover how to use past life regressions to make better choices in this life, see how the idea of reincarnation is increasingly validated by new discoveries in physics, and learn about Soul Groups and step-ins.

Part 2 gives you practical, step-by-step guidance for experiencing your own regressions. You will receive simple, powerful tools for discovering your past lives, learn what to expect, be shown how to conduct your regression, and explore how to validate your memories.

Part 3 is about reaping the rewards of past life regression, and is composed of case studies that explore such subjects as understanding and enhancing relationships, healing and vitality, finding your life's purpose and path, meeting challenges, and deepening your spiritual journey.

After each chapter, we offer a case study that illustrates some of the principles just discussed, and illuminates various facets and benefits of past life regression.

I honor your hero's journey through this fertile territory, and look forward to sharing it with you.

Case Study

Debby

Debby wanted to experience a past life in order to gain greater clarity about herself and her life path. I asked her subconscious mind to lead her to one or more lifetimes that would reveal information on these subjects.

Beginning with a relaxing visualization, she imagines moving down the hall to a door. When she goes through the door, she finds herself outside.

D: It is nighttime. There are stars, and I notice flat land. It's chilly, but it feels good. There is a dog near me, frolicking. There is someone behind me who I can't really see.

ML: Even though you can't see them, you know who they are and what they look like, just as you would know who I am and what I look like though your eyes are closed.

D: Oh. He's an older man, a Native American shaman. He's a medicine man. Maybe we are related. He is older than I am. He has feathers and wears leather. He's distinguished.

ML: What do you know about yourself?

D: I am eleven years old. I'm female. I am playing with the dog. The shaman laughs. We stroll and look at the stars. He is telling me tales about the past, the future, and the stars. I'm not really paying attention. We sit down, cross-legged, and he tells me tales of our ancestors.

ML: What happens next?

D: This reminds me of the movie *Dances with Wolves,* in the village scene. I'm walking with a bowl of grains. I'm talking to people in the village. I am married to a warrior. He is a wonderful man. He's brave, funny, and sensitive. We work from morning to evening gathering nuts, grains, and wood. We wash clothes, prepare food. It's a way of life. It takes all day to do what is necessary to exist.

ML: What else would she want to do?

D: Her dreams are to travel. She wants to explore other places.

ML: Move ahead in time. What do you notice next?

D: We were all killed in a massacre. Some of us were tortured. It was maybe the cavalry. It was a terrible commotion. It was all so dusty and brutal.

ML: As you look back over that lifetime, what do you observe?

D: I see how that life was. The family meant everything. She loved her people and her family. It was awful to see my loved ones harmed.

ML: If she could give you her words of wisdom, what would they be?

D: "Live each day to its fullest."

ML: Asking the subconscious mind to reveal yet another lifetime, where do you find yourself this time?

D: I'm in a hut, somewhere in the South Pacific. I'm a female in my twenties. I'm running. It's windy and cold. We have to prepare for a storm. The old people are scared, the children are crying. I'm trying to make the people feel better. I'm a teacher. The weather calms down and we survive the storm. The storm has passed. The roof leaked. We were terrified. It was cold and some people got ill. We tried to recover and take care of everyone. My mother has gotten sick. I am busy nursing the people. My mother died. I'm very sad. It is a terrible feeling to have no control, to be at the mercy of the elements, and to loose someone you love so much. It is exhausting to be strong for everyone. It is difficult to be a leader. You have to be strong and lead by example. You have to keep giving. You think you will be a heroine of sorts, because of selfless actions. It is worth it. To not do anything is worse. I don't begrudge it. I keep giving. I feel fortified from some higher source. I feel that others will give because of my actions.

ML: What advice would she give you?

D: Don't be such a crank all the time, and lead by example. Quit whining. If I did that, it would fortify me. It's like peeling an onion. If you dig deeper, good things can be found.

Debby received information and messages that will help her make the most of her present life and encourage a positive attitude. Both lives showed aspects of the same message—that time may be short and that each moment should be lived to the fullest.

2

What You Get: The Gifts of Discovering Past Lives

"You cannot dream yourself into a character; you must hammer and forge yourself one."
—James A. Froude

Before beginning any journey, it is good to be clear where we are going and what we want to get out of the trip. This chapter gives you a map of the benefits people have experienced as a result of past life regressions.

Like all heroes' journeys, discovering our past lives can be both uncomfortable, and tremendously fulfilling and exhilarating. Why undertake it? The rewards of past life regression are gifts we give ourselves—for our soul's ever-increasing capacity to experience joy, love, and esteem, and for our spirit's ultimate enrichment.

The benefits are seen and unseen, known with the mind and with the heart, spiritual, psychological, emotional, and material. Of course, the richest benefits will be those that are most important to you, and that you seek out deliberately.

What do you want to take away from this process? What gifts are most precious to you? If you could get anything you wanted from past life regression, what would that be? That is the gift you will give yourself. Add it to the benefits we cover in the rest of this chapter. Each section discusses a different family of rewards.

Richer Relationships

The better we understand our relationships with family, friends, colleagues, mates, and all the people in our lives, the richer those connections will be. The wisdom we gain from exploring past lives can make each of our relationships more enjoyable, fulfilling, and valuable. Every connection becomes a more abundant source of lessons that move our spirit forward on its hero's journey.

Mental Match-Making

Have you ever met someone for the first time, and known immediately that you could be good friends? Or known, without any proof or provocation, that you should stay away from that person? Very likely, these are people with whom you have related in a past life.

Each of us carries a similar energy pattern from life to life. Of course, that pattern changes with the growth or traumas that we experience, but we each have a unique energetic signature that allows us to recognize one another—regardless of the race, gender, body type, or other physical characteristics that we have selected for this life.

When the subconscious mind recognizes these energy patterns, the conscious mind races through its memory banks, searching for "files" that will provide contexts and labels. Sometimes the match is retrieved, and we remember who they are. Other times, we "know that we know them," but we never do retrieve the file. It just isn't something the conscious mind has stored away during this life.

The conscious mind contains only information that we have acquired in this life. The far more powerful and universal subconscious mind contains information from all our lives. It holds a record of all our experiences throughout the millennia. When that spark of recognition occurs in the subconscious mind, it may just as easily correspond to memories of past or future lives as it does to our present life. We may not know exactly who we were to that person, or who that person was to us, but we recognize that there is a connection.

I was curious about my past lives with a male colleague, because we hit it off so well as friends but had no romantic interest in one another. It turned out that I had lived as a man during the Gold Rush. I did not strike it rich in California, and headed home to the Midwest. In the mountains of Colorado, I came down into Central City and met a fellow miner. He offered me shelter in his small cabin and we became good friends. We were both solitary people who wanted to lead a simple life. We held similar goals of wanting to strike it rich, and so he invited me to stay. I lived there for the rest of my days. That man was my colleague. I saw in this regression that he and I had a history of deep friendship that was comfortable and trusting, but not romantic.

Even your encounters with strangers take on a new dimension when you think in terms of what roles you may have played in one another's past lives. The postman, grocery clerk, or doctor may have been your mother, your best friend, or the cause of your demise in another time. That person cutting you off in traffic may have been your endearing, but rowdy, best friend who simply wants to get your attention again.

Putting Information to Work

What can you do with information about your relationships with people in past lives? Say you were curious about your past relationships with certain family members. You did a regression, and discovered that you had played significant roles—for better or worse—in one another's spiritual development. How can you use that information?

Simply knowing that you have been together before, and that you are ultimately there to help one another, usually eases most difficulties. It places the relationship in a larger context. If there is no problem with the relationship and you just pursued the information out of curiosity, because you love the person, then the relationship should get even richer.

Past life regressions often help explain the challenges that cycle through a marriage, or difficulties that parents have with a particular child. The knowledge of past relationships can also explain why a mother and daughter may relate more as sisters or friends, while a pair of friends may take on the role of mother and daughter.

My clients often report that they feel and think differently about people after experiencing what their relationship has been in past lives. Almost always, the relationships become deeper and fuller. They have a better idea of why they are in the relationship, what lessons the other person may have for them, and what support they have agreed to give one another. They are inclined to value that other person more, and to have a stronger desire to resolve issues and respect the bond with that person.

Past life regression can also give you valuable information about your own patterns and behavior in relationships, and what lessons you need to learn.

Romantic Relationships

Your choices in mates, and your patterns in dealing with issues that surface within romantic relationships, may also become clearer after visiting other lives.

Whenever you meet someone with whom you will be closely involved—a mate, boss, children, in-laws—it is wise to look at who you have been to one another. Take the time to follow your memory of that energy back through the veils of time, and discover the depth and true nature of the energy between you.

This kind of information can deepen your relationship, explain aspects of it that have been puzzling, and help you know how to proceed from this point on. When you are clear about what you are here to do together, the relationship usually becomes less problematic and more fulfilling.

You may learn, for instance, that the person for whom you felt that strong, compelling energy—and later married in this lifetime—was a "villain" in a previous lifetime. Perhaps you interpreted the intense energy as a sign of your connection, and in the initial period of infatuation, didn't realize that the origin of that energy was a negative event. Often, seeing how you have related in past lives explains why certain people can trigger violent reactions in you so easily.

My client Alice came in for a regression in the midst of a divorce from her husband, Tom, who had been unfaithful to her. Before moving on, she wanted a deeper understanding of their relationship so that she would not repeat the pattern.

Alice discovered a life in which she had been the servant of a wealthy couple since birth. The man was Tom, and he was teaching her to read by studying the Bible. This gave them private time together, and she fell in love with him. He took advantage of her, and they began an intimate sexual relationship.

"My heart races when I think about that original home," Alice said. "There is fear, adrenaline. I am so afraid of getting caught. I remember him pushing himself on me. I was scared…and not…I was a virgin. I don't like the fact that I like it. The whole idea makes me feel disgusted with myself, and guilty." She described the guilt as a big, black hole in her chest and said, "If it were gone, I would be lighter, freer, unburdened, unchained."

Through visualization, Alice filled that hole with self-love and told me that the lesson from that life was: "Stand up for yourself. Take control and be proud…Believe in yourself. Don't be afraid of rejection."

Your Soul Group

Years ago, I engaged in a research project involving past life regression over a two-year period with about twenty-five peers. We would pair up and facilitate regressions for each other, targeting specific periods in time. We would then change partners, collecting information on several lifetimes, in many situations.

We discovered that many of us had incarnated together quite frequently. We were all members of two Soul Groups who had agreed to help one another through our various incarnations. During the regressions, we recognized one another from those other lifetimes. One person might recognize someone as their brother, sister, mother, or boss. With no prior knowledge of those findings, another person in a separate, private session would recognize that same relationship as well. We performed these regressions independently, and were able to corroborate memories of events, relationships, conditions, scenery, customs, clothing, and more.

We will talk more about Soul Groups in Chapter 6. As you begin exploring past lives on a regular basis, you will undoubtedly start meeting members of your Soul Group.

HEALING

Phobias, unexplained pains and syndromes, chronic pain and illness, birthmarks, depression, weight issues, and other health-related phenomena often reflect conditions or events from other lifetimes. Past life regression can be a powerful tool for altering the expression and magnitude of these challenges, especially when combined with proper use of hypnosis and neuro-linguistic programming techniques.

Gail's Neck Pain

Gail came to my office complaining of chronic neck pain. She had tried everything, and could not get the pain to subside. She also wanted to change careers, to move away from her office job and begin working in the healing arts—but each time she came close to making that dream a reality, she got very anxious and backed away from it.

I asked her to focus on the sensations in her neck. She described a vision of having a rope around her neck. I asked her how it came to be there. The vision opened up to reveal that she was being hung on charges of witchcraft. She had been accused of healing people with herbs. I asked her to remove the rope from her neck and heal that area of her body. When she did, I asked her to tell me how her neck felt.

Gail said the pain was still there. We went back, and this time she described being confined in stocks. Again, she was being punished and ridiculed for being a witch, and for using herbs to heal people. I asked her to step out of the stocks and heal her wounds. When she did, she said that there was still pain in her neck.

This time, she visited a life in which she had been beheaded! Again, for practicing witchcraft through her healing arts. I asked her to replace her head and heal the wound. When she did so, her neck pain subsided completely.

These regressions not only revealed the cause of her unexplained neck pain, but also illuminated her fear of pursuing a career as a healer. Through follow-up discussions, she was able to move past her fears and to manifest her true desire to be a healer, at last fulfilling her purpose for this life.

Barbara's Feet and Ankles

Barbara wanted to discover the basis for unexplained pain in her feet and ankles, and also to understand the sense of panic that she felt whenever she felt hungry. She visited three past lives, and got answers to all her questions.

In the first lifetime she recalled, she had been a man. She saw herself going up a staircase, and encountering another man to whom she owed money. The other man was wearing armor, and injured Barbara's foot with an ax—an injury that lamed her for the rest of that life. Barbara said that the lesson in that lifetime was about greed. Her past life counterpart had been unethical and unfair, and had learned through those experiences to be generous and to avoid making decisions based on financial gain.

In the second lifetime, Barbara had been a male slave whose ankles were shackled as a punishment for impulsive disobedience. In that life, she had learned that it was important to pick your battles, and to think about the consequences of what you were about to do. She realized that she did not always invest her energy wisely in this life, and saw that she needed to think more carefully before she acted or spoke.

In the third life, she had been a boy with twelve siblings. She saw a battlefield nearby. The boy was hungry, wet, cold, and tired—and eventually died of hunger as a prisoner of war. This explained her fearful response to hunger, and we were able to desensitize that memory.

From this one session, Barbara got powerful insights into the origins of her symptoms and experienced a great deal of relief.

Past life regression can give us information and experiences that help us understand and heal not only physical difficulties, but emotional ones. When we know the roots of the problem, we are in a better position to deal with it.

One common result of past life regression is a resurgence of a strong sense of self. This awareness may be accompanied by an expanded sense of the spirit, an increased depth of the energy reserves, and an awakened sense of personal power.

Understanding Our Choices

Before each incarnation, we have an opportunity to make many choices about our purpose, growth, lessons, circumstances, the people with whom we incarnate, and even our gender and body type. The ability to access our past lives gives us vital information about why we made the choices we made—and what we are supposed to do with those choices in this life.

Let's look at a few examples of these choices: genetics, body type, and gender.

Genetics and Body Type

Past life research reveals that we often have a coloring and body type that is native to our spirit. We will gravitate toward that coloring and body type, whether or not we have incarnated into a family that has those kinds of genes. For example, people who are large boned and who carry a lot of weight may do so because that is how they see themselves. It is the body type that is native to their spirit. They may have chosen that body type in many other lifetimes, and subconsciously drifted toward it in this life, regardless of their genetic makeup.

Another way of choosing body type is to incarnate into a family that has genes consistent with how we see ourselves. People who are by nature short in stature, for example, or who have dark skin, might choose genes that would likely give them those characteristics.

We all have much more genetic material than is apparent when we look in the mirror. The subconscious mind can select from this vast array of genetic material those traits that we prefer, or with which we are most comfortable. It may be that some traits manifest themselves, and others do not, because of subconscious choices we make. For instance, two people may have "alcoholic" genes—but one will become an alcoholic, and the other will not. Or a person's genetics may allow for either brown hair or black hair, and the person will subconsciously choose brown.

This may be what accounts for members of the same family exhibiting distinctly different hair and eye color—or provide an explanation for why two brothers may have a six-inch difference in their heights.

Gender

We can also choose which gender to experience in any given life, and can alternate between being female or male from lifetime to lifetime. Some spirits prefer one or the other, and therefore experience the majority of lifetimes as a particular gender.

When a spirit is attracted to one particular gender, that attraction may be consistent regardless of the body they choose. For instance, a spirit may prefer women, regardless of whether he chooses the body of a man or the body of a woman in a particular lifetime. This concept may offer an explanation for homosexuality, as well as for men who appear effeminate and women who appear masculine.

Gender may be chosen to fulfill a specific purpose, to be sexually available or unavailable to a specific mate, or to provide a different experience from the norm of that spirit.

In some cases, gender may be chosen purely by physical genetics and timing—and have very little to do with the soul's Life Purpose.

Personal Growth

We reincarnate in order to grow, expand, experience more, and become more fully conscious. That means becoming aware of our blind spots, any unconscious patterns or cycles of behavior that may be limiting us—and doing something about them.

This can be uncomfortable, but the process becomes more interesting and productive—as well as easier and more clear—when we can access other lifetimes as well as this one. Sometimes, when a particular pattern of behavior began many lifetimes ago, past life regression is the only way to make sense of it. By viewing our cycles of behavior over lifetimes, we gain clarity about our unique quirks, habits, character, fears, and choices. That can help us honestly assess our strengths and weaknesses, and show us where we need to make changes.

When we are working with information from past lives, we can also be more *objective* about ourselves. Experiencing a past life can feel almost as if we are watching a movie about someone else. We can observe ourselves and our behavior in a more clear and objective way than we can when looking back over the events of, say, the last weeks or months. When we watch that "other" person behaving in the same dysfunctional ways that we do, it is often easier to see what we want to change. The penny drops, and we "get it" in a way that isn't always possible from the perspective of only one life.

My client Sarah was in her thirties and lived in the Midwest. She revisited a life on the prairie as an early settler. In this former lifetime, she would wash the clothes and hang them out on the line to dry, always keeping her attention on the horizon. She was waiting for someone, or something, to come along and make her life exciting. This was an extremely dull lifetime, because no one ever came over the horizon who made her life the way she wanted it to be.

When I asked her what she could learn from that lifetime that would be relevant to the life she was living now, Sarah exclaimed that her current life was just as dull! She had a washer and a dryer and a condo, but she was still waiting for someone to knock on her door and make her life less isolated and more exciting. Sarah awakened to the fact that if she wanted excitement, she would have to generate it. She understood that she could not go on repeating the same pattern and expecting a different result. In the life on the prairie, she had died alone and unfulfilled. She was determined not to let that happen again.

Carryover Wisdom

We can bring the insights that we gained in a past life forward into this life—and also gain new wisdom simply from watching ourselves in a former life.

While visiting a past life, Adele saw herself as a woman who was not typical of her times. She had left home, and gone to the city to learn about people and write about her experiences. Adele said, "She never marries. I see her as much older now. She is a strong woman, more of a philanthropist. She spends her time helping people and understanding them, helping people to understand their identity."

The wisdom Adele carried forward was, "In that past life, I accomplished my goals. I learned that I must keep my creativity and expression open. I understand now that independence is not just about earning income, it is about being true to your dreams. Regardless of the times, I can be true to my dreams if I am creative enough. What I was doing in that life didn't feel like work. I was loving it and loving myself."

There were many similarities between that past life and Adele's current life. "I want to have a center to help people develop their passion and to facilitate their exploration of who they are and what their beliefs are," she said. "I have struggled with my identity and my decisions in this life. They were always based on the impressions and opinions of others."

Experiencing that past life gave Adele the wisdom and courage to go forward with her dreams.

Overcoming Fears, Blocks And Challenges

The roots of phobias, fears, blocks, and challenges often surface during regressions. If we drowned in a past life, for example, we may have an "irrational" fear of water in this life. Seeing where these fears and challenges originated can help us move beyond them and create the life we want.

Often simply re-experiencing events from a past life will unblock energy, or allow a breakthrough or healing—especially when we work with a qualified facilitator.

Bob wanted to experience a past life regression in order to better understand his intense phobia of heights. He was unable to enjoy mountain vistas or even beautiful views from balconies. When Bob realized that he couldn't even climb a ladder, he decided that his condition had become debilitating and was determined to put an end to it.

During the regression, he experienced a lifetime when he was moving across the country in a train of covered wagons with his wife. There were very few women on the journey, and three other men in the group were jealous and plotted to get rid of him. One day as they were traveling past a canyon, the three men engaged him in a conversation. They drew him close to the edge of a cliff—and in one quick movement, pushed him to his death.

Seeing that past life resolved Bob's subconscious fears. He realized where they had come from, and understood that the danger was long gone. He had nothing to fear from heights in this life.

The Power To Change

Past life regression offers us a unique opportunity to make deep, profound changes on many levels. We gain a new and broader perspective on life and on ourselves, and that makes greater change possible.

Seeing Through New Eyes

We know that our consciousness shapes our reality. How we remember and interpret events determines their effect on us. When we can change those memories and interpretations by looking at them from a broader and more mature perspective, we can literally change how we see ourselves and how we behave in the world. We can let go of limiting interpretations that have held us back, and move forward into more fulfillment and ease.

For example, when we revisit a childhood event in therapy and observe it with our adult eyes, it may seem entirely different from how it seemed when we were six years old. When Sharon was six, she tried one afternoon to get her mother's attention, and couldn't do so. Her mother was distracted and busy with other things. Sharon made a nonverbal decision, in that moment, that her mother didn't love her. Without being consciously aware of doing so, she had been operating all her life as if that six year old perspective were accurate. She acted like a person who thought she was unlovable. This self concept was beginning to cause problems at work and in her marriage.

When she revisited the event in therapy, with the wisdom and perspective of many decades, she saw it quite differently. By then, Sharon was a new mother herself. "Oh!" she exclaimed. "It wasn't that Mom didn't love me! That wasn't it at all. She was just trying to answer the phone, cook dinner, change my little brother, and deal with me all at the same time!"

When Sharon's memory and interpretation of the event changed, its significance and impact on her changed as well. She no longer had to walk around as a person whose mother disliked or ignored her. Her adult perspective and her willingness to revisit the incident in order to change something all worked together for a good change. The same principles apply to working with past lives.

Conversations With Our Past Life Counterparts

Regressions can help us change in other ways as well. When it seems appropriate, my clients exchange advice and wisdom with their past life counterparts, actually holding conversations with their "former" selves. Through these talks, they are often able to change their perceptions of and reactions to past events and experiences, just as Sharon did with her mother. They can actually diffuse any negative emotional charge around these events, and avoid being triggered by similar situations in the future.

These conversations may actually be helpful to our past life counterparts as well. Physics tells us that the very act of observing something, changes it. We know that electrons, for instance, behave differently when we are observing them. In the same way, we may actually change the dynamics of past life events simply by observing them in this lifetime. And our own "future selves" may be doing past life regressions to our present time—and affecting the outcome of our current life!

During those two years when I participated in the group experiments, we discovered an interesting phenomenon. When distinct changes occurred in our current lives, we noticed that certain events or conditions appeared to have been altered in our past lives as well. The shifts that we were experiencing in the present had a noticeable ripple effect into other lifetimes.

Access To The Subconscious

One of the enormous benefits of working with past lives is that it asks us to hone our skill in working with the subconscious mind.

We do not yet have ultimate, definitive answers about how the mind works—but most people agree that the conscious mind represents only a small fraction of our thought processes. The subconscious represents most of what goes on in our minds, even though it is not always seen or recognized—and it is far more powerful than the conscious mind.

The conscious mind is the part of us that thinks, interprets, judges, analyzes, and decides. It holds the information that is in our focused attention at any given moment, and generally accesses only memories from this lifetime. The conscious mind only holds one thought at a time, although it may oscillate back and forth between several thoughts so rapidly that it seems as if we are thinking several thoughts simultaneously.

The subconscious mind holds a far larger body of information. Since we don't know exactly how the subconscious works, the following discussion is simply a way to start our mental juices flowing and begin thinking about the subconscious.

In this work, *the subconscious refers to the mental body that stores all experiences and knowledge that the spirit has been exposed to on any level, at any time*. This includes memories, past and future life experiences, filters, patterns, habits, compulsions, aversions, emotions, dreams, inspiration, creativity, and extrasensory perceptions. The subconscious mind gathers and stores information continuously and without logical order. It holds all there is to know about us.

The subconscious may also be connected to all knowledge and awareness everywhere. If this is the case, we may be capable of accessing information about subjects and events far beyond our personal experience. This interconnected cache of knowledge about all that exists is often referred to as the Akashic Records.

The Iceberg

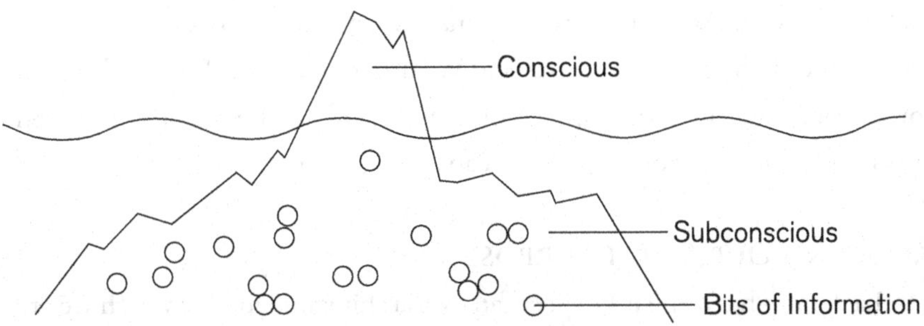

The most common metaphor for the conscious and subconscious minds is an iceberg. In this diagram, the tiny tip peaking out above the surface of the water represents the conscious mind. Here, information like our name and address are easily retrieved, along with many other bits of knowledge and memory that may be slightly below the surface.

Farther down the iceberg, in the subconscious mind, are the memories that are brought up with some effort, including those that can only surface with the aid of hypnosis, dreams, or the reviewing of evidence. Some recollections are brought to the surface easily; others are more obstinate.

Obviously, we are more likely to remember events that had a high impact on our lives. Examples might be a wedding, funeral, accident, or graduation. During these events, we are usually more focused and more aware of the sensory information around us (sights, sounds, smells, and other sensory data) than we are under normal circumstances. When an experience involves multiple senses and has an intense emotional or physical component, we describe it as a memory cluster.

Sometimes we can retrieve the entire cluster by focusing on one of its elements. A smell, for instance, can often evoke a memory cluster from long ago. Or we might recognize someone in a past life regression whom we know in this life—and that one piece of information may enable us to recall much more about that life. The subconscious can even be programmed to guide us to a specific time that we have shared a life with a particular person, or to a life that can give us wisdom about a choice we are making today.

Since we are still in the process of discovering how the mind works, and how extensive it really is, we need to stay curious and gather all the information we can. Are our minds ultimately connected to every piece of knowledge in the whole of existence? We don't know yet. But we do know for certain that our awareness is more vast, and working in more dimensions, than our conscious minds are capable of comprehending.

Knowing Our Spirit Purpose

Each of us has a Spirit Purpose, an overarching mission for which we are created by our spirit's energy and direction. Each of our aspects, souls, or incarnations contributes something unique to the fulfillment of this purpose—and each has a Life Purpose, a smaller mission that can be accomplished in one particular lifetime. Within that Life Purpose, there may be many other more immediate, short-term goals.

Here is how it works. Dave may have a Spirit Purpose "to discover the divine in all existence." To that end, his Life Purpose in one lifetime might be "to serve others." Within that Life Purpose, he might have an immediate purpose to pass the bar exam so that he can work to protect people in his community. Another immediate purpose might be to raise his children with love. Both of these immediate purposes support his Life Purpose, which supports his Spirit Purpose.

Knowing our Spirit Purpose is extremely valuable. It can help us make productive decisions and guide us along a path that supports our growth. This knowledge almost always brings a grander sense of our position in the larger scheme of life, a greater sense of responsibility toward the planet and its people, and a stronger sense of morality and personal value.

Since the life we are engaged in now is only one of an infinite array of lifetimes, we have a far better chance of understanding our Spirit Purpose if we can access more than one lifetime. We gain a broader perspective from which to approach the quest, and have access to a broader scope of reality in which to manifest it.

Seeing And Embracing Our Life Purpose

Do you know exactly what you are here on Earth to do in this life? Each of us has a specific Life Purpose, a primary mission that our soul wants to accomplish in this particular lifetime. Our other lifetimes may hold clues to the purpose of our current life. They can also show us, for instance, why we have a natural penchant for music, the arts, science, or healing—and why we enjoy particular occupations, hobbies, or sports.

When we have reconnected with the talent and skills we had in former lifetimes, we can bring those abilities, and that focus and knowledge, into our present life. Doing so may also generate ideas about our purpose in this life, as well as confidence in pursuing it.

Clarifying Core Values

Past life regressions have brought my clients not only a stronger connection to their Life Purpose, but a richer connection to their personal core values.

Jayne's goal for her regression was to be happier and enhance her perspective on life. The two lifetimes she visited had a common thread. In the first, she had been a male potter who sold his wares in a market during the first century A.D. He lived alone, never made much money, experienced poor health, and died young. Yet he had been very happy. He had never felt the need to impress anyone. He had simply enjoyed his own skill and knowledge, and appreciated an opportunity to fulfill a need in his society. He had known instinctively that life was too short to let anything cause unhappiness.

In the second life Jayne experienced, she was a woman receiving treatment for cancer. She died young in this life as well, and learned a similar lesson: Make the most of each day, because you don't know how long you will live. The message was not to wait for happiness, and not to think of it as something that might or might not happen in the future—but to create all the happiness she could every day. Jayne vowed to stop her negative thinking and stop "sweating the small stuff" so that she could live each day in more joy.

UNDERSTANDING THE BIG PICTURE

In addition to watching our own spirit's path unfold as we discover our past lives, most people experience an enormous expansion in how they see our awe-inspiring universe. We come to understand that we are not the only ones on a hero's journey. The entire universe is on its own quest for existence and consciousness. This broader perspective helps us see the big picture—and how we fit into it.

One result is that personal difficulties become less important, and therefore less troublesome. We see life not simply from the perspective of our own personal issues, but in the larger context of evolving our society, the planet, and all that exists. Our own individual hardships seem less overwhelming. We can turn our individual struggle into a communal process, becoming participants in—and contributors to—the greater flow of energy.

Appreciation

Through exploring past lives, people often find that they have a greater appreciation not only for their own Life Purpose, but for all of human culture and endeavor—for history, art, natural history, strategies of war, politics between nations, cultural curiosities, and travel. Everything takes on a new meaning and personal relevance, because they have been involved with these activities in past lives.

My clients also report loving the opportunity to travel to places they have been in other lifetimes. Touching the buildings, walking on the roads and sidewalks, visiting the cathedrals or mountaintops, and experiencing the foods and customs, stir memories and sensations deep within their souls. History becomes more than dates and names to be memorized. Geography becomes more than the study of maps and terrain. It is no longer "out there." It is part of their personal history.

Birth and Death

Seeing life in a larger context gives us new perspectives on birth and on death. We come to understand the choices we make as we approach birth, and have greater insight into the birth process itself. Having visited our deaths in past lives gives us far greater awareness of that process, and usually a great deal of comfort as we approach our own death or the death of loved ones.

What has been most remarkable to me, in regressing clients to pre-birth and early childhood memories, is their extraordinary knowledge and clarity in those very early stages of life. The embryo, the baby, and the child are acutely aware of their environment and the people around them, and of all the emotions that everyone is experiencing. These memories can yield extremely useful information about why the person chose a particular body or a particular set of parents.

While experiencing a past life, my client Maria described being in her mother's womb while the mother was walking on the beach. They lived in a primitive culture, so when it was time for Maria to be born, her mother simply squatted on the beach and gave birth. Maria remembered the entire process of being birthed—the acknowledgment that it was time to move out of the womb, the journey through the birth canal, and then being out in the air, and on the beach.

In her observations about how it felt to be a baby, she claimed that one of the greatest disappointments was the lack of information. Maria was craving instruction and understanding about her new world, even as an infant. She cried frequently, not from hunger or pain, but from frustration that her vast consciousness was not being filled with information about the fascinating world she had just entered.

Expanded Awareness

During the regression process, and particularly through the newer hypnotherapy methodologies, our awareness becomes more open and expansive. For some people, this expansion is dramatic. For others, it may be only slightly noticeable. In either case, the new and wider perspective helps us discover new choices, pathways, and possibilities.

Exploring our past lives not only gives us a broader perspective and a deeper sense of our place in the scheme of things, it also expands our capacity to experience what is around us. The very act of opening up to exploring past lives, and learning what they have to teach us, expands our awareness. We start seeing and realizing things we have not been able to see or comprehend before.

As we expand our view of the universe, we naturally expand our view of ourselves and our potential. Instead of shrinking fearfully from interactions with others, with life, and with the universe, we can let ourselves be grander, and more powerful and effective, than we thought possible. We widen our circle of influence, and our capacity to contribute.

Seeing The Divine In All Life

Perhaps the greatest benefit of discovering our past lives is that we begin to see the divine in all of life. We see it in ourselves, in everyone around us, in all times and places, in everything that exists. A life lived from that perspective is a life of bliss.

In the end, we are all part of one another. Everything that exists is connected with everything else. After experiencing a number of regressions, most people move closer to a genuine experience that each individual is a part of every other individual—and that we have all interacted with one another in many ways and taken various roles with one another throughout history. Our paths cross and re-cross. Our roles reverse. And then reverse again.

With the understanding that each person we encounter may have been our parent, child, sibling, or spouse, we come to recognize the precious nature of every human contact. Each person carries the potential of having served some important role in one or more of our lifetimes. Experiencing past life regressions encourages us to honor that fact, and the divine in every soul.

These are just some of the benefits that clients have reported to me from past life regression. You will discover your own personal benefits. They may include those we've discussed in this chapter, and they may be completely new and different!

For Audrey, the benefits were physical, spiritual, and emotional. The regression described below helped her deal with several serious health issues, including a seizure disorder. Her case study also shows that many different types of benefits can be gained in just one session, and demonstrates the kinds of healing techniques that you can use in your own regressions.

CASE STUDY

AUDREY

Audrey had studied philosophical topics for years and was interested in finding out more about her past lives. She also wanted to meet her spirit guide, learn about her life lessons, and resolve several health issues. Audrey had a seizure disorder that began soon after her marriage. Her medications made her inclined toward depression and self-destructive behavior. For several years, she had experienced a grand mal seizure once or twice a year, as well as several milder episodes each month. She complained of migraines that felt as if she were being stabbed in the side of the head with a knife.

This partial transcript of our session illustrates several aspects of past life regression. It shows the value of simply following your intuition, and how it is possible to extract illuminating information even from small incidents or details. It also demonstrates how a session may wander through several lifetimes, and address many different kinds of issues.

As the session began, Audrey saw herself outside.

A: I see grass and sticks. It is daytime and I am alone. I am about twenty years old. Now, I see tall trees, a rock, some hills, and a grassy area. I am picking up sticks and putting them into a sling to take them to other people who will use them for fire. I see myself going inside my home. I live with my parents. My mom is home and is preparing food.

ML: Do you know where you are or the date?

A: I don't know exactly where we are, but the date is 17 A.D.

ML: What else do you notice?

A: I am sitting, and working with my hands. Now I go outside. I am going up a hill, looking for a man. I'm happy. I sit down and wait. I want him to come with me down the hill. I sense there is something dangerous going on. He doesn't come. Other people are coming. They want to kill our people. I hide. Many people get hurt. Someone hits me and has their hand on my neck. It's a man. He shoves my face in the dirt. I'm scared. He hits me with a stick on my back and on my head. It's right where the migraines are. It's pulsating.

ML: If that sensation had a shape and a color, what would it be?

A: It is reddish pink, and looks like a long island.

ML: How could you change it so you could experience healing and relief?

A: I can change it to white and blue. That feels good.

ML: I would like you to ask your spirit guide to come and speak with you now. What do you notice about them?

A: There is one guide. He is male, a little older and he's smiling at me. His name is Brian. I ask him what I am supposed to work on, what is my purpose. He shows me someone who fell down. I'm helping them up. It is metaphorical for my purpose, to help people in general, as well as work with a specific person.

ML: Moving on to another lifetime that will give you information relevant to you at this time, what do you notice next?

A: I see a wooden door with an old tarnished handle. I'm outdoors, on a boat. It's large. I am a man. I'm on the deck, rocking back and forth. It's calm. A mild day. I'm on a merchant ship. I am making sure that people are doing their jobs. Now I see we are in port. We go to a tavern and are drinking and eating. Everyone is happy, but I'm nervous. I am waiting for someone to come in. A couple of big men come in and one sits down with me. The other stands. They are glad to see me, but I think they may be blackmailing me. It's about a deal that I've made. I want to give them what they want so they will leave. I want it to be done. I tell them to come to the boat. I will let them take something off the boat. They are laughing. I feel disgusted. I leave the people there at the tavern. I go to the boat. I'm walking around in the hold, thinking about what I did. I am waiting for them. They show up and surprise me. I was daydreaming.

I tell them to take what they came for and leave. They pull a gun on me. I'm not surprised. I suspected that it would end badly. They are laughing and they have a box. I said that I made a deal with the devil. Then they shoot me. They leave and I sit next to a crate. I am thinking of what I did. It was wrong. I was trying to take a short cut. I had something in the box and was transporting it to someone who wasn't supposed to have it. It was jewelry.

ML: As I count from three to one, you will know the date and the location of this scene. Three, two, one.

A: It's 1575. I'm an English native, and this occurred in Africa. There are dark people here.

ML: What have you learned from this experience?

A: There are no shortcuts. When working with people, you have to go through the process step by step. I have to be in charge of my own destiny.

ML: Move now to another lifetime. What do you notice next?

A: I'm in a Victorian house. I am walking around. It's my house. I live with my husband and two children. They are both boys. I'm thirty-five years old. I am arguing with my husband. I want to have some control in the marriage. It is a happy marriage, otherwise.

ML: What do you know about your husband?

A: He is a banker. I don't work. We are talking about finances and he says no to me. He won't see my point of view. I'm crying. We go on with life, but I am resentful.

ML: Move ahead in time. What do you notice next?

A: We are older. My son is there with his wife. She and I are talking. I'm telling her that I wanted control of something in our marriage but it didn't work that way. I have put it behind me. She wants more control also. She is having a baby. I tell her that it will be a full time job.

ML: Moving ahead again until the next relevant event, what do you notice next?

A: I'm old and in bed. I'm sick. I can't get out of bed. I am living with my son and daughter-in-law. I enjoy my grandchildren.

ML: Looking back over that lifetime, what were your lessons?

A: I found it hard to conform, but it is important to do so. I was supporting my husband in his career. We had social pressures. I lost a bit of myself in the process.

ML: Do you see any correlations between that lifetime and this one?

A: I am learning to do things for myself now. I am trying to stay in control. Seeing this helps me to not be resentful.

ML: Once again calling in your spirit guide, what do you notice this time?

A: I see an older female this time. I see two guides. Brian is there again. He is male, with a beard and dark eyes. Brian speaks: "You are on the right path." He shows me a scene. There is green grass, a shepherd, and a lamb. The boy is caring for the lamb, which is eating grass. The boy carried the lamb down a hill and gives it water. He also carries a stick. It is glowing with a yellow light. He holds it above his head. It gives him strength and power.

ML: What does this message mean to you?

A: I'm the shepherd, taking care of children. I'm supposed to take the power. It was mine all along. I didn't realize that. He wants me to be more open to his guidance. I need to keep meditating. I should keep learning. Read books. Write in my journal. He wants me to wear a gold ring, my wedding ring. I need to get it sized to wear it again. It is for security. He tells me to be happy.

ML: Thanking your guide for his assistance, I would like to ask him to show you yet another lifetime. What do you see next?

A: There is a curtain. It has warm red, orange, and brown colors. I'm in a small hut or house. There is someone ill in there. It's a young boy. The only other people there are his parents. They are worried and wringing their hands. I am a man and I am there to heal the boy.

I go to the boy and put my hand on his forehead. I'm calling down a type of energy. I am a conduit to help clear his blocks and give him a jump-start. I can sense there is something wrong with his stomach and intestines. The energy is trying to work. It is forcing some kind of bad stuff out of his feet. I know that he won't die.

This involves a lesson for his family. They need to learn to be less concerned with the material matters, and more concerned with family, and the wellbeing of the family as a group. At some level, the boy has decided to be sick so that they would focus on what is really important. He will get well. I can sense their frustration. They can't see past the illness to the deeper problem. I can see that the boy eventually got better, but they did not really learn the true lesson.

ML: What do you notice next?

A: I leave there and go to the temple. I am a man, in my thirties. I am maybe thirty-six or thirty-seven years old. I am single and I am a priest or holy man of sorts. I have a lot of responsibility for the people in my area. For their spiritual well being. There are other men who do the same thing. We are in South America, in the jungle. We are near the west coast of the continent. It could be either Central or South America. It is not a coastal town, but it is not far from the coast. Maybe a few days of travel by foot. I wear a robe wrapped around me made of a cotton-like material. I don't have a lot of hair, but what I have is pulled up.

ML: Moving ahead in time to the next relevant experience, what do you notice next?

A: We are celebrating a high holy day. I am sitting on my chair, or throne, during the ceremony. People from outside of the temple bring offerings. They give them to me, or perhaps it is a ceremonial gift to a deity that I represent. I'm not sure. It is the beginning of some season and it is hot. Today there is going to be a lesson of compassion.

During the day, someone does something wrong and a young boy is brought before me for punishment. I am in the position of a judge. I am to hand out a sentence of what should happen to this boy. Because it is a holiday, I am telling them that they need to be compassionate. We will learn compassion instead of punishment today. The poor people are happy, but the people who have more wealth are upset. They like the rules for the rules' sake. They like to enforce more than follow the rules. The celebration continues.

I retire to the living chamber where it is less chaotic. I speak with my friend, who is another priest and teacher. He is older than I am. He shakes his head and tells me that I like to cause upsets. I like to stir things up. He laughs because he knows I was right. In this life, he reminds me of my husband's boss.

ML: What happens next?

A: I am looking out over the river, from way above it on a cliff. The river stretches beyond where I can see. I am looking at it and thinking. It is my retreat from my daily work. I am searching my inner self for answers regarding my frustrations with my duties of being a leader. What is truly important seems to be bogged down in the daily life of the people who come to us. I need to learn patience. My job is to teach and guide people. I must be patient until they get to the level that they can understand these things. I also serve as a role model.

ML: Moving ahead, what do you notice next?

A: I am in an argument with someone. This leads to me taking on a student. He is a young boy who is to come into the priesthood. He is my novice, my apprentice. In this life, he is my son. I spend a couple of years teaching him. One day there is a solar eclipse. It is daytime, but it is dark. My student and the other people are scared. The priests know that this is a good sign. The eclipse provides energy to be used, energy that can be worked with.

We have a ceremony. Only the oldest, fully trained priests attend. We are gathered in a circle. We are connected, either by holding hands or it is an energy-mind connection. The group focuses on one thought. We make a ritual drawing on the ground that we stand on. They are trying to use the energy to raise the vibration or make some molecular patterns of the body move faster. There is a large group focusing this thought and intention at this time. It feels successful. We are pleased with the outcome.

ML: Moving ahead in time, what do you notice next?

A: I am about forty-seven or fifty-seven at the time of my death. It is time for me to go. My student is there. I'm lying on the bed, talking, and I just die. I feel a sense of satisfaction and accomplishment. I was a teacher. I was successful teaching a lot of people that love is more important than fear. I helped those I was supposed to help.

ML: What correlations do you notice between that lifetime and this one?

A: The lessons are the same. I need to teach love, not fear. I must teach not only the love of humankind, but also the love of self, so that people can relate to each other better. I am already doing it. I am helping them to feel better about themselves through my work. I need to take better care of my words so they feel even better inside. My work is to raise the consciousness of others.

Five years have passed since Audrey first started her regressions. She has had one small seizure and no grand mal episodes. Past life regression may not be the only cause of her improvement in health. However, she is happy and leading a normal life, free of migraines and serious seizures.

3

Life's True Purpose

"There is a theory which states that if ever anybody discovers exactly what the Universe is for and why it is here, it will instantly disappear and be replaced by something even more bizarre and inexplicable. There is another theory which states that this has already happened."
—Douglas Adams

We saw in the last chapter that exploring your past lives yields enormous benefits in terms of relationships, health, spiritual and emotional growth, wisdom and clarity, and expanded awareness and perspective. Yet perhaps the most important benefit is that it keeps us moving on our hero's journey toward the true purpose of all life—the holy grail beyond even our individual Spirit Purpose.

This chapter is about that great mystery, the purpose of all life. Before we explore how reincarnation actually works, and how to make wise choices in this process, it is good to know *why* we are doing it.

Existence And Consciousness

There are two basic components in any life—existence and consciousness. Existence means that we can place ourselves at a specific location in time and space. Consciousness means that we are awareness of our existence in that time and space.

These two basic elements depend on one another. Without *both* of them, there would be no spirit. Without existence, there would be nothing of which to be conscious. Without consciousness, we would not be aware that we existed.

The continuation of existence and consciousness is the fundamental purpose of every living being. In fact, our survival depends on the continuation, and enhancement, of our existence and consciousness. Everything we do is geared to support that survival. This is the overriding purpose that all spirits share. We have an instinct to perpetuate, and to expand, our existence and consciousness—and we will do whatever it takes to make that happen.

Sometimes this survival instinct can become twisted, and produce behaviors that are dysfunctional and self-sabotaging—fear, greed, jealousy, anger, the inability to love ourselves or others. Repeating these behaviors turns them into habits, and leads to chronic unhappiness. Yet they are simply reactions to our basic need for survival. As healing occurs, our behaviors and choices become more closely aligned with the glory and elegance of our true nature. Our responses become more supportive and life-enhancing.

Past life regression helps with this healing, and allows us to "untwist" the survival instinct when it becomes dysfunctional. We have access to more lessons, and so we can embrace our true nature more quickly and fully. The result is happiness, and the emotion it produces is love. (When we are not acting in alignment with our true nature, the result is anger—and the emotion produced is fear.)

When it comes to existence and consciousness, we are looking for *density of experience*. We are looking for rich, loamy lessons, for whatever exposes us to more of life and teaches us to experience it more deeply. That is what builds a spirit.

Each day, ask yourself, "How am I feeding my consciousness, my spirit?

How am I ensuring and enhancing my existence?"

The Tapestry of Life

Imagine your spirit's life as an infinite stretch of embroidered fabric. The warp and weave are your existence and consciousness. The threads that cross, twist, and wind their way above and below the surface are your experiences as you move through your various lives. Those threads, with all their colors, directions, and intricate twists, determine how decorative, bold, and meaningful your particular tapestry will be. *The denser the threads, the more the consciousness and existence are bound together—and the more they are enhanced and strengthened.*

The spirit's entire life exists in one eternal present moment—but we move our focus along the threads, becoming aware of one knot or stitch at a time, focusing on one lifetime and then another.

As we move our focus from one stitch to the next, we have the option of altering the tapestry. We can change the tension, the direction, or the color—and if we do so, all the other parts of the fabric adjust accordingly. Using this metaphor, how do you imagine your tapestry would look and feel? Are there any parts of your life fabric that you want to alter in some way?

One of the benefits of past life regression is that you can make those alterations with a great deal more information, insight, and wisdom than you might have with access only to the experiences of one lifetime.

Why We Incarnate

The ultimate goal of our hero's journey is to gather the riches of more existence and deeper consciousness, and bring them back to nourish our spirit. The more diverse and varied our experiences, the more we enhance our existence. The greater our growth and the wider our awareness, the more we enhance our consciousness. As our aspects, or souls, quest out through time and space over the millennia to gather these treasures, we become denser, richer, more textured spirits.

Whether we choose to be in or out of a body, for any length of time, depends on how well the experience we might have in that body serves our primary purpose—the maintenance, and expansion, of our existence and consciousness. There are no hard and fast rules about the frequency, or the length, of incarnations. At any given time, a spirit has the option of occupying a physical form somewhere in time and space, or remaining in a non-physical form on the astral plane.

Let's look at why we might make the decision to incarnate.

Our Laboratory

Imagine a science laboratory with a sealed, glass-enclosed space containing an experiment. The only way to enter this enclosed space is to place your hands inside gloves that extend into the sealed space. With those gloves, you can manipulate tools, move objects, and interact with other sets of gloves. Placing our hands inside the gloves, and extending them into the sealed space, is an apt metaphor for incarnating into a physical body.

Are the gloves in control of the action? No, they are vehicles that allow action to take place in that enclosed world. The true manipulator of the experiment is the brain of the person who has his or her hands in the gloves.

In this metaphor, the person is the spirit. The hands entering the gloves represent the soul, the part of the spirit that enters the physical body. The spirit puts an extension of itself into a physical vessel so that it can interact with other similar vessels and with the world in which it resides. Placing its hands into the gloves and extending them into this contained world expands its range of experiences—its range of existence and consciousness.

Without occupying the gloves, it could only look at that world. It could not truly experience it. In the same way, we can observe the physical world from the astral plane, but we cannot interact with it fully unless we enter a physical body.

What might happen if we adjust some factors within this metaphor? Consider, for instance, what would occur if:

- The gloves had desires of their own and did not fully respond to the movements of the hands

- The hands lost nerve connections with the brain and acted contrary to directions and instructions
- The hands chose to disobey commands and acted with free will, even when doing so was self-destructive
- The other gloves in the contained space had opposing goals and fought hard to prevent the gloves and their hands from fulfilling their mission
- The other gloves completed a task that destroyed the instruments that our glove needed to use to fulfill its directives
- The hand followed the directives of the other gloves, and forgot that it was attached to its own body
- The body became so tired of its work that the hand and glove fell into disuse

These are hypothetical examples, meant primarily to amuse but also to create curiosity. If you were the person in this metaphor, what do you think would be the state of your brain, body, hands, and gloves?

To use another metaphor, the body is a vehicle. Like a car, it gets us to our destination faster. We know that the body is not the spirit, but having a body promotes our spiritual growth.

Spirit Purpose

We spoke briefly of Spirit Purpose in the last chapter. Each of us was created with energy that operates in a unique and special way. Some spirits have energy that attracts, and some have energy that inspires. Others have energy that leads, directs, heals, teaches, or manages. Some are seekers; others are gatherers of knowledge or resources. Our particular energy operates in a way that is unique to us.

To get a closer look at your own Spirit Purpose, go into a state of meditation in whatever way you prefer, and consider the following questions.

- Over your lifetime, in what ways have you naturally used your energy?

- When you consider many lifetimes, what are your general proclivities?
- Do you typically:
  - Draw people into groups?
  - Disseminate information?
  - Create and share love?
  - Break things down to examine their parts or structure?
  - Create chaos in order to shake things up?
  - Heal things that are broken or out of balance?

There are many other choices as well. Reflect on how your energy operates in the world to get a sense of your Spirit Purpose. Occupations, hobbies, and other activities may help suggest your basic dominant pattern.

Life Purpose

Within the grander cycle of a Spirit Purpose, each individual soul has a Life Purpose. This purpose, in its truest form, supports the Spirit Purpose. Yet the Life Purpose is more directed toward the activities and environment within one particular lifetime.

A Life Purpose might involve:

- Learning a lesson such as overcoming a negative pattern or habit (greed, jealousy, violence), or gaining positive character traits (courage, compassion, loyalty)
- Assisting another person, particularly someone in your Soul Group. When others in your Soul Group are moving forward, it is easier for you to move forward as well. Helping them always brings a personal reward, in addition to the fulfillment of supporting someone close to you.
- Gaining knowledge about the universe from various perspectives (poverty, royalty, warrior, artist, etc.)
- Furthering your range of experience to fulfill your Spirit Purpose. Being a healer at the level of your Spirit Purpose might manifest as

a Life Purpose being an herbalist, a shaman, a dentist, a nurse, a massage therapist, etc.

There are many, many other Life Purposes. Past life regression is a good way to discover yours, if you have not done so already. During a regression, you may explore your decision-making prior to coming into this life. That will probably illuminate both your Spirit Purpose and your Life Purpose. You may also meet spirit guides who can give you valuable information. Everything that happens in the regression can shed light on your Life Purpose.

Other clues of your Life Purpose may be revealed through examining your childhood desires and games, hobbies, interests, and concerns. Do you recall a sense of urgency about wanting to accomplish a particular goal? Were you frustrated when you couldn't access or realize certain talents or abilities?

Remember that your Life Purpose may not be tied directly to your occupation. Some occupations are simply what you do for a living, or what you are good at doing, and are not necessarily your purpose for coming into this life.

Do you know what your Life Purpose is? In what ways do your occupation, interests, talents, and relationships support that Life Purpose?

Doing the Work

We need to shape our own personal Life Purpose each time we incarnate. We do not simply get our marching orders and show up for a body with all the decisions already made for us. We need to do some planning. Part of the planning involves asking ourselves these kinds of questions:

- What Life Purpose best serves our Spirit Purpose at this point in its evolution?
- What circumstances will best further that particular Life Purpose?
- What kinds of parents will work best? What economic situation?
- Are there any physical attributes that would be beneficial?

It is crucial to develop our Life Purpose, and to stay connected with it. We want to know where we're going when we get to Earth, and what this life is all about. When people fail to do this work, their lives lack purpose and passion. They tend to drift. The life may come to an end physically, or they may find themselves just going through the motions. If nothing is done to correct the situation over the course of several lifetimes, a spirit can languish and even be extinguished.

If we forget our Life Purpose, we can always go back in a regression and review our decision-making process before entering this body. If we feel disconnected from our Spirit Purpose, we can go back to earlier lifetimes. One way or another, we need to be in touch with our purpose in order to keep the juices flowing.

Compatible Life Purposes

Our various Life Purposes are usually connected by the thread of our Spirit Purpose. Knowing about our past lives, and Life Purposes, helps us stay clear about our Spirit Purpose.

Sam was a white male musician and visual artist who sought out past life regression to clarify his connection to the arts. His experience is particularly interesting because he was able to carry a directive from one lifetime to the next in order to fulfill his Spirit Purpose.

Sam first regressed to a lifetime when he had been a black jazz musician. In the 1930's, he had been in a car accident that impaired his vision, but he continued to perform until 1952, when he was in another traffic accident and died in a Chicago hospital.

"I look down at my body. I see the room better than ever. It's so beautiful," he said. "There is color everywhere. When I see my body, I see a black man in his forties, slightly graying and a little overweight. I notice broken limbs and a beat-up body. There are flowers everywhere. But no one is there. I'm floating away. It's okay."

Sam said his lessons from that life were about expression, tolerance, modesty, having fun, and helping people through his music. The next lifetime was his present life. I asked him to go back to the time just before he incarnated and access information about how he chose his current lifetime.

On his deathbed in the Chicago hospital, he had been imprinted with the message to "Remember what I know." He heard the words, "Let it flow. Let it go," and understood that he needed to "do what I could and make it good." He was to be careful with his body and always "find the right note." He could learn from others, but he was to do things in his own way.

I asked Sam what the older black man's intention had been, and he replied, "The old man would be happy if he could come back as a white person with great vision. He had a joke. He'd say, 'I think I'm going to be an artist.' He wanted to make paintings because he had never been able to see. He would construct beautiful scenes in his mind. He wanted to go to Hawaii and California. I am not supposed to forget him. He had terrible grief around being left behind when all the others in his group kept on performing, and he had to go."

Immediate Purpose

Immediate Purpose refers to shorter-term goals within our Life Purpose. They support the Life Purpose, just as a Life Purpose supports a Spirit Purpose.

Immediate Purposes are all about gathering the tools and character traits that allow us to accomplish our larger goals. They may involve getting the grades we need to go to college, relationship skills, doing what it takes to hold a job, becoming self-sufficient, and so forth.

Our daily activities provide the "playground" in which to procure these skills. What everyday activities are you engaged in that indicate an Immediate Purpose? These may include punctuality, living up to your word, learning to relax, overcoming limitations to prosperity, and so forth. Several lessons may be occurring simultaneously. Or it may be that when one is mastered, another one takes its place.

We are constantly moving through lessons that advance and expand our ultimate purpose—existence and consciousness.

Death Is Not Required For Advancement

Some people claim that they have completed their purpose in this lifetime and are "free to go on to the next level." If that were true, they would go. If they are still here, there is probably something more for them to do or learn in this lifetime. The irony is that there is always more to learn, and always more ways in which to grow! The spirit is always hungry for more experience, thirsty for more consciousness.

Contrary to what some people believe, *we do not have to die in order to graduate and start at the next level.* (If we stop learning, however, we are as good as dead.)

Carolyn confided to me that she felt she had never wanted to be born, and that she constantly resisted having to stay in a body. Through hypnosis and past life regression, she went back to the decision-making process just before this incarnation and discovered herself arguing with her spirit guides about the virtues of entering her present body. She really did not want to experience another physical lifetime, especially the one they were suggesting. They finally convinced her that she needed to do this for the fulfillment of her higher purpose.

She reluctantly agreed, and entered the embryo. Carolyn spent a lot of her time in the womb projecting out into the astral plane. When it was time to begin the birth process, she remembers deciding that she would prolong it as much as possible. She turned her body and tried to hang on, thinking it would be best if her head stayed in the womb until the last possible moment. Hers was a breach birth, something she had not known about previously. After the regression, Carolyn's mother confirmed that she indeed had been born breach!

Carolyn's entire regression is given at the end of this chapter. Here is a short excerpt in which she explores the reason she incarnated and the lessons she was to learn:

C: I am told I need the experience. I am to help lead.

ML: Lead whom, for what reason?

C: The evolution of change is hard and the strongest souls have to lead the people through the changes. I'm strong and have to be one of them here. The changes are much more subtle than what I've been waiting for.

ML: What do you mean by that?

C: I have been waiting for something terrible to happen to the world. This is indicating that it will be different. It will be subtler. It will be a lot of little terrible things.

ML: What else do you know?

C: I had no choice. This is bigger than my soul. I don't know what to call it—destiny, a master soul, a universal plan? I don't know. But I couldn't resist. My soul didn't want to be here.

As much as people may resist incarnating, and hope to escape their difficulties by leaving the physical plane and never returning, it is in this realm of physical existence that we have our hands in the gloves—and acquire the capacity to learn lessons that fulfill our Spirit Purpose.

How Long Do We Stay Here—and There?

Again, we go back to purpose. How quickly people return to a physical body depends on how well a return would serve their growth—and also on the strength of their decision-making abilities.

When we are in balance and making rational choices, the frequency of return is based on the purpose that a life on Earth, or in a physical body somewhere else, would serve. If our growth would be served by returning to the physical realm immediately after a death, then we will do that. If our purpose will be better fulfilled by remaining on the astral plane for a length of time, then that will be the proper choice.

Occasionally, the desire to return to Earth is based on an addiction to drugs, alcohol, cigarettes, food, sex, or some other compulsive habit. If this is the case, we may find ourselves returning more often based on those urges, rather than on rational choices.

Bottom line, there are no rules or limitations. The length of time out of a body will vary, just as the length of the life in a body will vary.

Do We Have a "Last Life?" (And Would We Want one?)

Is there ever a time when a spirit stops incarnating into physical bodies? And is this even a desirable prospect?

Some people seem to think that the purpose of life is to evolve to the point that "we no longer need to incarnate." We hear a lot of talk about "This is my last life" and "I'm working to finish up so I won't have to come back." But is that really how it works? And would we want it to work that way? In order to answer these questions, let's examine the pros and cons of incarnating.

What Incarnation Buys Us

Incarnating into a physical form gives us access to worlds that are otherwise unavailable to us—and lets us have experiences that we simply could not have if we stayed in non-physical form. It gets our hands into the gloves, into the sealed container in the lab, where all the juicy experience is.

Taking physical form also requires us to exercise and use our consciousness—so it stays strong and alert, and keeps expanding. If we don't use a muscle, it deteriorates and eventually atrophies. In the same way, our consciousness deteriorates if we don't exercise it. Over time, it atrophies. If we allow it to atrophy long enough, it can shrink to nothing and extinguish itself.

Incarnation also builds our base of experience. In order to grow, learn, and expand our awareness, we need continuous input from a variety of experiences. It makes no difference whether these experiences are pleasant or unpleasant. We learn and grow from both.

The "Escape Hatch"

If a spirit chose never again to experience physical form, it would remain forever on the astral plane. This might seem like a pleasant option to people who are having a hard time with life on Earth, and who may even have had a whole lifetime of difficulties. It might have a momentary appeal to people who are in pain, or who are disgruntled with the way things have turned out. These people sometimes "can't wait to get to the other side."

Other people believe that a "last life" with no more incarnations would represent a sort of graduation. They would have "gotten off the wheel" and elevated themselves beyond lowly physical experience.

But let's consider a few things.

Our body, mind, spirit, and emotions are all parts of one grand consciousness and existence. One is not more important, or more advanced, than another. Is your hand more important than your eyes? Could your liver be more important than your kidneys? Each part serves a different function and is valuable in its own right. Being in a physical body is not a lower condition than being on the astral. On the contrary, it is a powerful extension of our spiritual essence.

Everyone who has consciousness and existence has a spirit, yet not every spirit has a physical body at all times. A body is something to be treasured, something that adds dimension to a spirit, rather than something that holds it back. If having a physical body were undesirable, why would beings continue to be reborn? Why would spirits be determined to come into a body? Why would we fear or resist dying?

In truth, we enjoy our physical experiences. It is exciting to interact with the physical world. We enjoy hugging our loved ones, eating tasty foods, playing sports, and having sexual encounters and other sensual experiences. These are not available in the same way on the astral plane.

The Limitations of the Astral

We have seen that on the astral plane, there is only energy. This energy has patterns, movement, intensity, and other qualities. When our consciousness encounters energy on the astral, it tries to make sense of what it "sees" based on what it already knows. It interprets the energy based on its own memories, experiences and filters. Therefore, our experiences on the astral are only as good as the information we have stored in our knowledge banks, and only as sharp and vivid as our imagination and memory allow.

How good is your imagination? Do you have a difficult time picturing a red apple with a stem? Can you make the picture revolve or rotate?

How accurate is your memory? Can you remember the taste of something you have not eaten since you were a child? How clearly can you remember someone's face whom you haven't seen in years?

If your imagination and memory are not sharp, your experience of the astral may be somewhat dull or faded.

Extinguishing the Spirit

When spirits have been without a physical body for hundreds or even thousands of years, their ability to recall details from the past diminishes. Their consciousness has fewer and fewer reference points, or key experiences. It begins to degenerate. Eventually, it deteriorates completely. The spirit finally loses consciousness and is extinguished.

Yes, a spirit can extinguish. When that occurs, it is no longer located in any time or space. It no longer exists at all. This is rare, but it does happen.

What would it be like to be extinguished? It would not be like dying, or like spending time in the astral. You would not just sit on the sidelines, observing other people making their way through life. If a spirit were fully extinguished, it simply would not exist. It would have no consciousness, no energy or aura, no form whatsoever. It would not even be aware that it ever had existed, or be able to experience total nothingness.

To Incarnate or Not to Incarnate?

Does it sound appealing to stop incarnating? Are the trials and tribulations of physical existence so traumatic that total annihilation is more desirable?

Not wanting to incarnate is similar to turning your back on loved ones and saying that you no longer want to be with them or help them. You are saying that you have no desire to interact with or help your Soul Group—or anyone else. When we are honest, that is not what most of us really want.

Even if you took an exceedingly long break from incarnating, what is the likelihood that you would remain a non-participant forever? Would you not want to have influence, interject opinions, or feel purposeful?

If a spirit chooses not to push forward or expand its consciousness through incarnation for long periods of time, and yet does maintain a limited existence, it might experience what could be called hell or purgatory. Mistakes would be made over and over again. Lessons would have to be repeated continuously. It might be like falling in a deep, dark well and living there indefinitely.

A spirit has the choice to reverse its path at any time. If its existence has been a great downward spiral, it only takes one decision to change that course. But that decision requires action. Making this kind of turnaround requires courage and conviction, but it is possible to reverse even the most desperate and anguished path.

When religions and philosophies extol the virtues of Nirvana or some other final resting place where souls exist infinitely in peace and harmony, they may well be talking about a continual state of mind that we earn through learning lessons—rather than a particular location in space and time.

When people speak of experiencing their final incarnation, they may be referring to the last lifetime that they will experience in a given physical plane. Our Earth plane, for instance. We know that there are places other than Earth where souls can incarnate. Whenever we complete all the lessons that any given world can provide for us, we are free to move on to another world. There are countless worlds to explore, and the odyssey of reincarnation takes place in infinite realms.

Case Study

Carolyn

We mentioned Carolyn earlier in this chapter. She had claimed that she wanted to "get out of here." Although she would not commit suicide, she admits to flirting with danger and death, in the hope that an accident would occur to end her life on Earth.

In her session, she wanted to discover her purpose for being in this life, so that she could understand her time here. Perhaps with that information, she could begin to relax into the experience, or at least understand the reason for it.

To access information on a person's Life Purpose, it is useful to target the time just before he or she enters the body. During that time, the spirit is contemplating choices and decisions concerning a particular family or set of circumstances. These choices and considerations help us see and understand the person's Life Purpose.

I asked Carolyn to imagine moving down an imaginary hall, and to choose a door that would lead her into the most appropriate past life for this quest. She described her door as plain brown wood, with a round brass knob. As she opened and stepped through the door, she could not determine whether she was indoors or outdoors. She knew only that it was dark.

She begins to notice her clothing, which was confining and in many layers. In her past life, she was wearing petticoats, a skirt, and an Amish style hat. She continued:

C: There is a feeling of contentment in whatever I am doing. My clothes feel confining. I see now that I am inside. There is a wood stove, and I am heating water. I'm humming and waiting for the water to boil. There is a baby in the other room, crying. The baby is wearing many layers, too. She is wearing a big hat that looks like the sun with ruffles. She has on a big sleeping gown. The baby is in a fancy cradle, homemade from wood. We live comfortably for that time. I'd say upper middle class. We have everything we need but we're not in a giant castle, or anything. Now my humming stopped and the baby is crying.

ML: Then what do you notice?

C: I make my tea. Now I'm sitting on a rocker made of the same wood. There is no real kitchen. The heat for the house comes from the same place where I make food. There is a separate room for sleeping.

ML: Do you notice anything else?

C: My heart is heavy. The humming is a cover-up. It seems my husband is at war. I see an image of him carrying a big gun. He loads it himself, like the old powder guns. I worry so much about him. There is no means of communication—no television, no radio, no newspapers, and no phones. He's just gone. And I'm here taking care of the baby. I rock in the chair until I fall asleep.

ML: Move ahead in time to the next relevant experience.

C: A soldier comes to the house on a horse. I'm feeling very heavy. I'm already crying by the time I open the door. He gives me a flag. It only has maybe thirteen stars. It's folded so I can't tell, but it doesn't have fifty stars. Oh, this must be the American Revolution. He says to me, "Your husband died forming our new country." I go to the baby. I can't tell if it's a boy or girl. Oh, it must be a boy, because I say, "You'll follow in your father's footsteps. He was a great man. You'll be a great man too."

ML: What else do you notice about that?

C: I don't seem to be worried, just very sad.

ML: When you think of your husband, picturing him in your mind, and feeling his energy, do you recognize him as anyone you have known in this lifetime?

C: (Pause) He's my dad in this life.

ML: And do you recognize the baby as anyone you know in this life?

C: (Pause) He feels like both my cousin and my daughter. Their energies are very similar.

ML: Moving ahead now to the next relevant experience in that lifetime, what do you notice next?

C: I'm in a place that is candlelit. It is big, with open windows. It is much different from the first place that was dark and felt closed in. My son is now sixteen or seventeen. I am worried about him. He is of the age to serve in the Army, and I don't want him to. He's so easy going and comforting to be around. He reassures me that I'll be okay, no matter where I am. It is clear now that he's definitely my daughter in this lifetime.

ML: What else do you notice about this?

C: I'm very worried. He is in a uniform, and going out the door. I'm left crying again.

ML: What happens next?

C: He comes home. He's a man. I don't know how much time has passed. I'm so relieved and happy to see him. I don't know my age. He moves me to another town. We travel by horse to get there. I am wearing giant skirts and I ride sidesaddle. It doesn't feel good.

ML: What else do you notice about this?

C: He has a wife now. She's pregnant. I feel like I will die before the baby is born. The wife feels like my son in this lifetime. Oh, so, my children were married! She's angry about me dying before the baby was born. She needed my help. I feel her hurt, even though I'm dead. It also feels as though he (my present son) brought some of that disappointment into this lifetime. I feel I have to make up for it.

She (the daughter-in-law then) felt I abandoned her. We weren't even blood related and I didn't know her that long. We had just met—but I guess not so recently on the soul level. And now I'm dead.

ML: What do you experience as you leave the physical body?

C: It's freeing. It's like light. As I leave, I notice the people there, and I see my indigo aura, surrounded with a rose color, leaving. I see my aura floating up and becoming part of the universe. I free-float. It's like being in a vast ocean.

ML: As you left the body, did you notice anything else?

C: I feel the emotions of my son and his wife. They are both crying. I try to send them my essence, to let them know that I'm at peace. I can't get through to them. I want to move on, not stay there and dwell in this. I'm part of the ocean of the universe. It's really wonderful, comforting.

ML: Allow yourself to move ahead in time and space toward the 20th century, to the moments before attaching to the body in this lifetime. What do you begin to notice about that experience?

C: The water is getting rougher. It's as if a whirlpool is forming. I'm resistant. I want to stay holding on to the smooth water on top. My drop of water is being sucked down. I'm being told that I need this experience. The message is given in thoughts, not in words.

ML: What do you notice about being sucked down?

C: It operates like a whirlpool. There's no way out. I have no choice. Then I notice being in my mother's womb.

ML: Going back to the moments when you are experiencing the whirlpool, what else did you know about the reasons for being sucked down?

C: I am told I need the experience. I am to help lead.

ML: Lead whom, for what reason?

C: The evolution of change is hard and the strongest souls have to lead the people through the changes. I'm strong and have to be one of them here. The changes are much more subtle than what I've been waiting for.

ML: What do you mean by that?

C: I have been waiting for something terrible to happen to the world. This is indicating that it will be different. It will be subtler. It will be a lot of little terrible things.

ML: What else do you know?

C: I had no choice. This is bigger than my soul. I don't know what to call it—destiny, a master soul, a universal plan? I don't know. But I couldn't resist. My soul didn't want to be here.

ML: And you said that you noticed being in your mother's womb. Can you tell me more about what you notice there?

C: It's peaceful, warm, and cozy in there. I feel loved and wanted.

ML: What else do you know?

C: It's so warm and comforting. I don't have my negativity and resistance in the womb. It's okay there. It's even safer than floating in the universe. It's contained, but comfortably contained. It's so much fun moving around. And I can move more and more. I don't want to come out.

ML: What do you notice next?

C: I see my mother in labor. She's being pushed in a gurney. I don't see my father. They give her drugs to put her to sleep. I'm thinking, "No, no, I don't want to leave here." I see forceps. I didn't know that I was delivered with forceps, but since my mom was drugged, she may not remember either. However, I see the doctor pulling me out with a tool on my head. I'm resisting.

ML: What do you do to resist?

C: I see myself in a headstand position – not really breach, but digging in with my legs. I tie myself in my umbilical cord…no I just tangle it around my feet because I don't want to die. Yet, I also don't want to leave. They get me out, and I'm screaming. I see my father smiling, but he's looking at me through glass. The doctors and nurses hold me first, and I don't want them. I want my parents.

ML: What else do you notice?

C: I'm screaming. I recognize my father right away. I'm not sure I knew my mother from before. However, I feel safe with her. She'll take care of me. It's obvious to me that I really know him. I feel the energy connection between us. I see a color dance—our auras—and the sense that "we're back together again." It's hard to describe. I just had a flash! I had that dance with both of my kids at their birth. I was the recipient of their energy dances. They came early; they wanted to be here.

ML: What else do you notice about your birth?

C: My mother is glowing when she wakes up and gets to hold me. The connection is still not clear, but it feels like she will be my protector.

ML: So does this experience help you to understand why you are in this life, even though you always have felt the resistance to living?

C: It answers the question. Yet, it doesn't make it any easier. I now know that it's bigger than I am. Now I can remember that fact when things get difficult.

This regression not only answered Carolyn's questions about the reasons for coming into this life, it gave her a view of experiences between lives and during the birth process.

4

How Reincarnation Works: The Nuts and Bolts

"A journey of a thousand miles must begin with a single step."
—Lao-tzu

We have seen that reincarnation nurtures the spirit, and brings enormous benefits in this life. This chapter is about how that works—the mechanics of reincarnation, if you will.

To review... We all live one long lifetime as a spirit. Our purpose is to maintain and enrich our existence and consciousness. That long life is divided into parts, much like the chapters of a book, which we call lifetimes or incarnations. From our earthbound perspective, we call the time between these incarnations being "dead." However, we are alive both when we are in physical bodies, and when we exist on the astral plane without bodies between incarnations.

We usually confine our memories when we are "alive" on Earth to events that have occurred since our current birth—but we can choose to remember other lives through the vehicle of past life regression. We can do this easily and regularly with a bit of practice. To begin that process, let's look in more detail at how reincarnation works—beginning with the astral plane, where we exist when we are not in a body.

The Astral Plane

The astral is where spirits who do not currently inhabit a body reside. When we die, our conscious awareness moves to the astral plane. We can also project our consciousness there intentionally while we are still in a physical body. The astral plane acts like a freeway or thoroughfare, surrounding and connecting all planes of existence. When we travel to another plane or dimension, we do so via the astral plane.

Even when we are in a physical body, a part of us is seated in the astral plane. This is called our astral body. When we are focused in the astral plane, either by astral projection or by death, our consciousness is embodied in the energy field or aura of this astral body.

Actually, the astral body is just one of several layers of bodies that we all possess. Various schools of thought label them differently, but they are essentially:

- *Physical:* the body
- *Astral:* consciousness, self-awareness
- *Spiritual:* raw energy
- *Mental:* cognition, mind, some conceptualization
- *Emotional:* reaction, assessment, capable of fears, guilt, and feelings
- *Etheric:* imagination, electrical current
- *Preternatural:* power, as the energy in a martial arts punch or when a woman can lift a car in an emergency

When we are "alive" in a physical body, our consciousness is manifest in all of these bodies. When we "die," we have all of them except the physical body. During astral projection, the astral body leaves the proximity of the physical body and travels on its own for a short time. At death, the physical body is permanently vacated by all the other bodies.

Life Between Lives

In most past life regressions, after my clients have experienced a particular past lifetime, I ask them to move to the time of death. This is so that they can understand their situation at the end of that lifetime. When they have determined the age at which they died and the cause of the death, they release from the body and experience the death process itself. After that, we begin delving into what happens between lives.

On the astral plane, there is nothing physical. There are no physical bodies, houses, modes of transportation, or vegetation. There is no need for food, clothing, or jobs. Everything in the astral is sensed as an energy field that may have patterns, colors, direction, speed, and consciousness. It can appear that objects are floating through us, or that we are floating through them. The energy we experience in the astral may be part of a conscious being, or not.

When we encounter other energies in the astral, we seek to make sense of them by searching our minds for something familiar, and then imposing that image or interpretation on to the energy. We want to define and describe it in terms that explain our experience—and these descriptions are shaped by our beliefs, opinions, and other mental filters. If we "see" a deceased relative, for example, we are actually sensing their energy field, and then projecting the image of their familiar face on to that energy. This helps us relax into the connection, and that strengthens our memory of the interaction.

All communication in the astral is telepathic. A spirit, or energy form, has thoughts—but no organs for speaking or hearing. We identify people much as we do during life on Earth. Some people we know, and some we don't. We are drawn to some people, and not to others.

Whatever we imagine to be true in the afterlife, that is what we are likely to encounter. So when we sense that a male energy has come to guide us, we may choose to label him as Jesus, Mohammed, father, brother, or friend. Christians may report seeing or speaking with Jesus. Buddhists may describe passing through Bardos. These may be only our interpretations, based on our beliefs. The more we learn, and the better we become at deciphering reality, the more accurate our interpretations become.

Arriving On The Astral

When my clients go through the death process during their regressions, they frequently experience a calm, detached, floating feeling. They often express delight at being free from the physical body, especially if the body had been experiencing a lot of pain or disease before the death.

We have seen that our experience as we arrive in the astral depends on how we interpret the various energies we encounter. Some people describe seeing a bright light, and gravitating toward it. Others see their spirit guides or loved ones who have preceded them in death. Or they may find themselves in a classroom, learning something new. Most people are content with whatever vision or sensations they experience, and frequently prefer the post-death state to being in a physical body. Rarely do they regret dying, or dislike their experience in the astral.

When there is regret, it usually involves a purpose that was unfulfilled in that lifetime, or a premature separation from their loved ones (typically their small children), a recognition that they made choices that did not further their growth, or a suicide. In the case of suicide, the astral plane gives them perspective. They realize that no circumstances on Earth were as insurmountable or devastating as they may have appeared. Released from their physical confines, these people have the opportunity to see the many options they had and the actions they could have taken to improve their situation and complete their purpose on Earth.

People who have not been practicing their sight or their ability to astral project can find themselves somewhat disoriented when they arrive in the astral. They need a period of adjustment which may be brief or lengthy, depending on the flexibility of their awareness and the amount of guidance they receive.

Next comes a period of assessment. What experiences will provide the most growth? What can be accomplished while out of a physical body? What are the benefits of returning to a body? What course of action will best serve the spirit? Some put off decisions about their next incarnation until after they have had a long period of rest or adventure in the astral. They use their time in the astral to explore, learn, rebalance, and make plans for their next incarnation. Some even serve as spirit guides for loved ones. Other spirits decide to reincarnate rather quickly.

But the astral plane is not always the blissful Nirvana, the place of complete enlightenment, that many believe it is.

Being Alert

Just as it is wise to shy away from certain streets at night, it is important to learn which places it is safe and unsafe to travel in the astral. Our newspapers are filled with stories of people who lie, cheat, steal, rape, murder, take unfair advantage, tease, play tricks, and harm others. Those people eventually wind up in the astral. We all go there when we die, regardless of the kind of lives we have led.

When people arrive in the astral, they do not necessarily transform from a negative orientation to a positive one. Their characters remain intact. If they are hiding from the error of their ways, they will not suddenly be willing and able to face those truths just because they no longer have a body.

Many of my clients have not wanted to think about negative spirits. They try to will them away, pretend they don't exist, or ignore them in the hope of not attracting their attention. If society denied that crime existed in the streets, would that make this world safer? Has the world situation gotten any better when governments have ignored inhumane atrocities around the globe? No.

Ignoring negatives only makes us blind. It doesn't change the nature of reality. What each individual chooses to do regarding the negative aspects of reality is a personal option. Balance comes with experience, and through striving to be stronger, brighter, and more capable of handling any situation that arises.

I say these things not to alarm, but simply to point out the existence of negative spirits in the astral. Be alert, and proceed as you would in a similar situation in the physical world.

Just Because You're Dead, Doesn't Mean You're Smart

I often hear people say, "Oh, I can't wait until I get to the other side, so I'll understand everything." They believe that all they have to do is die, and they will escape whatever may be bothering them and attain complete enlightenment. Moreover, they are certain that they will never make those same mistakes again. They believe they will have perfect vision and omniscience in the astral, perhaps because their spirit guides are present with them. If you're with your guide, then you'll know everything, right? Truthfully, it doesn't work that way.

My work with numerous clients has convinced me that we are not suddenly enlightened, just because we have "passed through the veil" and find ourselves in the astral. In fact, we gain only a slightly broader perspective of reality and our place in it than we had when we were in a body. We may have greater insight into the consequences of our choices, and be more aware of the larger patterns of our personality and behavior—but we do not suddenly gain access to enormous wisdom that was not a part of our consciousness before death. Our psychic vision is only slightly clearer than our capacity for insight was when we were in a body.

The best strategy for gaining wisdom and enlightenment is to work hard while in a physical body. The best investment is to learn lessons that help us clarify our vision, strengthen our morals, heal emotional baggage, and acquire knowledge. This world is our proving ground. It is through the experiences in this physical world that we make the greatest progress.

If all it took to gain enlightenment were death, wouldn't we all be enlightened by now? After all, we have died many times. If it were that easy, there would no longer be any crime, or lessons to be learned, and we would have only other enlightened souls with whom to play.

Eventually, most spirits choose to leave the astral and incarnate into a body. While it is possible for a spirit to learn while in the astral, the testing of that new knowledge happens during a physical manifestation. It is meaningless to be morally upstanding in your consciousness, unless your behaviors in physical reality reflect those choices.

Possibility And Probability

What determines the kind of lifetimes we experience? Let's look first at what is possible, and what is probable in this area.

As you look at a circle, it appears to be finite. It looks as if it is limited by its perimeter or circumference. But according to the laws of geometry, an infinite number of points will fit within any circle. In this regard, a circle is actually infinite. The same is true for a spirit. Each spirit has infinite possibilities for experiences and lifetimes—infinite possibilities for its own expression.

Within this infinity of possibilities, certain types of lifetimes are more probable than others. You can see in the figure below the darker, smaller circle of probabilities within the larger circle of possibilities. The circle that represents our probable lifetimes can shift at any moment, based on our choices and actions. When we choose to commit violent crimes, for example, our circle of probability shifts to include increasingly more negative, dangerous, painful, and deadly experiences. When we choose to live by a healthy, life-enhancing moral code, the probabilities shift toward positive opportunity, health, kindness, gratitude, and acceptance.

The movement of this circle of probabilities, within the larger circle of possibilities, is controlled by our conscious and subconscious spiritual focus—which includes our character, personality, emotions, intentions, and actions. We can shift it at will by shifting our focus, intentions, consciousness, values, and decisions. This may be one explanation of the creation and resolution of karma. It may also help support the concept of the Law of Attraction. It looks like this:

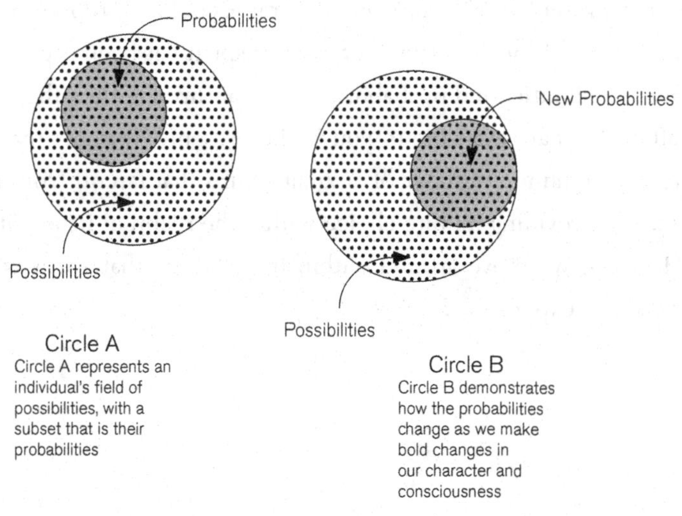

Probabilities
Possibilities
New Probabilities
Possibilities
Circle A
Circle A represents an individual's field of possibilities, with a subset that is their probabilities
Circle B
Circle B demonstrates how the probabilities change as we make bold changes in our character and consciousness

Our Infinite Universe

But wait! If all of us have circles with infinite numbers of points in them, does that mean that we have all been everybody else at some point? No. We all have our own circles of possibilities, and our own circle of probabilities within it. My circle contains an infinite number of points, and so does yours. But none of the points in one circle are the same as the points in someone else's circle. Both are infinite, but they are not the same.

We do not know how many lifetimes a spirit experiences over the course of its existence. The number is probably different for each of us—and we can also incarnate on an infinite number of planes other than the Earth plane—but we do know that the possibilities are infinite.

CHANGING THE FUTURE—AND THE PAST

Another way to look at our past lives is on a grid.

First, imagine that each column on Grid A below represents a roll of film. As we know, film consists of a length of contiguous freeze frame shots. Each frame exists separately and simultaneously, but when the film is rolled through a projector very rapidly, we see one moving picture—not a series of individual freeze frames.

Now imagine that one column of pictures is your current lifetime, and that one particular frame is you, now, at this particular moment. The frames above it represent your future, and the frames below it represent your past. Each moment of the entire history of your spirit has been captured on film. All your possibilities and probabilities, are captured in the other columns—and all of them are available to you in the present. Not only that, but each frame has an infinite number of auxiliary films that fan off from it in every dimension, providing infinite choice within the realm of its possibilities.

How can we move around within the grid, so that we maximize and optimize our experience?

These grids demonstrate the concept of infinite lifetimes—past, present/parallel and future. Each column is like a film strip with the future moving upward, and the past downward.

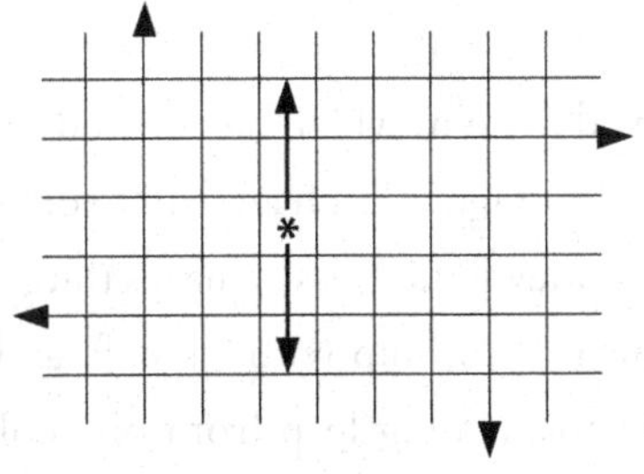

Grid A

Grid A shows a person moving along their present path.

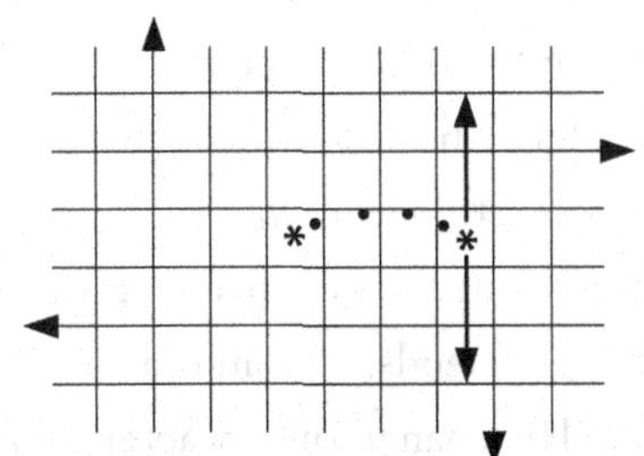

Grid B

Grid B demonstrates what happens when a bold change is made, altering the future, and therefore altering the past.

The Pebble in a Pool

Imagine a still pool. A pebble drops into the water, creating waves along the surface that radiate out in concentric circles.

The same thing happens when we make changes in our lives, whether in our character or in our choices. We might decide to change careers, or to work on our anger so that we can express more kindness. We might have children, or stop smoking, or become a Big Brother or Sister. We might make negative choices as well—taking advantage of someone in a business deal, or being intentionally cruel to someone.

Any energetic shift radiates out from us on many levels. These radiant waves affect all other aspects of our spirit, and even touch our future and our past lives. The stronger the changes we make, the greater the shift.

Changing Tracks

Looking at Grid B above, we can see that making a significant change puts us on *a whole different column of film*. A small change might put us on the column next to where we were. A huge change might put us on a column way over to the right or left. In either case, we are on a whole new strip of film. A whole new track. We have a different future, and we also have a different past!

Since all time is now, and since we have an infinite range of possibilities, we have always had this new future and past. It just appears new because our point of reference has changed from where we have been, to our new position on the other track.

Here's how it works. Suppose Ed has lived a life in which he cheated on his wife, stole from his employer, and took advantage of his friends. At some point, he decides to change. He returns the money to his boss, squares things with his friends, and finds a way to honor his relationship with his wife and kids. His change of character allows him to make a big leap from one column to another.

Obviously, his future is going to be a lot better than it might have without the changes. But his past will improve as well. On one level, he will see everything in his past differently—and probably a bit more responsibly. He will be less likely to blame his parents and others, and more likely to see his own part in what had been his descent. On another level, he will actually be living a different life. That life will be lived on an entirely different strip of film, and will have its own past.

We need to look at time a little differently when we think about reincarnation, since we are dealing with possibilities that we don't usually consider.

Time And Reincarnation

Here on Earth, especially before we become aware of our past lives and begin exploring them, we may think of time in a sequential way. Events occur chronologically, one after the other, in an apparently logical order. We pick the apple, *then* we eat it—not the other way around.

Time is a dimension experienced on Earth, even though we cannot see it in the same way that we can see length, width, and depth. It allows us to measure speed and distance. More importantly, it gives us sanity. Without a sense of progressive time, we would perceive that all things were happening simultaneously.

However, physicists are beginning to hypothesize, and some even assert with certainty, that all time is actually occurring simultaneously. *Now!*

All Time is Now

Imagine that there is no beginning or end to time, and that an infinite array of events and lifetimes are all occurring simultaneously. Our minds have to stretch in order to contemplate such a thing, because we are used to thinking in terms of chronological time, but it is a fascinating meditation. I invite you to expand your consciousness, and open up your imagination, while we pursue it for a moment.

In other planes of existence, time is experienced differently from how we experience it here. On the astral plane, for instance, it is possible to move around in time quite fluidly. We can go into the future, into the past, and back again. Time can also be warped on the astral plane, so it is possible to spend several years studying with your spirit guides in the course of one night's sleep here on Earth.

This idea that "All time is now"—that all events, in all lifetimes, are happening simultaneously—includes the notion that we can focus our conscious attention wherever we choose. Each moment, each event, is just waiting for our attention. Whatever moment we choose, that is our "now." Most of the time, we are focused here on Earth, on the aspect of our spirit that is in this particular body now.

Point of Focus

All aspects of our spirit exist simultaneously, but our "point of focus" is the one to which we are paying attention at the moment. Our point of focus becomes very important in a universe where all time is occurring simultaneously. Without a primary focus, we would be in all moments of our infinite experience at the same time. Although all those moments actually do exist at one time, in the present, our capacity to focus on one moment at a time gives us continuity, adventure, learning, curiosity, discovery, opportunity for choice—and ultimately, sanity.

Our point of focus is the only place where healing and change can take place. It is only in this very moment, where we are focusing *now,* that change can occur. At the same time, it is important to remember that when we visit past lives, or alternative aspects of our spirit—or even memories of this life—

because they are the object of our point of focus, we alter them to some extent. The degree to which they are affected by our focus depends on our intention and the intensity of our contact with them.

Time and Possibilities

As we think along these lines, we must consider the possibility that we do not have to incarnate "chronologically," by our Earth perspective. The next time we incarnate, for instance, we can choose to focus on a lifetime that we think of as occurring earlier than our present lifetime.

It is also possible that we could repeat any given lifetime, if we chose to do so. We could return to a lifetime and attempt to do things differently. (This may be one of several possible explanations for the phenomenon of "déjà vu.") If we did this, what would it mean to the people we knew in those lifetimes? What would they experience if we were to relive, and change, our part in what happened?

If we repeated a lifetime, bringing with us deeper understanding and making new choices, we would not follow exactly the same "film strip" that we were moving along previously. We would have made significant changes, so we would be moving along one of the infinite parallel paths, where the other people from that time were also making different choices and having different reactions to us. Along this new path, there might even be new people with whom to have relationships, and we might not encounter people who were in that life previously. Making big changes would have altered the path, and our experience of it, very significantly.

Old Soul, New Soul

When we consider that all time is now, we have to rethink the idea of "old souls" and "new souls."

When people use these terms, the implication is usually that "new souls" are less evolved or advanced than "old souls." But according to our new, expanded idea of time, no soul or spirit has been around longer than any other. The spirit that may appear "more advanced" does not necessarily have a longer existence than any other spirit. It may have a greater density of experience, awareness, and knowledge—but it is not "older."

People also tend to think of "new" or "old" souls strictly in terms of spiritual focus. "Old souls" are more interested in spiritual matters and seem to have acquired some wisdom. "New souls" tend to ignore their spiritual nature, close down their thinking and emotions, and pay little attention to personal growth and development.

This way of measuring a soul's progress is not necessarily valid. It could be that someone gained great power and wisdom, but then experienced a severe trauma in a "recent" lifetime. That person might choose to shut down for awhile, and therefore appear "young" or "new"—when actually, he or she might have been quite advanced.

Forgetting And Remembering

Clients often ask, "If it's so great to have these memories available to us, why do we forget our past lives?" Some even argue that we aren't meant to remember our past lives, and that regressions should be taboo.

I believe that exploring our spirit's path through ever deepening and widening experiences is our birthright—and also a vital part of our hero's journey toward self-awareness and growth. We have experienced every moment of that journey. It is a record of our own existence, and it is ours to have and use.

So why do we forget? There are three main causes of amnesia concerning our past lives:

Life's Distractions

We arrive here on Earth with a lot of information about our past lives—but things get very busy, very quickly. We have a lot to do when we first slip into our bodies.

In the womb, we may be fully conscious of our past lives, our purpose, and our reasons for coming into this life. Then comes the moment of birth, which is tremendously stressful and sometimes even life-threatening for both mother and child. Once we emerge from the womb, there is a period of adjustment that is more or less traumatic, depending on how it is managed. We have to deal with bright lights, cold air, breathing, learning to drink our mother's milk, having people handle us, and a host of other trials.

When we go home, we may encounter mean or jealous siblings, doting grandparents, and household pets. Then there is the struggle to get our thoughts, desires and needs communicated in a world inhabited by people who are not telepathic, and perhaps not even sensitive. We also have to learn how to operate the physical body—grabbing, sitting, standing, and walking. Then, after a couple of years, we begin the process of learning language. It's a wonder we can remember anything, let alone our past lives or time in the astral.

By this time, much of our pre-birth knowledge is forever locked in the recesses of our subconscious mind. We've simply been too busy and distracted to deal with it—and we haven't even started school, made friends, been asked to attend any meetings, or acquired our first PDA!

Societal Norms

At around age four, we may be able to communicate what remains of our memories of other lifetimes—but our words are often ignored. We may be patronized, told that our stories are fantasy, and urged to run along and play.

The memories recede into the shadows, locked away from the conscious mind, like acts of shame. Years later, if we become curious to regain those memories, we may have to invest money and time in recovering them.

Most spiritual belief systems include some version of an afterlife, but in some cultures and religious beliefs, these memories are seen as unreal or evil. People who are subject to these systems may never learn what past experiences have contributed to their present selves.

Avoidance

Another reason that people forget the experiences of past lives is that they want to escape negative memories—which may elicit shame, horror, regret, remorse, fear, boredom, or grief. They had hoped that when that life was over, everything that happened would just go away. In the current life, they may use phrases like, "It will all be over when I'm dead," and "You are born with a clean slate."

We all have painful memories. Who hasn't had their heart broken, lost a loved one, endured a painful experience, or deeply regretted something they said or did? Difficult experiences are part of the human condition. They are part of our hero's journey, and serve as measures of our character. They bring tests and lessons that accelerate our growth. When we are in pain or crisis, we tend to examine our choices and behaviors more closely. We become more creative about seeking solutions. We "work on ourselves" and strengthen our character in ways that we don't always do during the easy times because there is nothing to "fix."

Yet all too frequently, people's attitude is, "Leave the past in the past." This implies that it is better to bury difficult memories than to draw them out, value the lessons they teach us, and use them to build our character.

Putting Down The Burden

The other side of this coin is that some people *cling* to painful memories, using them to define their reality and their sense of self. They "can't possibly succeed" because they were mistreated by their father in this lifetime or a past life. They "will never be loved" because their mother didn't love them. They give up on life, and use past occurrences—in this or other lifetimes—as an excuse. They are willing to bring up the unpleasant memories, but not willing to resolve them and let them go.

They are like the guy who goes to the gym and works out strenuously to sculpt and shape his muscles—but then, when the workout is finished, carries all the equipment around with him to work, to lunch, and home at night. True bodybuilders leave the weights in the gym, and simply enjoy the results. The purpose of bringing up painful memories is to face and resolve them so that we can move forward unencumbered by them—just as the purpose of working out is to enjoy the sculpted body, but not to carry around the weights.

We don't have to drag every difficult, stressful, or traumatic thing that ever happened to us around with us wherever we go. Past life regression helps us see that carrying those burdens only causes stress, pain, blockage, phobias, and dysfunction. We can use visiting past lives to heal the residue of those difficult episodes, and leave them in their rightful places, while bringing with us into the present all the wisdom and growth that we earned from them.

When we heal issues from other incarnations, it becomes easier to do the same for painful events and experiences of our present life. As new traumas and stresses occur, we have the tools and understanding to release them, so that we don't carry their effects into the future.

REFRAMING

One of these tools is reframing. Reframing is a way to use difficult or painful experiences from past lives, and from this life, in positive ways to move us along our hero's path.

Duke Ellington said it best: "I merely took the energy it takes to pout and wrote some blues." That is a classic description of reframing. Instead of pouting and complaining, he transmuted that energy into music that was an expression of his soul.

People sometimes say they are afraid of experiencing past lives, because they might see that they have committed some atrocity. They don't want to find out that they murdered or raped someone, or that they cheated or lied.

Most of us have done things that bring shame or regret, in this life and in past lives. The question now is: What will we do with that experience? Will we let it drag us down forever, using our energy to keep it under wraps, or will we use it to grow?

When people are afraid of discovering negative characteristics, it is likely that the characteristic is already in play on some level in this lifetime. If the anger, jealousy, or other negative characteristic were completely foreign to them, they wouldn't fear it. They might not want to see it in action during a past life—but in fact, looking at that past life may show them how much they have grown, and how far they have come, since they demonstrated that characteristic or behavior! If that is the case, it definitely works to their advantage to uncover that past life and take a look.

If they have not made progress, all the more reason to bring out the negativity and work on it. The negative emotions and behaviors we most want to block or deny are precisely the ones we need to examine, as soon as possible.

Blocking painful or frightening memories requires a tremendous amount of energy. This creates stress, which can lead to premature aging and disease. Furthermore, there is a risk that we may act out those negative characteristics or repeat the negative behaviors if we have not faced and resolved them.

How It Works

In my early years of facilitating past lives, a lovely, spiritually oriented woman came to my office for a regression. As she went into trance, she became very curious about her experience. She described the feeling of sneaking down an alley. Then she felt she was actually stalking someone. She realized, to her horror, that she was a serial killer, much like Jack the Ripper. She was astonished as these events unfolded in her mind.

After her regression, our discussion centered around her revulsion at the memory. Since she would never consider such behavior in this life, it was important for her to recognize and appreciate that she had learned many lessons and grown significantly in the time since that life.

For this client, *the reframing was taking an experience that she had considered negative, and looking at it from the positive perspective of how much she had grown.* Reframing difficult memories means not only measuring the distance we have come, but also extracting the learning, wisdom, and other benefits from those experiences. Reframing may not change what happened, but it helps us see events in a different light.

Beth's case offers a poignant example of reframing, and learning the lessons that painful events can offer us.

Case Study

Beth

Beth came to the office wanting to resolve several issues around the abuse she suffered as a child. After the usual induction and preparation for a past life regression, we proceeded.

B: I'm traveling in a carriage. There is a man in a hat with me. I'm a woman. I'm feeling scared. I think we are getting married. I'm not exactly sure. But I know that I'm nervous. I am thinking, "What am I getting into?"

ML: What do you know about the man?

B: He's relaxed. He is assuring me by saying, "We'll make it. We're almost there. I'll take care of you." I'm wondering why he doesn't recognize my beauty. He keeps strategizing, saying things like, "How can I (trails off)... She's beautiful, talented and attractive." It becomes obvious that he possesses me to help his position and lifestyle. He expects me to always be the belle.

ML: Move ahead a short ways into the future. What do you notice next?

B: I get pregnant. He has turned mean and abusive. My dress is tattered. It's a dusty lifestyle. I have a boy, like his father. I feel alienated. I'm exhausted. I'm filled with grief. I feel trapped.

ML: What else do you notice?

B: There are ladies who come. They make me feel better. They are used to the prairie. I feel like I might as well die. I do die early. I feel like I'm sixty-five, but I am more like thirty-two. My son is thirteen.

ML: Do you notice anything else?

B: That's all.

ML: What did you learn from visiting that lifetime?

B: I learned to not stray from the path ever again. There is a place for me. It's not wrong to be me. I am feeling guilty. I know that I don't have enough self-esteem.

ML: If the aspect of you in that lifetime could share her wisdom with the aspect of you here, what would she tell you?

B: "Don't do what I did. Harm will come." She tells me to marry for love, not for the wrong reasons, like change or escape. Don't listen to promises or to people who say they know better how to live my life. I have to provide my own certainty. Solidity is an illusion, if you aren't walking the path. She's glad that I came by and wishes me well. She says, "Don't ever marry out of comfort. Be who you are. You'll fit in. Fit in for yourself. Don't leave your Self behind."

ML: Is there anything you would like to say or do for her?

B: I hold her. I want to take her away from that lifetime. She's horrified to leave. "What will I do; what will I be?" I put her in bed, to be nursed and re-educated. Her boy says goodbye to her. He might have been my ex-fiancé from my early twenties in this lifetime.

To reframe Beth's difficult childhood, we decided to request information concerning her purpose in life and her choice of parents. We started in an imaginary hallway, choosing a door that would lead us to the pertinent information.

B: The door is framed with a big clear glass mosaic heart. It's almost like angel wings.

ML: When you are ready, open the door.

B: It's creaky. It opens into dark, deep space. There is no landing. No stars. It's two-thirds open now. I'm not sure of going out there. It is a soft nothingness. It would feel good on my skin. I wouldn't have to do anything. It's the ultimate hibernation. I want to let go. I let go. There is nothing. I'm caught by an invisible puffiness. I'm not falling into oblivion. I wonder, did my subconscious set up the support?

ML: What else do you notice?

B: I'm passed from one place to another, bouncing gently. I lie down. A being comes, as though through cellophane. His face and hands come out through this membrane. Now, I feel like I am being held in the branches of a tree. It's a solid tree, with firm branches. I'm afraid they will break. It appears that a stork comes. There is a rattle shaped like a plastic safety pin. The stork is wearing a captain's hat. Am I a baby now?

ML: What do you notice about that?

B: I am feeling a tugging at my pelvis. I'm being rocked by my limbs. They are preparing me to be born. It seems someone is saying that I've rested enough. "It's time for her to get ready." Huh? I feel like I'm coming out of a sleep. I start to sit up. I say, "Where do you want me to go?

ML: What is the response?

B: I have resistance to what they are telling me. It's not easy. They are being soft with me. I start to panic. I get rigid. I now seem to look like me as an adult, with this body and face.

ML: What do you notice next?

B: There is a pulse of light, an energy, through the tree. It's getting me going. I'm being nudged away. It's hard; I'm really resistant. They want me to go away. They tell me, "Sorry, its time." I'm baffled. What? Why?

ML: What do you know about that?

B: I notice a long tunnel. I'm being shown where I will be going. Oh no. This does not bode well. I notice a striping, then stars. There is a light at the end. I notice fuzzy white or gray. I'm resisting so much. My body doesn't want this happening to me. There is a fuzzy light. It comes to me. Now I am sitting in a cloud. I'm still attached to the previous place. Someone reaches out from the clouds. Is it me? They give me something to come into. I don't know what this is. Anyway, I let go of the tunnel. It's dark now. I'm in the clouds floating, in an angel outfit. Someone points at the tunnel, reminding me I can't go back home. This is not good news for this body.

ML: What else do you notice about this?

B: I hear a message, "You are going to go through a lot of paralyzing, overriding emotions. You'll forget who you are many times over. There will be glimmers that will seem like a speck. You will feel separate, abandoned, and lost. You will go in through your mother and not remember.

ML: What else do you know about your situation?

B: I'm thinking, "My father is crazy. My mother is reaching out to me. I can't believe I am being born to these extremely toxic people.

ML: And then what happens?

B: I want my own voice. I shake my head silently. I resist. Now I'm here in this body. In that moment of transition, I forget. I'm sunshiny. I take on a vehicle of sunshine. I keep myself from crossing over to their world. Instead, it made them want me more. I do that so they think I am incredible and will want me. I want it on my terms.

ML: Then what happens?

B: I am given over to my father, by my mother. She knows we're connected. Energetically it feels bad, and she's terrified, but she does it. My father takes me on as if I'm his trophy. He's waiting for me. I'm full of light. He wants me sexually. There is no time to grow up. No time. I'm given to him, like in other cultures. I'm two years old or less. There is no chance to get my bearings. I see my grandfather in the perimeter.

ML: Let's go back to before you connected with this body. Go back to the time before this started, before the beginning of this story you just told me. What do you notice about that time?

B: Again, I'm in that tree. That being has facial features that are distinct and beautiful. It's attempting to help me. It's time for me to rest.

ML: Then what happens?

B: I'm being jostled around. I'm flipped like a pancake. Why is that being so angry? It hurts to be prepared. It makes me wake up and get ready. My body is not happy. I'm being tortured in a way. I go along. I offer no fight.

ML: What else do you notice about the being?

B: He is like my grandfather, but in that place he is so evil, so disgusting. I also notice another being in spirit form. He says, "Look at this one. We got her. I told you we could do it. I wouldn't have believed it."

ML: What else do you notice about that?

B: They were tracking me down. They are negotiating with each other for me. Who gave me up? I thought there was more to me. I let them pull me in. I thought I was tricking them. It seemed like a good deal. I thought I could do God's work, in disguise. I thought I would let them think they got me. It was cruel for me to do that to myself. It was unfair. I set it up to come into danger. That wasn't nice. What happened? Who led me to this?

ML: What do you notice about the answer to those questions?

B: I'm floating in space. The evil faces are uncloaked, in blips. They are watching, grinning. Who did this? It is so not okay. Then the process began. It's as though they are licking their chops. There is the tree there. It is a respite for strength and rest.

ML: Then what do you notice?

B: They picked my mother. She wouldn't stop it. They were thinking, "But you'll be of our lineage." To me it is like being bacteria on a sponge. Someone was masquerading as God. Who sent me? Was it a false god?

ML: I would like to ask your subconscious to take you to an experience that will help you to understand the answers.

B: I'm experiencing happiness. I'm out of my body, but connected to a human form. It feels like maybe this took place in Atlantis.

ML: And then what do you notice?

B: I'm drawn into a vortex. It's powerful. I seem to come too close and then I am pulled in. I can't get out. I spin. I'm out of control. There is confusion. It's a whirlwind, down, down. I see my grandfather, and then the tree. I'm dizzy. I am whacked up so much that I'm totally off center.

ML: What have you learned from experiencing this regression?

B: I'm not supposed to be here. This is not good. I shouldn't have had to come through like this. I want out of this mess. I'm like Dorothy, with the evil witch. There are so many illusions and she tries so hard. Still she's taken from her home. I'll never be the same.

ML: What is it that has changed in you?

B: My innocence was trashed. I'm trashed. Now a force wants to pull me off my path. This is not good.

ML: Now that you are grown, and with the knowledge that you gained today, what wisdom did these experiences give you?

B: I can see well. Not a lot gets past me. I don't always choose to go with my intuition, but I generally know things. I carry my religion in my heart. I understand it somehow. Was it branded in me? I didn't die and I won't die. I see why I have always felt I had to fight for my life. I was never free to be. I understand an enormous amount about human motivation, greed, fear, and avarice. I see why things happen on this planet. A big piece was missing. Now I understand. I am a spiritual being, with compassion and depth. I can look at the dark beings. Sometimes there are evil beings, and I can take a stance.

ML: How will this information change the way you do things in the future?

B: I need to take my soul and hold it. I need to just hold it. I can feel the direct connection to God. It is never ending nor will it ever stop. I need to be strong and energetic. I need a cellular healing and never fall prey to that energy. That was my weakness.

ML: Is there anything else?

B: It was not enough to know that I'm a high energy being. I need to surround myself with people who see me and adore me. I can grow, like a skyscraper. I need tenderness, nurturing, and to be held. There is an exchange—the old for the new. I am giving up my entire way of looking at my self. People are lured to die before their time because of this force.

ML: If you are to live fully now, in your highest energy and purpose, what have you learned that you need to do?

B: The highlight of what I do is to see people come alive by something I've done. I enjoy being able to see a shift in them. It gives them hope, a jump-start, and activation. Then they can go out and be, and do what they are to do. I'm a purpose activator. I wake people up when they are ready.

ML: And what is the purpose of that?

B: To populate the planet, and help in the balance between those that are asleep and those that are awake.

ML: And the purpose of that?

B: The world naturally heals without chaos. I help God. Now I'm not sure God needs or wants that. Maybe I'm not supposed to help God.

ML: Where are you in all this? What are you doing for you?

B: I'm not. My friends always say, "You need to take care of yourself."

ML: What would be different if you were taking care of yourself?

B: There would be sensuality. My body, my skin—I'd nurture and pamper myself, and I would be more feminine. I would enjoy that. Things would come naturally. People would contribute and help. I would be a reflection of my feminine soul. I'd enjoy bodywork, massage, oils, baths, and affection.

ML: How would your soul feel if you were to do that?

B: She needs life. She needs my life. She needs to be able to play in me and wants to be able to express herself. To have what she wants. She would have fun and live in joy. It's who I am. She is showing me my

> human self. I'm worth it. If I had worth, I would be doing my work on the planet. Life would be pulsing through me. My soul is dark, feminine, magical, and transformative.

Beth discovered information that put to rest many questions that she has had concerning her choices and experiences in this lifetime. She learned that she cannot obtain her ultimate goals if she abandons herself for the sake of others.

5

MAKING GOOD CHOICES

"They always say time changes things,
but you actually have to change them yourself."
—Andy Warhol

Many of us were raised with the idea of a supreme being who looked down on us from above and kept a scorecard of all our good deeds and bad deeds. It was a formidable task, since he was doing this not just for us, but for billions of people all over the world—and conceivably for beings on other planes as well.

We have no evidence that such a punitive scorekeeper exists, but we do know that we keep our own very accurate, if subconscious, records. Our tally is the sum total of all our positive deeds, thoughts, actions, and states of mind—minus all our negatives. The conditions of our lives, at any given moment, reflect that balance.

That balance sheet is all about the choices we make. Are we choosing thoughts, actions, and words that have a positive impact, or a negative impact?

One of the most powerful gifts of past life regression is that it helps us make good choices. We aren't stuck with what we have today, or what we had yesterday. If we don't like what we have in our lives today, we can make different choices. If we like what we have, we can make it even better. Exploring our past lives yields a treasure trove of information that helps us shape our lives in more positive ways, accomplish our goals, and cherish our connections with others.

The clearer we become about our own nature, and the nature of the universe, the better our choices become. This chapter is about making choices that enhance our spirit and contribute to all of life.

Our Elegant Internal Teacher

We all have within us a magnificent system of teaching and internal justice. Our subconscious mind compels us to create exactly the life conditions that we think we deserve, based on our balance sheet of positives and negatives. It also prods us gently into situations that give us the lessons we need. The elegance of this system is that *these situations are usually the same.* If we feel we "deserve" a negative situation or condition, being in that situation will usually prompt us to learn the lesson and turn around the negative that put us there—so that we can stop the pain!

These situations are not always the most comfortable, but they are the ones from which we learn the most. They help us grow into our fullest selves, and align us with our purpose. Karen's situation is a wonderful illustration of how this elegant system works.

Karen's Lesson

Karen didn't think she deserved to be loved, so she wound up with two husbands who abused her and one who left. At that point, she did some serious self-examination and internal work. Past life regressions revealed that this was not the first life in which she had experienced abusive relationships, and she was able to see her current situation more clearly in the context of examining several lifetimes. She saw that in this life and in past lives, she had suffered from lack of self esteem and had been motivated by fear.

Karen realized that she needed to make different choices, both internally and externally. She had to change the way she thought about herself and about men, and she also had to break the habit of choosing men who would not treat her well.

It took courage, but Karen set about making these changes very deliberately. She did further work with her past lives, and with neuro-linguistic programming. She changed how she saw herself, and what she thought she deserved. Her priority became to love herself and to love others, and she did the work necessary to see herself as a valuable and loving presence. She thought about the kind of man she wanted and deserved, and she chose not to associate with other kinds of men. Her conscious and subconscious minds worked together to bring her what she truly wanted—loving and supportive relationships.

Karen learned the lesson that was hers to learn. Being in that situation—negative relationships that reflected what she thought she deserved—pressed her to start making different choices. The result was that she grew, and began to attract loving relationships not only with men, but with her colleagues and family as well.

Making Corrections

One very obvious way that past life regression helps us make better choices is that we can see the consequences of our behavior. If lying, cheating, or saying hurtful things brought pain in a past life, we are less likely to repeat those mistakes. If we can see the growth and joy we brought with love and kindness, we are more likely to gravitate in those positive directions.

Heaven and hell are conditions we create for ourselves, both here on Earth and in the hereafter. It all comes down to the choices we make. If we are making choices that create a hell, the pain usually motivates us to examine those choices and start making different, more life-enhancing ones. Remember that if we don't like where we are, the most important questions to ask are, "What must I do to achieve a different result?" and "What different choices must I make?"

Our impulse is always to learn and grow. Our hero's journey forever compels us to seek more experience of existence, more consciousness, more wisdom. The subconscious mind is always at work on that quest, whether or not our conscious minds are aware of what is going on.

OUR FOUR DIRECTIONS

Our spirit is always moving in one of four directions. Each lifetime has an overall direction, and each specific thought, action, and choice has its own direction as well.

The four directions are:

Moving toward death. These thoughts, actions, and choices involve harmful, self-sabotaging intentions and behaviors. They may include drug and alcohol use, violence, and criminal activity.

Moving away from death. These activities are based on fear, on avoiding disaster or punishment. They may include giving in to personal or political pressure, and making choices based on the lesser of two evils. "Victims" often move in this direction, as do people who spend their time reacting to whatever circumstances come their way, rather than creating the life they want to lead.

Moving away from life. These actions lead us to avoid lessons and experiences, to sabotage the fulfillment of goals and purpose, and to get involved with deprivation, denial and suicide. People moving away from life often give control of their thoughts and decisions to other people, and tend to be escapists.

Moving toward life. In this direction, we find the proper pursuit of happiness. Spirits on this path engage in purposeful activities that contribute to their growth and promote the survival of their consciousness and existence. They face their lessons directly, and are happy to learn them. They consider their choices, and opt for those that support life. As a result, they enjoy great creativity and self-determination—and greater happiness.

Decision-Making Skills And Strategies

We make our first decisions about any given life in the astral plane. Those decisions are:

- Is it time to return to the physical plane?
- If so, what circumstances shall I choose?

The decision-making skills and strategies we use in the astral are not very different from the ones we use here. They both reflect our inherent core values, desires, priorities, and styles. Take a moment to analyze your own decision-making strategies.

When making decisions, do you systematically weigh all the possibilities, or do you act impulsively? When choosing whether or not to come into a body, some spirits listen carefully to their counselors. They try to anticipate the consequences of their choices, to determine what lessons might be possible, and to examine the overall gain that a given lifetime might provide for them. They observe the parents, calculate the effect of the siblings and the environment, and extrapolate the opportunities and the challenges available. They then use this information to arrive at a rational decision.

Other spirits find themselves conflicted in the decision. There are pros and cons to coming into a body—and to coming into the particular body they are considering. They may not want to incarnate again, yet are being advised to do so because the lessons will be valuable, or because they have a particular purpose to fulfill. They may half-heartedly agree to experience a certain lifetime, but actually feel they are being pushed into the decision.

Still other spirits move blindly through the process. They do not think clearly about the details, or pay much attention to their options. They have specific desires or needs that they want to fulfill, and they don't always look ahead to the consequences. Perhaps they have unresolved addictions, and simply crave any opportunity to return to old habits. These addictions might include drugs, alcohol, sex, relationships, food, shopping, or various physical body sensations.

Other spirits are in a hurry to incarnate because they are running away from some experience in the astral, rather than running toward life in the body. They may be uncomfortable out of a physical body. They may be afraid of what they are experiencing in the astral, and just want to return to something familiar as quickly as possible.

What are your decision-making skills and strategies? Are they developed enough that you can rely on them when it is time for you to make your next choice about a lifetime? How do you think those skills have served you in choosing your present situation, parents, opportunities, and challenges?

Choosing A Life

If we have decided to incarnate, we must then bring all our decision-making skills to bear on choosing the time, location, people, and circumstances we will experience. The best guideline for making these choices is to look at what supports our overall purpose: To nurture and expand the breadth of our existence and the depth of our consciousness, so that our spirit becomes richer, denser, and wiser.

Choosing the birth time and place can be complicated. It involves selecting not just location and date, but parents, an environment, siblings, opportunities or lack thereof, and many other factors. It may be important to consider the parents' health and genetic make-up. Some spirits may be concerned about the astrological influences and the numerology of the date or name they choose.

Strategies for making these choices can be as complex as a game of chess, or as simple as picking a lottery number and crossing your fingers. Ultimately, it is up to you. Here are some things to consider when making that choice.

Sense the Situation

Most people who recall the pre-birth period report having had some sense of what they wanted in terms of parents and the environment into which they would be born—and they continued to rely on this "sensing skill" even after coming into the body.

They remember their time in the womb, and recall sensing both their mother's and father's emotions toward them. They have embryonic memories of conversations, arguments, activities, events, and situations—both pleasant and unpleasant. They are clear whether or not they felt wanted and loved. They also remember sensing any fear or anger that existed about the pregnancy, and any desire for, or attempt at, an abortion.

Choose Lessons, Not People

Sometimes we want to incarnate just to share a physical life with certain people. This can be pleasant, but the richer choice is to focus on an opportunity or lesson. The lesson may involve choosing specific people—but it is wise to focus on what we are to learn, rather than the individuals involved.

Choosing our circumstances based on a purpose or goals may lead to a life that holds challenges, but it also promotes our spiritual growth. In the short term, we may be severely tested. But the growth we earn from those tests ultimately leads to a more enjoyable and valuable existence, and a richly expanded consciousness. Living with our shortcomings and failures may be a form of hell—but when we learn to overcome them, we create heaven.

It can be daunting to consider having a difficult or challenging lifetime. Yet avoiding our lessons only prolongs the process, and usually creates even more challenges. We know, consciously or subconsciously, which lessons we need—but sometimes we have trouble getting our minds around what those lessons are. That is when spirit guides can be brought into the discussion. Wise spirits defer to their guides for assistance in making choices about incarnation.

We have to learn all of our lessons eventually—and pass all our tests. We can only do that in physical form. If we claim we have learned a lesson, we need to incarnate in order to test our mastery of it. If we don't do it now, we will have to do it later. One way or another, our own internal teacher will make sure we get it right.

Can We Make A Mistake?

First, it is important to remember that most "mistakes" can be fixed. We just have to learn the lesson, and then come back and pass the test. Or repeat the lesson!

We all want to choose the most productive and instructive life possible, but sometimes we fall short of the mark. We may make our choices about incarnation impetuously, without much consideration. We may simply not be paying much attention. We see a body, or a set of parents, and we choose without much thought or planning. We just slip into the first available body because, for whatever reason, we want back on the physical plane.

Even with careful consideration, it is possible to make mistakes. Perhaps the parents were attractive to us; they were doing just fine without a child. We thought they would make a great family for us, but the stresses of having a baby caused their relationship to fall apart. If that were the case, we might experience tension, abuse, financial struggles, divorce, or other problems. (Or, we might choose the situation precisely because we *would* experience those difficulties and learn from them.)

My client Nancy had a difficult family life, and wanted to understand why she had chosen to be a part of it. She learned that she loved both the parents deeply, and wanted them to learn more about love. She knew that they were not getting along very well, and she had high hopes that she could make everything better. They would focus on their love for her, and that would override their own dysfunctional relationship. She incarnated as their child.

The plan backfired. The birth of the baby only precipitated deeper problems between her mother and father. Worse, they took out their anger on the baby girl, and abused her. Understanding what had happened didn't make Nancy's life experiences any less damaging, but it helped her see her choice as a heroic act of love and purpose, even though it may have failed in some respects.

Mistakes can occur when spirits have their values confused, even if their decisions are based on love. They may want so desperately to be with a specific person, for instance, that they attach themselves to a newly forming embryo regardless of other factors. They haven't considered that the mother, the person they want to be with, is at this point only a child herself and got pregnant by accident. She may be far too young to give the spirit what it wanted when it chose to incarnate with her.

It is possible to correct mistakes, but we can avoid them entirely with a little forethought and consideration.

Losing Our Way

What if we lose our way, and make a choice that sets us on a path that has nothing to do with our purpose?

Moving off course may slow us down, but there is always something to be learned. We might examine what motivated us to move off course, and learn from that. We might learn something about our value system or some other aspect of our personality. Wherever we find ourselves, there is something to learn if we just look around.

Whatever lesson we are experiencing in the moment is valuable, whether or not it is the one that was "next on our path." We would have to learn that lesson at some point anyway, and now we can simply check it off the list. If we are learning generosity instead of loyalty, then we can learn loyalty another time. Generosity is still a good thing to learn.

The only real mistake is to stop learning or growing. Like our bodies, our spirits thrive on being fed and nurtured.

Do People Choose Violent Families?

Some people think they are choosing a good situation, and it goes sour. Others choose a lifetime they know will involve violence—usually in order to fulfill a particular purpose. It is rare that people want to experience violence for the sake of violence; there is usually a deeper lesson involved.

What might that lesson be? They may want to learn how to triumph over violence with love. They may choose that difficult situation in order to teach the parents the consequences of violence. Those consequences might include incarceration, regret, or karmic repercussions. Sometimes people choose a violent situation in order to better understand the pain it causes, or to learn compassion, strength, independence, non-violence, or fairness.

In rare cases, dysfunctional spirits incarnate into difficult situations with the express purpose of reinforcing negative behaviors, and giving themselves a justification for future violent behavior. This may seem extraordinary, but it happens. These dysfunctional spirits include souls who incarnated and became serial killers or war mongers like Charles Manson, Jeffrey Dahmer, Adolph Hitler, Osama bin Laden, or Saddam Hussein.

We only have a few case studies of these kinds of people, since typically people who are interested in past life regression are also interested in spiritual growth. Dysfunctional spirits would probably not choose to face the information that would surface during a hypnosis session. If they did agree to participate in such therapy, they would be well on their way to making positive changes.

A Personal Experience: My Father

A few years ago, I received the gift of being involved with my father's transition from being a vital, active man, through his death, and then through his re-entrance into this world as a healthy baby girl.

Within a year of being diagnosed with mesothelioma, a deadly cancer related to asbestos exposure, my father was dying in a hospice center. My brother and I had a chance to talk everything through with Dad before he left us, and to make sure that everything was resolved between us.

Dad was curious about any information that might help him during the final phase of his life, and I shared with him everything I could about reincarnation, past lives, and journeying between lives. He wasn't certain that he believed in reincarnation, but he said, "I hope you're right." I told him it didn't matter whether or not he believed, that he should just file the information away in case it served him at some point. It comforted me to know that I had done everything I could for him, and had given him something I considered valuable from my particular area of expertise.

Three weeks after going to the hospice, he died quietly and comfortably. The rest of the story comes from the experience and intuition I've gained over the past twenty years, from meditation, and from information given to me by my spirit guides.

Both my guides and my father's guides were present when he died. They took his hand and comforted him as he made the transition. He seemed somewhat surprised that there really was more to life than his physical existence. Because he was a bit disoriented, he was taken to a place in the astral where he was surrounded by friendly spirit guides who watched over him, conversed with him, instructed him, and protected him.

For some unknown reason, my father had amnesia about this most recent lifetime. This happens occasionally. People simply forget one or another lifetime. When I visited Dad in the astral, he did not recognize me as his daughter, Mary Lee. Instead, I was at some times his daughter Annabelle from the 1700's, and at other times his teacher from a more ancient lifetime. For two months, he stayed in that condition. He did not recognize his family or remember anything about his most recent lifetime.

My spirit guides were able to give him a great gift. During only one night in our Earth time, they warped his experience of time and gave him the equivalent of three years' instruction and healing. After that experience, he regained full memory of this lifetime and was able to visit us. When he visited me, I always felt a distinct low-level electrical vibration moving through my right hand. It was very unusual, and so pronounced that it drew my attention away from whatever I was doing at the time.

Despite all the instruction he was receiving and his companionship with me, my father was not content to remain in the astral plane. He wanted to return to a physical body as soon as possible.

On a Wednesday morning in mid-February, three months after his death, I woke up teary-eyed and missing my dad. My heart was just breaking. My spirit guides told me that Dad had decided to incarnate into a baby the following weekend. I would have only a couple of days to say my goodbyes for this lifetime. In meditation, I discovered that he was born the following Sunday morning, a baby girl.

Within a day or two, however, he began to get a much better sense of this baby's path, what would be available to him in that life, and what its limitations would be. He did not like what he saw, and began to regret having selected that body. The baby developed severe complications and died.

He immediately chose another baby girl's body, only three to four days after the first birth. He is doing well on this new path, and his astrology chart is very spiritual and adventuresome. This time, he seems very satisfied with the path before him.

It is wonderful to think of my dad now, in his new body, enjoying the love of his new parents and the prospects of his next life in the physical world. His gift to me is that this experience revealed even more information about the death and rebirth process.

Lessons Learned

My father's story illustrates some crucial points. Among them are:

- An individual's spirit does not have to attach to the fetus at conception. My father did not make the final, permanent attachment until two days before his birth. (How might this information change the public's opinion about abortions?)
- He was only between lives for three months before choosing to reincarnate.
- He did not become omniscient upon death; in fact, he experienced amnesia.
- He was consciously present around me for only a short period after his death. He did not instantly become my spirit guide, or a permanent advisor on the other side.
- He will not necessarily be present and waiting for my mother when she returns to the astral. Although some people may choose to wait for their spouses, it is not guaranteed.
- He will now be focused on his own life, as we are on ours, rather than being concerned about his loved ones who remain here. We don't necessarily spend a lot of time and effort thinking about people from our most recent past life. Instead, and fortunately, we move on.
- Even after being born, he still had the opportunity to change his mind. (How might this bring new understanding about infant deaths?)

My dad had led an honorable life, free from addictions or abuse. His choice to reincarnate quickly was more for the sake of personal comfort than the result of a compulsion. He simply did not enjoy his time in the astral plane, although most people report enjoying it very much. In fact, a significant number of people report that they are reluctant to return to a physical body because they prefer their experiences in the astral.

The Three Wise Men

Tracking a spirit's movement, as I did with my father, brought to mind the story of Jesus and the Three Wise Men. Perhaps the Three Wise Men did not just follow a star. In many stories, they are not simply wise men but Magi, or magicians. They may have been from a druidic-style lineage. If so, they would have been able to read stars. They would have been adept at astrology, and also capable of psychic vision, astral projection, and communicating with their spirit guides. This would have given them access to a great deal of information.

They may have known the spirit of Jesus from the astral, or from previous incarnations, and already have been aware of his plans to incarnate. They could have determined his general location on a certain date by psychic sensing. From there, they could simply inquire about recent births, and then look at the astrological chart of the child to know his identity.

Of course, when they actually found the child and were in his presence, they would have known immediately that this particular child held the spirit they were seeking.

These kinds of speculations keep us inquiring into the nature of the universe, and past life regression is a powerful tool in this endeavor.

Adam's regression illuminates many aspects of reincarnation, including the process of making choices while in the astral plane.

CASE STUDY

ADAM

Adam is on a path of soul seeking, and wanted to gain deeper understanding of his Life Purpose and the nature of his spirit. He also yearned to be united with his Soul Group, as well as to understand more fully his connection with his wife in this life.

After guiding him into a deep relaxation and down an imaginary hallway, he noticed a thatch door.

ML: As the door opens and you move through it, what do you begin to notice?

A: I'm indoors. There is a dark floor. It's a small building, a hut. There are household items around. Someone is coming in. It's a child. She is running, excited. She wants me to follow her out of the hut.

ML: Are you male or female?

A: I'm a female. She is my niece. There is some kind of activity in the center of the village. People are coming back from a hunt with an animal on their shoulders.

ML: What do you notice next?

A: I wake up in the night to a commotion. There is a fire elsewhere in the village. I am going out. There is a hut on fire. I run to it. I run in to the hut to see if anyone needs help. I grab a baby and run out. I'm crying and the baby is too. Other people are standing around, and some are trying to put out the fire. There is not enough water, and the hut burns down. Someone needs to care for the baby. I feel a connection to the baby, as though she is mine. I am grateful this life was spared. I have a great appreciation for life and those we love, especially little ones. I take her for walks in the forest. Because of the fire, I am worried that something may happen to her. I am very protective of her. I always want to nurture and protect her.

ML: Do you recognize her as anyone you know from this lifetime?

A: I think she is my wife now. We have a really close connection. She has the same vibrancy in her eyes.

ML: Move ahead in time to the next relevant experience. What do you notice next?

A: I am very old. I am lying in bed, in a thatched hut. I can't get up and do much. Sometimes people come and talk to me. I spend time looking at the ceiling and thinking about life, and the beginnings and endings of things. I think about those I love and how their lives will be. I think about life, and what I know and don't know. I think about what it might be like after I die. The girl comes to see me a lot. She's about fourteen now. She is very excitable. Her energy makes me happy. She's too restless for too much talking. I am content knowing that she has some happiness in life. I will miss her when I move on.

ML: What have you learned from viewing that lifetime?

A: It was a good life. There were struggles, but I had a place in that group. I had someone to love and be valuable to. It was a good life. There is cruelty in life, but it was a good life.

ML: Go ahead and release from that physical body. What do you notice as you experience the death?

A: It is kind of nice. I didn't want out of the body, so it's not achy. I just slid out, calmly. I was ready to go forward after I said goodbye. I was met by someone. They are there to escort me. I go give the girl a spiritual hug, an embrace. She doesn't know yet that I have died. She feels my presence. Then she knows, and she gets sad. I stay with her for a while, maybe a couple of weeks. Then I'm done. I go upward and diagonally as I leave. It is not up in the sky really. It is like I am being escorted somewhere. It feels funny. The feeling isn't tingly, but a little bit cold. It feels kind of good, but I'm kind of nervous. I'm somewhere I haven't been in a while. I'm not sure what to expect.

ML: What do you notice next?

A: I arrive, and there is someone there. He seems very familiar. He greets me with a big smile and a hug. He is proud of me. I have a strong hug feeling and we talk a little bit. I still have the feeling of the previous body on me. He escorts me to a different place. It is like a courtyard of a temple. There is a garden. We walk together. He holds my arm. There is an altar, in a circle. We walk the length of the garden. There are big arches over the pathway. It is a big garden with big stones. We walk up and stand in a circle. It's a couple of steps up. A light comes down like I'm taking a shower. Parts of me from before are being washed away. It is nice to be there. I feel refreshed. It is a familiar place. When we are done with that, it's like after a shower when you put a robe on and feel all clean. It's not that I think I have a robe on, but it's the feeling that you get—kind of vulnerable in a way.

ML: What happens next?

A: We go from there. We travel again. I'm not with the same person now. I have another chaperone. I know this one so well. Now we are in what appears to be a line, like riding an escalator. There is a whole bunch of people, all moving. I see across the way. It appears like a big circular place with tubes going in carrying people in. There's a huge crowd. The chaperone knows where he is going. I don't know exactly how we get there. It seems cool that there is a huge crowd of people who know where they are going. We go out a different tube. It's weird. I just came from a life. It's weird because it is not the same as having to go to one place after another. Places just exist. It feels like you are moving, but you don't know how you got from one place to the other. Now we are going to more familiar territory. It's like when you go to a neighborhood where you grew up. When I recognize where I am, the chaperone leaves me. I thank him.

ML: What do you experience next?

A: I am taking my time getting where I am going. There's a lot to see. It sounds odd, but it's like a neighborhood. There is a particular house. I don't know if it is yellow or red. It feels like I belong in this house. There is a wooden gate, a cobblestone path, and the door is open. Everyone in the house cheers when I come in. They have been waiting for me. There are hugs and smiles. It is a big family.

ML: Do you recognize anyone there that you have met in this life?

A: Yes, my friend Jake is there. I am glad we are here together again. Maybe there's someone else, I'm not sure. It's nice to be here. I know this place, and it feels like a big family. I feel I have a place here. I am comfortable with most everyone. I have a place to stay. We don't have to eat, but we eat together anyway. It's like we play house. It's a group tribe. I like to experience the closeness of the family. It is funny there would be a big house in the spirit world.

ML: What we experience as physical in the spiritual world is our projection of the experience. Your experience is real, but the way you perceive it is imagination.

A: I spend a lot of time resting because I just came home. I sleep a lot. Some of my friends come and visit one at a time. We talk about life, and my previous life. I realize how much I have missed them. There are about nine people in this house. I see the house color as pale yellow with red trim. Kind of stucco, or an adobe feel to it. Earthy. It feels more comfortable. I like earthy houses. A couple of the people in the house are a little more mature. We sit around the table and talk about life. They are not pushy, but they have a strong presence. They know a lot. They tell me I did really well. I did a good job with expressing love to the child I raised. I could learn to forgive in my heart more. I did a good job coping with stresses, and the burden of my role in the tribe. They ask me a little about where I will choose to go for my next life. That makes me anxious. I want to take a break. I don't want to think about what to do next. I want to play. I understand. They are not disapproving, but I feel, not weak, but that I really look up to them. They know so much more. I am not feeling very capable. I'm intimidated by them. They have a lot of personal power. They are solid on the inside. There is a groundedness I don't have yet. It is nice to have that kind of strength. I'm working on it. They pat me on the shoulder. I know they love me. There are two of them. One is thicker than the other. Denser and grounded and strong. The other one is female. She is still more mature than I am. She's nice. They are not parental, just older, like older siblings who watch over me and give me good examples. Maybe he is my guide. The name "Allen" comes to mind. It's probably short for something. We have table talks once in a while. Not pressure, but to share ourselves. I think I am known for being child-like, mischievous and extremely curious. Curious and mischievous go together. I like to sneak up on people, not to scare them, but as a little game.

ML: What else do you notice about this experience?

A: We talk about whether I want to be a woman or a man next time. It depends. Being a female can sometimes be so much harder. Maybe I want a break and take a male body. But maybe I will change my mind before I leave again. The experience is so rich in the way that love is experienced and the way you feel in community. It feels richer, fuller, and emotionally broader. I know it depends, speaking from experience. I need to learn more about emotions and how to deal with them. He opens a book. He is showing me stories, like faery tales. I like to imagine. There is a story about a dragon. It's not mean. It's an imaginary place in another dimension. I think he is showing me places I can go. It's like a travel brochure. He likes to show me because he knows how curious I am, and I like good stories. If I want, I can be in this story, this place. We tell each other stories. He teaches me to make better stories. I can practice, too, being in the story. I get to go experience what I like. I don't know whether the others in our house do this also. I think they like stories too. Funny, in this life I've played role playing games. We do that there. Life is like that. It's funny to see someone you know in a different role. My guide learned a lot this way. You can do so much in the spirit world, create so many things. It's not the same as the Earth experience, but you can learn a lot about yourself through the roles. Not all stories are so much fun. We explore different kinds of scenarios and roles. That is what it is, we see different perspectives. We play different roles so we know the whole story, the many layers. It's multi-dimensional. It is a good way to develop a sense of empathy. Funny, when I was reading books on regressions, I wondered whether I was a beginning or advanced soul. I am not that advanced, but I am not a beginner either. I don't care, really. It doesn't matter. I'm just me. I do a good job and have enthusiasm. Some of those Earth lives are really hard. They can be frustrating because you don't remember. Maybe this is not a house, but sort of. It is a good picture with an earthy feel. I really love the souls in this house. I have lived some other lives with the souls in this group.

ML: Would you like to ask your guides whether these are the members of your Soul Group?

A: They said, "Yes, for the time being."

ML: Would they clarify that?

A: They said, "All things are temporary." He says that this is my Soul Group. However, he teaches that there is that which is permanent, that which changes, and that which takes a long time to change. He focuses on that which never changes. So, by saying "for now" he reminds us that it is not eternally permanent. While we are a group, we aid each other. Our individual journey will create our own growth. When we move on and join another group, we have strength to know that that group was perfect for that time. It was lovely in that we share a connection with other souls and have experiences together. We connect with that which never changes, deep within us. It's like the stories. They come and go. They are beautiful, but deep within us resides who we are. So there is a kind of loneliness, an achy-ness. It pulls us toward them, while knowing that it is transitory and they are playing roles. We are with others and also alone.

ML: Move forward through your experiences in the spiritual world, to just before you chose this body. What are your experiences at that time?

A: I am excited about this one. I get to be the youngest child. I am alone. It's like a sphere. It's not a screen, but a substance, a means of projecting and amplifying thought into manifestation. There is nothing to see, but a three-dimensional magnifying glass. There are a few spirits watching. They are not doing anything, just there. I can project out to different places. It's like shooting along a rainbow, but not having gone anywhere. It is amazing there are so many different kinds of lives to be lived. What I really want to do is bring the knowledge of the connection, the knowledge of that which does not change. I've tried before. I'm not as dense or hard as my guide, but I have confidence I can do this. We'll see…

ML: What else do you notice?

A: I have to pay attention to the type of body that I choose. The circuitry will be important. Each body is different. One of the reasons I chose this body is that has the capability for powerful projection and imagination, extreme sensitivity to the energies around it and of other people. It is able to relax, although there are times when it has difficulty with that. There are more reasons why this body is suitable. Sensitivity is one reason. I can use that to show people things on their insides. I can use it to communicate. It makes life harder because it is so sensitive. There are so many signals, it gets distracted and overwhelmed. There were other bodies I could have chosen. None had this sensitivity. I can't force someone to recognize what's on their insides. I can't take an intimidating body and have them recognize what's deep down inside them.

ML: What else do you consider?

A: I also get a lot of sensitivity exercises, working with heavy energies. I have to be alone with them and deal with them. It is touch and go for a while. I thought I was going to get stuck. Perceptions of the mind can be hard. I kept it flexible. I'm balancing flexibility with hardening my thought processes. My personality finds the extremes frustrating. But it is going well. Maybe I will manage to help a few people in profound ways. That makes me happy.

ML: What happens next during this process?

A: I go to the viewing room. I see these lives. It's a rich experience. Because I played so many roles it is the perspective in the Earth mind that can be so difficult. The family I chose is so rich and bright on the inside, yet so dense everywhere else. I found the juxtaposition amusing. So much brightness and then the density. The rest of the community is not so impressive. I don't hold anything against the souls. It's just the story, the lives. They are so closed and small, it seems so little. The only reality they know. But it's good for me. I want to open up the patterns. Get them to see their patterns. It's easy to be compassionate because they are not to blame, it is just the way they are. I watch them and feel their patterns. I open them up and allow their souls to make other choices. I feel young as a soul goes. It seems scary, like a long road ahead. There are exercises I do in this life. Any advantage we have in a body, there is also a drawback. I can go out into my imagination, far, but I can't get imbalanced. If there is a fear that comes in, my body gets full of negativity. I've had my trials.

ML: What else do you notice?

A: Maybe a lot of what I thought were issues were issues of the personality. I was so self-conscious. I didn't like the way I looked, but it is just the natural playing out of this personality in this society. The body is trying to process it all.

ML: What do you notice about your purpose for coming into this body?

A: I knew there would be a certain hardness, a density of the family, the body, and society. I made a hard choice. I don't like to do boring things. I wanted to make progress. I chose this body because of so many possibilities. I talked to my spirit guide. He gave me warnings. He advises not to be scared, but is implanting me with a trigger to help find my way out during dark times. He assures me that he will help me if I need it. He says, "Do your best. Whatever happens is okay."There will be an emphasis on that which never changes. There is security in that. It allows us to do things we would otherwise not do. He infuses me with something that helps give me strength. He is a really good teacher.

ML: As you prepare to enter this body, is there anything else that you notice?

A: I went and said goodbye to my Soul Group. It feels like my other friend, Jess, is there. He feels small, so I don't know. I say goodbye. Each soul gives me a little gift. I see them like boxes. They are gifts for my life. I can open them along the way.

ML: What do you know about the gifts?

A: They are like story weaving. I have the access to weave some things into this life from the pre-life experience.

ML: Like what?

A: Books that would come to me at various times, such as *The Artist's Way*. A presence of joy, like a chunk of energy that would trigger when I wanted to experience joy. Shoes that make me more sure-footed. Stories, giving me the ability to travel to certain places with my mind.

ML: What else happens?

A: I say goodbye. I am so happy that I have so many good friends. The last person I see is my spirit guide. He gives me reassurances. I am ready to go.

ML: What do you notice as you connect with the body?

A: It is like sliding down a long tube. It reminds me of a water slide. I glide down. I feel I am external, though attached. I can watch my mother. She is gentle about the way that she goes about things. I don't like the meanness of my dad. It is like I am taking notes, as I have to deal with him in the future, too. Mom takes care of what she eats, likes herbs. That is soothing and reassuring to me. I have a lot of work to do. It is important this body is prepared in a way to do what I want to do in life. Mostly in the brain. The body is set up. But the brain will be changeable. I will be guided. I will change its flexibility later. I hone in on things that need attention in the body. I must do something with my voice. I am not sure what I am doing with the voice. It is in the throat. Preparing it somehow. It has to do with communication. Being able to communicate inner energies. It's spooky being in the womb. It is soothing, but it is an enclosed space. Later, when I am in the body, I have to...I have memories of other past lives and associations. I am excited, but there is a certain amount of dread, because of memories of other lives. It is good for me to experience this time. But also it is kind of boring. There is only so much you can do. Even while in the body, I am creating. It is like I am entertaining the infant brain with stories. There is something about my feet. I don't know. Something with groundedness. My feet crave to touch the ground.

ML: What else are you noticing about this experience?

A: The throat. I am working on it so it will be flexible. Not only physically, but in control. The whole body is prepared to take on other energies, really feel them, and experience other people in their words and language. I'm pleased so far, but I don't appreciate being jostled around.

ML: What else can you understand about your purpose for your life?

A: What is confusing is this personality and life. There is a purpose that is large, about grounding myself and changing. My mind is rigid at times, and that causes more suffering than is necessary. Regarding the purpose, it is hard to pin down on an action. It is not an action. It is the experience of this body and the overwhelming experience of every one around me. The purpose is to help others and reach in where I would like to reach. The biggest frustration is fear. The biggest drawback of this body is the fear that is magnified in the powerful imagination. So I have held myself back. It is a matter of relaxing and accepting the talents and the limitations. The experience I have had has been in wanting no limitations and having high expectations of any soul influence and my spirit guide influence. He tells me it is okay. I'm where I am. It is enough to be here. The irony is that I chose this life because of all the different possibilities, yet the different possibilities have driven me nuts.

ML: Is there any advice that your guide can give you about this?

A: The best advice is to be balanced and pursue that which brings me joy. The tendency is to be obsessed, to be one way or another. So questions about what I should be frankly don't matter. I have the talent to do any of those things. The key is to not limit, or avoid, those things by thinking that "I am this, or I am that."

Adam discovered the answers to his questions, and much more. What a descriptive tour through the afterlife experiences, plus sound advice that is pertinent to all of us!

6

Soul Groups

"The meeting of two personalities is like the contact of two chemical substances: if there is any reaction, both are transformed."
—Carl Jung

Have you ever met someone whose energy seemed as familiar as an old friend, even though you had never met him or her before in this life? That person may well be part of your Soul Group.

What Are Soul Groups?

Soul Groups are sets of souls who were once an individual spirit, or conscious energy unit, and have subsequently divided into a number of apparently separate souls. They remain connected at some greater level, and yet are now capable of incarnating into their own separate physical bodies.

How does this happen?

In The Beginning...

Imagine what it would be like to be God. You would be all that existed. There would be nothing and no one outside you. You would be all knowing.

Everywhere. Eternal, with no beginning and no end. You would have nothing to learn or discover, nowhere to go that wasn't already a part of you. No one to meet, no one to get to know, no one with whom to relate because you already were everyone.

What would that be like?

It wouldn't be powerful. Power implies power over something outside you, and God already is everything that exists. It wouldn't be interesting. That implies that you could satisfy some curiosity, and God already knows everything. It wouldn't be sensual, because there would be nothing outside you to see, taste, hear, smell, or touch.

Perhaps it would be lonely to be God. It might even be boring.

What would you do under those circumstances? There is speculation that at one time, eons ago, there was one massive unit of homogenous energy. At some point, it split apart into many pieces. From each piece's perspective, they were now separate. They had become individuals, capable of incarnating into their own bodies. Now they could play the fascinating game of rediscovering all the other pieces of their original Self as they manifested into a multitude of interesting forms.

Of course, this is speculation. As with many metaphysical concepts that are beyond the range of our physical senses, it and the rest of the information in this chapter is based on observations and on perceptions gained while in trance or astral projection.

Spirit Splitting

What happens when a spirit's consciousness has gained such expansion that it can no longer function properly within an inhabited physical life form?

It divides again. This allows each resulting piece to develop its own set of aspects and incarnate into a separate body and continue the journey of learning. This may explain global population growth. As spirits become enlightened, and then split, there are more souls available to inhabit bodies. Another reason for the growing population may be that souls can come here from other planes and from other galaxies within our three-dimensional plane.

The split portion of the spirit does not lose any of the growth or progress that it has made. If anything, it has advanced farther along its path. However, the split allows it to have even more opportunities for a variety of experiences to feed consciousness. Remember the metaphor of the spirit being a hand attached to the central nervous system, and souls being like the fingers stretching out into the universe to gather information and wisdom.

Soul Groups are clusters of souls who can trace their origins back to a common spirit. That is why we recognize one another, and this is an important reason for lending each other support.

A Return To Oneness?

Many philosophies and religions proclaim the virtues of returning to oneness, of every piece of consciousness finding its way back to that one original spirit and merging again—just as it was "in the beginning." This is an interesting concept, one that may sound better on paper than it works in actual practice.

We imagine that it might feel wonderful, much like uniting with an old friend. But in fact, there would be no friend if we returned to oneness. There would be no separation between any consciousnesses…no relationship, no sensual contact, no conversation.

Consider why the spirit divides in the first place. It wants to gather knowledge and experience, more existence and consciousness, in pursuit of surviving and thriving. It craves ever-increasing facets of reality to discover and explore, and is constantly engaged in and fascinated by this learning. Splitting also gives it "others" with whom to share the experience.

On a stressful day on the Earth plane, returning to oneness can sound appealing. However, imagine locking yourself in a closet for a year or two without stimulus, change, or contact with other people. That is the metaphor for the return to oneness.

Finally, if oneness were to occur, each soul's individual consciousness would extinguish. Rather than peace, a return to oneness would mean oblivion.

Better Than Oneness

Rather than yearning after oneness as the source of ultimate happiness, we might be better off cultivating balance and joy in our individual souls.

What is the best way to do that? We have seen that we create our own "heaven" and "hell" in this world and in the hereafter—and that we can experience both on a daily basis, depending on our behavior, our environment, and the state of our consciousness. We do not find heaven, or ultimate happiness, by running from challenges or taking shortcuts. When we follow a course of action that is harmful to ourselves or others, our lives reflect that behavior. We call it "a living hell." When we die under these conditions, we are filled with sorrow, regret, remorse, and a negative sense of ourselves.

When we live our lives aligned with positive, life-affirming principles, our experiences may still be challenging, but they are also fulfilling. They build and support a positive self image. This is "heaven on Earth." When we die, we carry that same sense of self with us, along with the confidence we earn from knowing that we can stay the course.

Rather than repudiating life and seeking to merge back into oneness, we serve our spirit better when we engage each moment fully and enjoy it completely.

Incarnating With Soul Groups

Now that we have seen how Soul Groups come into existence, let's look at how they work.

When we are in the astral plane, making choices about coming into a body, our Soul Group is often a factor in the decision. We are energetically connected to the individuals in our Soul Group—so what affects them, affects us.

If members of our Soul Group are progressing slowly, perhaps even starting to slide toward oblivion or extinction, their backward movement creates a drag on our own growth. If we notice that members of our Soul Group are experiencing difficulties, we may want to be born into a body that will interact with them so we can lend assistance. Or we may see that someone in our Group is going to engage in a quest that we find interesting.

That can be another compelling reason to incarnate with them.

Sometimes we simply love someone so much that we will overcome any obstacle to experience, once again, the physical sensations and pleasures that we have shared with them in other lives.

Can You Be Your Own Ancestor?

Family members are sometimes part of the same Soul Group, but can you be your own ancestor? Is Aunt Josephine from the eighteenth century really *you?*

There is no way to determine how often people incarnate as one of their own descendants. Several of my clients have remembered being a part of their own family tree, perhaps their own great grandmother or a great uncle. Clients have also reported recognizing that their deceased grandparent, or some other ancestor, has reincarnated as one of their own children.

This is not common, however, and it certainly is not necessary. The history of our own soul, including our past life "lineage," generally has nothing at all to do with our genetic lineage or family ancestry.

Recognizing Your Soul Group

People carry the same energy pattern, or aura, from life to life. It may change in some ways due to growth from mastering lessons, or due to experiencing traumatic events—but the distinct nature of each person's energy allows us to recognize one another fairly easily.

Sometimes there are physical or behavioral clues as well. We have already noted that people often take on similar physical attributes like body type or coloring from lifetime to lifetime. They may also bring certain behaviors, or a certain demeanor, with them from one lifetime to another.

In addition to these ways of recognizing members of your Soul Group, you can simply extend your own energetic sensors out to "feel" their energy. Look into their eyes. It is true that the eyes are the windows of the soul. Keep in mind that a person can incarnate as any race or gender, so these are not reliable clues.

You will know on an intuitive level when you encounter someone in your Soul Group.

Old Soul Versus New Soul

We have already discussed some aspects of what people refer to as "old souls" and "new souls." We saw that, since all time is really now, this is an artificial distinction from the perspective of chronological time. Let's look at this issue again, from the point of view of Soul Groups and spirit splitting.

Suppose that the original spark of consciousness divided into separate aspects or souls—and that those souls eventually became spirits with their own set of aspects incarnating into physical form. Suppose that this process continued. As each soul reached a certain maturity, it split into more souls. If this is the case, then some individuals have probably split more times than others. Some souls may still be closer to their original form, while others may have gone through several metamorphoses.

In this context, which are the "older" and which are the "newer" souls? One soul might have gone through many more "splittings" than another. In that sense, it might be considered older. But because it has split more recently, perhaps it is newer! And what about the soul that has reached a certain maturity, and is about to divide again? It may be "old" today, but very "new" tomorrow. When a soul is about to split, it may appear to have a greater depth of character—but it is about to get very "young." Are the old souls the ones that have remained closer to their original characteristics, or the ones that have divided more frequently?

These are all fascinating things to ponder—but we need to focus back on what lessons we can learn. If we spend all our time pondering whether we are an old soul or a new soul, we may not get to those lessons!

Amy's regression shows how we often meet up with the same people in various lifetimes.

Case Study

Amy

Amy wanted to have a deeper understanding of her relationships with her daughter and her dear friend. I asked her to close her eyes, breathe, and imagine a hallway. She came to a rustic log door with a rope handle.

A: It's dark. I'm comfortable. I am in a crib that swings on a brass stand. If I move I can make it rock. I am a female. I notice pink lace. I like the swing, maybe too much. I am happy. I like this space. I am not frightened.

ML: What else do you notice?

A: I have a nanny. She wears a black uniform with crisp white things. Now I am on a rocking horse. I'm really going for it. I like the rocking motion. The nanny is my friend, and maybe my teacher. I don't get to play with other children much. Maybe she is my governess.

ML: What do you notice next?

A: Now I am outside on a swing. I am going as high as I possibly can. She doesn't say I can't, but she makes sure that I don't get hurt. It is hung from a big tree. I like to climb this tree, too.

ML: What is the next memorable event?

A: I am a teen now. I am being sent away to school. I am really sad. I don't want to be separated from my governess. I don't really know my parents. She is the one who has raised me and taught me everything that I know.

ML: Do you recognize her energy as anyone you know in this lifetime?

A: She feels like my daughter in this life.

ML: What happens at school?

A: It is made of brick. It is cold and there are rules, conforming, bad teachers, and dorm sleeping. I have trouble socializing and conforming. I am not happy. I sneak away and take long walks. I sit by the river a lot. I write and sketch. Later I travel.

ML: How old are you when you travel?

A: I am eighteen or nineteen years old. I don't travel alone. That would not be right. I travel with my governess. We go to Greece to see the statues and buildings. All that we had looked at in books growing up. She is still my best friend. We go to Rome. We giggle, laugh, and learn. I hate wearing the dresses. They are so hot.

ML: What is the year?

A: 1890.

ML: Where is home for you?

A: Edinburgh.

ML: Move ahead in time. What happens later in your life?

A: I have married and have two girls. The same governess lives with us, but she is too old to be their governess. She is more like a grandmother.

ML: What have you learned from viewing this past life?

A: Let your kids experience life, and learn through those experiences. Learning is fun and it is a gift. Knowledge is power. I didn't want to be like my parents were in that lifetime. They had zero connection or affection.

ML: What was your governess' name?

A: Mary. She gave me affection and connection that I needed.

ML: How will the knowledge of that life affect this one?

A: It shows me a deeper relationship that I have with my daughter, and why we are so close now. She is so vibrant and eager to learn. She is her own person at six years old. I need to give her plenty of space and love. She will always have a solid boundary. Just because she runs in one direction doesn't mean that she won't come back. There is always a place where she feels love and is accepted.

ML: Going back into the hallway, choosing another door that will lead to yet another experience. Three, two, one. What does this door look like?

A: It is white with nine panes of glass. There is a brass latch.

ML: As the door opens and you move through, what do you notice?

A: Light. Bright sunlight. I have overwhelming joy (tears). It's a really nice spot to be. It's like being free. A free spirit. I don't see anyone, but I feel connection. I believe that I am between lives. I am downloading my experiences and also getting information back too. Fast forward. I am almost connecting with…there is an exchange of experiences and ideas. I feel light, airy. I am told it is time to go now. I am excited, curious, and interested. I am wanting to learn. Now I am watching a big screen. They are suggesting, no I'm being encouraged to go to Japan. I will not start as a child. Is that possible?

ML: Yes. We call that stepping in. What do you notice about that experience?

A: I will be a female. I will be twenty-three when I enter the body. I will be a wife with no children. My life will be my husband. I will be submissive. I see it on the screen. I am not thrilled about going there. I am told that I need to learn how to fight for, overcome, being dominated and submissive. That sense of duty. Oh, my feet hurt.

ML: Is that during the time when they bound the women's feet?

A: Yes. I am there now. My feet are bound. I am not happy about being there. As I go about my chores and duties I have to learn how to… It is the simple things. There is a rhythm of repetitiveness, of doing dishes and how to get through that on a daily basis. It becomes meditative, almost spiritual. They are mundane tasks that I had hated. Now I take pride and strength from that whole day to day pattern. I look at things differently. Now I am not doing dishes. I have turned it into something way beyond that; into what I want it to be.

ML: What else do you experience or learn in that lifetime?

A: I notice a female that I greatly admire. I knew of her and then saw her speak. She is strong, yet Japanese. She considers herself to be equal to all. Just because she is female doesn't make her less or lower. She is not afraid to speak out. She does it so eloquently. She gently nudges society slowly in her direction. She has gained their confidence and respect.

ML: How has she influenced you in that lifetime?

A: She gave me courage. I started painting. I looked within and listened to myself. I could be myself. I can be myself and still be responsible to my other roles. As a female in that culture I did not register as high, and was not listened to.

ML: Do you recognize that woman as anyone you know in this lifetime?

A: She is my friend.

ML: How will that lifetime influence you in this lifetime?

A: I will find joy in the simple, mundane tasks and be in the moment. Life doesn't have to be complicated. Instead of looking at dishes and laundry as a pain, I can see them as a gift. I have three people in my life, as part of my journey, to help guide and care for. I don't have to be negative about my responsibilities if I approach them from a different angle. I will take delight in the simple things. I will appreciate and observe.

In this session, Amy not only discovered past life connections with her daughter and her friend, she had the opportunity to experience the time between lives. She saw first-hand what it was like to make a decision to come into a particular body, and discovered that a soul can enter a body midway through its life.

There is one other interesting note concerning this regression. Amy's friend is the same person who, in a case presented later, saw herself in Japan as a female confidant of the Emperor. Now they have both confirmed that lifetime from two separate experiences, with the sessions occurring about two weeks apart.

7

Stepping In—and Out

"Everything you've learned in school as 'obvious' becomes less and less obvious as you begin to study the universe. For example, there are no solids in the universe. There's not even a suggestion of a solid. There are no absolute continuums. There are no surfaces. There are no straight lines."

—R. Buckminster Fuller

When people begin exploring past lives, they sometimes encounter a fascinating phenomenon. They discover that they started one lifetime before another one ended! The body they had been inhabiting continued its life, but they found themselves in an entirely different body. Perhaps they were mistaken about the dates. Or perhaps they did not stay in that particular body for its entire lifetime!

Other people have the experience of beginning a life at some point well after the body's birth. Their memories of that body's early life may be a bit vague, or they may feel rather disconnected from these memories. It is as if they "stepped in" to the second body midway through its life.

These phenomena are known as stepping out, and stepping in.

What Are Step-Ins?

The term "step-in" describes a soul who comes into a body after it has already been born, often when its life is already well underway. In order to do this, another soul has to be willing to "step out," to leave the body before it dies and allow the other soul to step in and take its place.

The "step-in" concept can be confounding, and even scary, for some people. First impressions of this phenomenon range from disbelief, to anxiety, to relief that a confusing experience has been explained and is working to everyone's advantage.

When we understand how stepping in works, we see that there is nothing to fear. We even realize that the concept has a certain elegance.

The Ground Rules: Both Spirits Must Agree

Most people's initial fear about step-ins is that some soul can just come along and snatch a body, unbeknownst to the occupant. Quite the contrary is true. In a step-in situation, both parties must agree to the arrangement. At a subconscious level, they have determined together that this exchange will be mutually beneficial, and have created a pact with one another.

Why It Happens

Let's say that one person decides, at the subconscious level, that she had completed what she came into this body to accomplish. Her present mission is finished, and she wants to exit so that she can get into position to enter a new body—fulfilling yet another task, in another time and location. She could choose to contract a fatal illness, get involved in an accident, become the victim of a fatal crime, or in some other way cause that body to die.

Or she could leave the body intact and allow another soul to enter and take over its operation. The incoming soul would have a particular mission as well, one that did not require her to experience infancy, childhood, and adolescence. The new soul might see that her mission could be accomplished more quickly, easily, and efficiently if she got together with the first soul and created a pact to use the body when the first soul was finished with it. She would have seen that the body's situation, personality, lifestyle, and location would support her in accomplishing her mission.

How It Happens

The exchange might take place during a "close call" accident, a fright of some sort, an operation with anesthesia, a fainting spell, or during sleep—although there are reports of souls stepping in while the person in the body is awake and alert.

As the departing soul exits, the incoming soul "slides in" and anchors herself in the body. The two souls often take turns in the body for awhile before the final switch, in order to acclimatize themselves to the changes they will both experience.

It is highly unlikely that either soul will remember the event of stepping in. However, my friend Susie recalls her experience quite vividly. Susie is a highly intuitive woman, and a musician. She is the step-in, and calls the soul who left the body Susan. Susan was also a musician.

Susie says, "Susan had been having some health problems, and her condition was weakening. One night while she was on stage, singing with the band, she collapsed. At that moment, I clearly remember sliding down into Susan's body while she was slowly moving up and out. We engaged each other's attention and exchanged a type of energetic embrace as we moved past each other. It was the most beautiful moment in my memory."

Susie also remembers the pre-exchange conversation with Susan, which included the agreement to make the switch. After the exchange, Susie was bedridden for three days while she healed the body and recovered her strength. Because they were both talented musicians, Susie continues their singing career.

This is an unusual case, in that Susie remembers the transition. Most people do not remember it happening, and remain oblivious to the change.

Stepping In Versus Possession

Stepping in is very different from possession. The step-in arrangement is agreeable to both parties, done in order to fulfill specific purposes for both souls, and leaves only one spirit remaining in the body in the end.

When a person is possessed by a disincarnate being, it is generally not by conscious agreement. Further, both spirits are residing in the body simultaneously, which typically sabotages the host's process and purpose.

What Happens To The One Who Leaves?

The soul who leaves the body is free to:

- Explore the astral for awhile
- Become a spirit guide, if they are prepared and inclined to do so
- Take a rest
- Learn something new
- Locate another body into which they can either enter or be born
- Fulfill some other mission or adventure of their choice

People sometimes get upset or confused when they suspect, or confirm, that they are step-ins. They may feel an attachment to the soul who has left, and worry about what they have "done." Or they may mistakenly think that they are the person who has left, and become paranoid that another soul has entered "their" body. Once they understand that they are the one who entered the body, and that the other soul agreed to the switch and is off doing something else, they begin to relax.

If you suspect that you have been involved in a step-in situation, then *you are the one who has stepped in*. You have chosen to enter this body and experience the remainder of this lifetime. The soul who vacated the body has also chosen to move on, and is carrying out their own purpose in a new location. You agreed between you to do this. Step-in situations should not cause alarm.

My client, Paul, discovered that he had been a musician in his previous life. He witnessed himself walking out of his manager's office at the end of an evening after a concert, and simply floating out of his body. He remembered floating up, and observing the scene below. He did not remember returning to that body, although he continued to observe his body walking and living life.

In the next scene Paul recalled, he was about twelve years old in the present life body, sitting on his bed and playing a guitar. He looked around and remembered thinking, "Oh, here I am." Curious and relaxed, the twelve year old went back to playing his guitar.

After this hypnosis session, Paul mentioned that before age twelve, he simply could not get his fingers to play the guitar well. But from the age of twelve forward, he began playing with ease and talent. At the time of our session, he was in a band and had made several CD's.

Paul had never heard of stepping in, and this was his first past life regression. Being a step-in explained not only the sudden appearance of his musical talent, but also his lack of connection to his early childhood. This episode further explains any overlap of chronological time between that past life and his present one.

Why Step Out?

The best reason to step out of a body is to position yourself strategically for the next incarnation, in the furtherance of your goals.

Other reasons for stepping out might include:

- To leave a disagreeable situation or to move toward a more favorable one. For instance, a soul might leave an abusive relationship, or even a situation that had become boring or meaningless.
- To move closer to a Soul Group or some particular individual. The soul may be attracted to another space or time where new and different lessons can be learned, and therefore draw away from the present incarnation.

Why Step In?

Again, the most important reason for stepping in is to further a purpose or learn an important lesson. Other reasons may include a desire to be near a particular person, wanting to experience a physical life while avoiding the early childhood phase, or taking advantage of a situation already created by another soul.

Three of us who know one another in this present life remember being part of the same soul exchange in a past life. Through regression, I remembered being the daughter of royal blood in Spain during the time of the Inquisition. The atmosphere was tense. People all around me were being tortured and killed. I felt at great risk, especially because I had made a dangerous alliance with a foreign freedom fighter who had invited me to escape from the country with him.

A male friend of mine in the present lifetime—we will call him John—independently remembered being the cavalier man who had fallen in love with me. He recalled that there was something odd about my energy in the final months of our lives, but he had been so determined to be with me that he overlooked the changes. On the day that we two lovers were to meet and escape the persecution of the church, the Inquisitors located me and ended my life. John waited in our secret meeting place until he, too, met his demise.

A second woman I know in this life—we will call her Emma—remembered the end of my previous life well. She was the one who actually experienced it! I had been so dismayed by all the cruelty and torture that my soul had chosen to leave that body several months before its untimely death. Emma had not experienced a physical body on the Earth plane for some time. She wanted to immerse herself fully in the harsh reality of the religious wars, in order to gain an important lesson that would provide a lasting impression on her consciousness.

I wanted out; she wanted in. And that is why John experienced me so differently in the last few months of our lives. All three of us witnessed and confirmed the soul exchange of that lifetime through independent past life regressions.

Who Keeps The Personality?

Your personality is shaped by the nature of the soul combined with life experience, and an imprint of all the initial soul's memories and experiences is left with the physical brain. When a step-in transition occurs, almost everything that has been logged into the brain remains. The new soul will remember childhood events, as well as familiar people and places. From the outside, very little will appear to be different—but certain dispositions, habits, quirks, and interests of the new soul will begin to show through in time.

If the personality of the incoming soul is stronger and more dynamic than the personality of the outgoing soul, there may be more striking changes immediately after the transition. The person may "pick up" new habits, or "drop" unwanted ones. They may even decide to leave long-term relationships. That makes sense, in light of the fact that they did not choose the relationship and it really wasn't theirs in the first place. On the other hand, some new souls come in specifically to partake in an existing relationship.

If the personality that has been imprinted on the physical brain is the stronger of the two, the new soul's personality may not show through very clearly. People may hardly notice any change. Sometimes when this happens, the new soul has trouble realizing their intended purpose. It is just too difficult to overcome the old personality and redirect the path toward the incoming personality's goals. This inability to manage the personality can cause substantial subconscious frustration. The soul who has stepped in may choose to complete that lifetime, or may arrange to step out again.

Stepping In Is Rare

The process of stepping in does not occur very often. It is the exception, rather than the rule. We address the subject here because it does happen, and so we need to be aware of the possibility. Knowing about the phenomenon of stepping in also helps us understand several other aspects of past life regression.

First, it helps clarify the situation in which people remember two lifetimes with overlapping dates. For example, some people dismiss the validity of past life memory if they hear themselves say, "One life was from 1735 to 1795, and the other was from 1750 to 1810." I always recommend carefully examining and researching any information that you recall from a regression, but remember that when there is overlap, there may be a step-in involved.

Second, we know that stepping in is not to be feared. In fact, it provides both souls with additional freedom and choice. A body is never taken by force in this type of trade; it is always exchanged by mutual agreement for an alternative experience more conducive to each soul's goals and desires.

I knew two young women whose souls were so closely linked that they chose to exchange bodies back and forth throughout their early lives. Interestingly, their lives were quite similar. They both had one younger sibling and divorced parents. They both had stepmothers who were abusive. They also had similar hair, height, and body types. Even their interests were the same. They each received the same gift from their fathers for high school graduation. Neither they nor their families ever met face to face in this physical life, yet these two young ladies were both part of the same circle of friends at different times in their lives. Every few years, they would simply exchange positions and try out the other body.

This information was revealed through trance work with one of the young ladies, who was able to recall experiences that she had while residing in the body of her counterpart. This client is now deceased, but the information was verified by members of the social circle who knew them both.

Helen's case illustrates some interesting aspects of stepping in.

Case Study

Helen

This profound series of past life memories reveal the source of Helen's many present-life issues—including pain, multiple physical ailments, and previously unexplained emotions and dreams.

Helen came from a fundamentalist Christian background and was not confident of her belief in past lives. She was not entirely sure at the onset of our sessions, for instance, whether undergoing hypnosis and visiting past lives would be a sin. Despite her apprehension, she felt compelled to get to the roots of her various disorders, visions, and emotions. She was on anxiety medications, and was referred to my office by a medical doctor who understood that she needed something beyond what they were offering her.

Warning: Some material contained in this regression may be offensive. The purpose of including it here is to show the understanding and healing that can emerge from this work. Because of the length of this material, my comments will be limited to only those that seem necessary to help the context of her monologue.

As we begin the regression, she describes the door that she is viewing.

H: It is a steel door. It is big, with a silver knob. It looks like a hospital door. As I go through it, I notice a hospital bed. It is a room full of light. It is too bright to see anything. When I become accustomed to that light, I notice people. There is someone in the bed. She is old and female. She is almost not human. She says that she is ancient. Her work has been to heal with herbs. She says, "You come to me when you are sick and I help you." I don't like her. I am not sick, but they say that I am. There are others in the room. They say that I need health. She says, "Would you rather be in this bed?" I say, "No." She helps me to get better. She tells me what to do and what to eat. She tells me how to care for myself. I don't listen always, but now I don't feel as afraid. Maybe she is okay. She is so stern. She is a spirit. She is hard with me. She has been telling me these things for three weeks and I have been doing it. I have begun to walk more so that I can sleep at night.

ML: What else do you notice about her?

H: She is not dead. She is alive, yet not in a body. I, too, am not of the dead. At least not of the evil dead. I should have a memory of her. She says that she was my nurse. She says, "I did everything for you." I see her with her white starched uniform, hat, and scissors hanging at her side. I even told her to use white bobby pins. If someone had cut off both my arms, I wouldn't have missed them, because my nurse did everything. I told the nurse to keep both her arms, because there were certain things I wouldn't do.

ML: What do you know about who you were in that lifetime?

H: I was an unconventional man, about thirty-seven years old. I think I was German, and I performed experimental, hideous medical procedures for the Nazis. I was very brave, a doctor. I would stand up against them. The nurse tells me, "You thought that you were the reincarnation of something evil, not just brave. But you kept us alive. You saved lives. You were brave. I want to help you through all your lifetimes. To help you with the things that you are required to do. You prayed for them before they died. You would cover them."

ML: What else do you remember?

H: I didn't love her, but I needed her help. I would medicate her to help her through the pain of an abusive relationship with a German officer. He was aware of all the things that we did. He would look over my shoulder. I could have left, but I wouldn't have known the exhilaration of scientific discovery that would help the world in many ways. I wasn't evil, but I was there. I could be guilty. She tells me I shouldn't hold it so deeply. My health problems in this life are from then. There is no need for the anxiety and fear. She said I was brave.

ML: What health problems stem from there?

H: I have such a depression. It is like a vice squeezing my chest and head. It comes from the memories.

ML: Do you know of any benefit in keeping that vice squeezing your chest and head?

H: I have to remember. I have to repent. I remember the blood. I see myself operating on a man in third level starvation. He had scurvy and rickets. I operated on his brain with no anesthesia. His eyes watched me as I removed part of his brain. I was possessed with the quest for knowledge. People were expendable. They look like sheep to me. I hate myself. I was one of God's chosen. I did this. I will never die. I will live forever.

ML: What else do you remember?

H: We thought the Jews had a special cell within them, an entity that made them so strong. We never found it. We took living tissue, cells, and put them in other people and animals. We would do complete lobotomies to desensitize the pain. We only had primitive life sustaining systems, and manual operations. We made some of the people keep others alive. When I see the stories now, I feel I was a monster. Some of the people that I worked with then I know now. They are the same now. My spirit guide says that I have to part with them. I never had any friends in that life. I only had my work. I didn't want friends. I was obsessed. I remember laughing and having a drink with blood under my fingernails. Sometimes I would see people and know what it would be like for them to die. I would look at people's hands to see if they had blood under their nails. I would chew my nails so there would be no blood. I could cut someone open and perform surgery if I had to, right now. Not to hurt them, but because I could. I can tell what's wrong with people now. I was a doctor before that, too. That was in the 1700's. In that life, I died on the battlefield with a bullet in my shoulder. I acquired gangrene and an infection. It was hot the day I died. I hated the heat. I saw the bloody mess that I left behind. There had been a skirmish on the border between Germany and Austria. I was English. I heard about it and I went to help. I left my wife and two children at home. She begged me not to go. In this life, I have a husband like that, who goes his own way. I hate him for that. I know how she feels now. I never knew what happened to her until three years ago. When I met her, in this life, I told her that she had been my wife in another lifetime and she believed me. Now she comes to me with her problems. I enjoy her and am compelled to help her. I've always been so driven.

ML: What else do you remember about the German lifetime?

H: I just want God to know that I am sorry for all the despicable acts that I was involved in. I had no conscience. I was so enthusiastic about science. I have been punished this lifetime. I feel more than I should now. It is atonement. I'm sorry. Now, I wouldn't take one life for any reason. Then, (in the Nazi life) I had some fear, but I was brave and outspoken. People were afraid of me, and they are even now. Those people would have been killed anyway. But that doesn't make it right. If God could only know. I am ashamed that I am so brilliant, and that was carried through lifetimes. I just couldn't wait for technology in order to learn it in a dignified manner.

ML: What else are you noticing?

H: The vice on my head and chest also relates to sexual irresponsibility. It is about the Italian women. I hate them. They are whores. They would intrigue and seduce us. I used them. I never enjoyed and loved them. We did things to them so they wouldn't become pregnant. It was painful. I'm sure that I do not deserve to love this lifetime. I am not lovable. I am incapable of love. I want to feel something. I feel lust and infatuation. I test being in relationships, then hate again. I never thought of the Italian women as human. I had no compassion for them. I wouldn't even kiss them. I didn't want their taste on my mouth. I am reaping what I have sowed. I wonder if I can ever love someone—someone who loves me for who I am.

ML: What would it be like to be lovable?

H: I would wear white. I would feel clean. It would be peaceful. It would be with a peaceful man. My spirit guide says that love is right here. He has been telling me for a week that I know something, but I don't. It involves one of the men around me now. He won't divulge too much. That would be too easy. I feel I can't choose because I have made bad choices before.

We continued to discuss Helen's present day relationships and choices. She said that, even though she was married, she felt a compelling, driving force to find a man—that special one. We went on to another past life.

H: This door has a rounded top, is wooden, and is hanging on big hinges. It is heavy with a window. I see six steps. Now I am in the clouds. It is sunny, but I'm in the clouds. I am flying. I notice the mountains and hills below, and a breeze. I hear the sound of an engine. It is coming from a small plane. It is peaceful and pretty. I'm a female in my thirties. There is someone flying this bi-plane. The pilot looks like my father or my friend Phil. Down below I see the land, green grass, people walking and being happy. Women are in long dresses. I'm in pants.

ML: What else do you notice?

H: Now I am in the house. I have a daughter. The man is going away. He is my husband. I think he is my father in this lifetime. He married me in a garden. I have one daughter and one son, as yet unborn. My husband is flying away. He is going to war. He mustn't go. We are in

America. Indiana in the 1930's perhaps. He leaves. I'm on the street, pulling the children in a wagon. It is a small town. Now I see us shopping. I'm afraid. It is hot and dusty. It's been so long with no word from my husband. I want to go to the post office across the street. I'm afraid. When I go, there is no letter from him there. There is a man bothering me. It is the deputy. I don't like him. He calls me Widow McCain. I'm not a widow. I dream of flying with my husband. I know that he lives. We eventually learn that he is missing in action. Now my daughter is fourteen. I continued to wait for him, but he never came back. They sent me his jacket and his watch, which was broken. I would sleep with the jacket. I can smell him on the jacket. Finally, I died of pneumonia. As I lift off that body, I see him. He looks strong and healthy. He sees me coming. We turn into bright light. There is no pain now. We are one. It is Phil.

ML: What do you notice about that encounter?

H: He wants to kill someone, in retribution for the war. He is going to kill a man. He made a pact with the Devil in Italy regarding more war in the future. It has to do with the Nazis. He is going back. He is going to kill him. I have to help. I can't go as a woman because I would have babies and I would be alone. I can be a strong man. He tells me, "We will get it over with quickly and come back to the light." I tell him, "We better." He wants to kill Hitler. He needs my help, and that of others. He said that I'll know him. I will smell him. He eats raw garlic. You will never forget how he smells. I don't know why he wants to do this. Why couldn't he just be my husband again? He is the only man who loves me.

ML: What happens next?

H: We accomplished our mission of getting into bodies, so we were separated again. I was the doctor that I talked of earlier. I didn't see Phil for a while. He went underground. He was a war criminal. I died first. I injected myself with poison. He told me to do that if he didn't come back. But when I did, he wasn't dead yet. I waited on the other side for him. I thought he had died, but he was a prisoner. He eventually died of starvation. Yet, he was still strong. He had a purpose.

ML: What else do you remember about that experience?

H: I didn't like being a man. I won't be a man again soon. He asked me, "Could you live without me in the next lifetime?" I tell him no. "Half a lifetime? I'll come to you when half the life has passed."

There was more discussion about their relationship in this lifetime. In our next session, we continued to explore her relationship with Phil.

H: I see a cot. There is a man laying on it sideways, asleep. He is a peasant. There is a cook stove, and four brick steps at the end of the room. There is a curtain to separate the bathroom area. There is a rocking chair behind the curtain. It is clean. I am a spirit here. I can't hear him, but the man has a wish. He wants his grandson to go to America and be prosperous. He says he is dying, and he wants me to know his wish. He says, "Find my descendants in America. Help them."

ML: What else do you know about that scene?

H: This is in Holland. I go out the window into the bright light. I am flying. I can see the ocean. It is beautiful. I land on a boat. I am looking for someone. I find a young man wearing a brown jacket and cap. He is the grandson of the dying man. I travel along with him. He is smoking a cigar. He is only eighteen years old. He sort of looks like my father in this lifetime. He gets off the boat. There are lots of people everywhere, and it smells bad here. He is running. He is hungry. After a while, I see him looking at a farm where he could work. There is a girl there, but he doesn't know that yet. Her name is Rebecca. I see the wedding. Now I see he has become a soldier. He is the son of the grandson of that dying man in Holland. Now, I have come into a female body and I marry him. It is 1916 and we are in Tennessee. We have an automobile. We go to Memphis. Oh, this is Phil again. He wants to have fun. It's our honeymoon. He scares me because he has so much energy and is so intense. Now, it's later and I see our daughter running across the floor to him. He hugs her and she says, "Squeeze me." So, he calls her "Squeezie."

ML: What do you notice next?

H: Now I see the hospital. I had another child. The nurses help me bathe. I'm crying because my husband went to war. It is WWI. I'm given a flag and a metal, but not his body. He starved to death on the ground in Germany or somewhere in Europe. His plane had been shot down from the ground and two children found him. They couldn't understand him. When they laid the flag down, I fell forward. I went down, and then came up and up. I saw a mountain. I left that body right then.

ML: What do you notice next?

H: Phil stepped into the body of a soldier, in 1942, and is smoking. I am right in front of him and I can't touch him. I must become human. Phil says, "Come to me," but I can't. So, I stepped into a young man. He was dying. He is hurt and scared. He has been shot and feels beaten. My spirit is on his body. I tell him, "Give it to me. If you want to go, go." He had a wife waiting on the other side who took his hand. I got in and I woke the body up. I am shot. I know what to do. I have to remove the bullet from my own shoulder, and I have to stitch my abdomen. I don't understand the language. I speak Russian, and I am in Poland. The Germans want me to go to the hospital. They tell the officials that I did it; I performed the surgery on myself. They say to me, "You know what you are doing" and they hand me a black bag. They say, "Is this yours?" I have never seen it before. It is the bag of the young man that died, whose body I am now in. Therefore, they think that I am a doctor. I say that it is my bag. It seems my hands know what to do with the medical instruments. My captors take me to a building and put me in front of a man who is told that I am a prisoner with skills. I am given a command and told to do what I am told or be shot through the head. I look around and I sense Phil is around here somewhere. My own brain is mixing with that of the man whose body I am in. I am beginning to think like him. I want to see Phil before I fall into forgetfulness.

ML: What happens next?

H: The man in front of me says that he is going to shoot me. He is joking to see if I am afraid. I say, "I am not afraid of your bullet, I am afraid of your dog." He says, "So am I." I am losing my vision. It is becoming more like that of the body I am in. I had never had the feeling of being a man. It's not right. I miss being a woman. I know that I'm going to lose my perspective now, and completely connect with the body. I am forgetting my spiritual vision.

ML: What do you notice next?

H: Now I am in the astral. I am traveling through time. We are always together. We are bound from centuries ago. Now we are two, experimenting with being separate. We must stay together. One cell, one life. Not male or female. One spirit. We had never been "bisected," until centuries ago. We wanted to feel it. But we can't be far from each other. The spirit that is Phil is becoming stronger. He can't be his own entity, but he is trying. He will perish if he tries. We must pool our fluid energy this life. We must be one again after this life. We must touch, agree to become one, in these bodies. We must not resist. If we do, they will die. The spirits will join. I am willing, but he is not.

It was fascinating to witness the two souls moving in and out of bodies, their lives crossing, making contracts, learning lessons, and trying to make their way through the experiences of the physical and spiritual worlds. This series of regressions gives a great deal of information about traveling in the astral, soul contracts, split spirits, the motivations for negative behaviors, and the karmic repercussions that follow our actions.

In later sessions, we called in the spirits of the patients worked on in the Nazi hospitals. Forgiveness was achieved, and the victims shared that they, too, had learned from the experience.

8

Our Infinite Potential

"Not only is the universe stranger than we imagine,
it is stranger than we can imagine."
—Sir Arthur Eddington

When we begin to explore our past lives, we come in contact with worlds and dimensions beyond what most of us experience in our everyday lives. We begin to see that the possibilities for where, when, and how we incarnate are virtually infinite.

This chapter touches on just a few of those possibilities.

Where Can We Incarnate?

According to the United States Geological Survey (www.usgs.com), scientists now believe that the universe is 11-15 billion years old. Our Milky Way Galaxy is 11-13 billion years old. Earth is about 4.5 billion years old. Even if we began incarnating on Earth the minute it was formed, that only represents about one-third the number of years that life could have existed in other places. It would be illogical, even arrogant, to imagine that our planet or galaxy are the only places where life could develop.

Further, the above only takes into account our universe. We have no idea how many universes there are. The number could be infinite—creating infinite choices of places for an individual to take physical form.

For these reasons, we must consider the likelihood of incarnations on other planets, planes, universes, and dimensions. From this perspective, the age of a spirit, and number of possible lifetimes that spirit could experience, becomes greater than we can fathom.

Dimensions and Planes

Mathematicians and scientist are starting to verify that there are many more planes and dimensions than we had once imagined. As they explore such concepts as the quantum universe, string theory, and beyond, they are finding mathematical proofs of ideas that seemed strange just a few decades ago. Here are a few thoughts on this information as it applies to reincarnation.

Geometry teaches us that planes are defined by dimensions. Our Earth plane is defined by the three dimensions of length, width, and height—but mathematicians now believe that there are about a dozen dimensions. Any combination of three or more of them can produce a plane. Any plane has the potential of creating inhabitable worlds.

We know that each of the three dimensions of our physical world is perpendicular to the other two. Think about a square box, a cube. Its width is perpendicular to both height and length. Its length is perpendicular to both height and width. Its height is perpendicular to length and width.

Now imagine that our three-dimensional cube casts a shadow on a table. That shadow is two dimensional. It only has length and width. If we could turn that shadow so that we observe it along its edge, the shadow would appear to be a one dimensional line. It would only have length. If we turned that line on its end and looked down on it, it would appear to be a zero-dimensional point.

So a point can be thought of as the shadow of an inverted line; the line as the shadow of an inverted plane; the plane as the shadow of a cube. Is the cube the shadow of something four-dimensional? What do you imagine that would look like?

Now imagine the process continuing until you are dealing with twelve dimensions. It is extraordinarily difficult for the "rational" part of our three-dimensional brains to think about that question. We need to rely on our imagination, our intuition, and our capacity to sense realities beyond what our eyes can see on this plane.

The same is true as we consider our infinite potential to incarnate.

Developing Our Dimensional Sensuality

Humans are capable of *sensing the effects* of more than three dimensions, yet typically we do not see those dimensions in the way that we see length, height, or width. With some practice, however, we can learn to perceive other dimensions—either while astral projecting out of our physical bodies, or after we die.

If we actually lived in five dimensions, in physical form, we would not be on Earth. We would need a substantially different physical reality. Making that change would require a fundamental understanding of those dimensions, and a bold expansion of our minds to encompass them. There are beings who are naturally capable of perceiving at least seven or eight dimensions, and any one of us may have lived in more than three dimensions at some point. But when we are born into three dimensions, our minds become accustomed to those limitations.

Choosing Earth

If we can incarnate in so many places and dimensions, why would we choose Earth? From many accounts, the Earth plane offers a wide range of vivid sensual experiences that are simply not available elsewhere.

Imagine a place where there were no colors, only shades of gray. Or a place where no creature, including you, could perceive sounds. What if all conscious life forms were flames of fire? What other possibilities for worlds and creatures can you imagine?

It is reasonable to expect that if you are reading this book, you are presently experiencing a life on Earth. The natural laws of our world dictate that life forms here are those that have survived, or adapted to, the environmental factors of Earth. We have created, or have conformed to, this environment. It is comfortable, and many spirits have grown very accustomed to experiencing lifetimes here. At some point, they may choose to incarnate elsewhere—but until they have touched all there is to experience on Earth, this is a familiar and inviting place.

Choosing Other Places

That said, we are certainly not limited to Earth. Not only can we take physical form in places other than Earth, most of us have probably done so.

Earth is relatively young, and the range of other possibilities is infinite. The likelihood that we have existed in other planes and places is overwhelming. (At the very least, we have all been on the astral plane between lives—and quite possibly, we have projected there while living on Earth.) In each place, we would take on physical configurations appropriate to the conditions found there.

When regressing to other planets or planes, it is important to remember that we are seeing only a small slice of time, out of what is probably a long history. That does not give us a full picture of the place or its history, any more than we would get a full picture of Earth if we regressed from another plane to one lifetime here. What if we landed in Africa at the height of the slave trade? Or in New York during the Depression? Or in Mongolia or Antarctica? None of these perspectives would give us the whole picture of Earth.

The same is true of visiting a lifetime in Atlantis, the Faerie worlds, or the Pleiades. Be aware that other planets and planes may be vastly different at various times, and in various locations—just as is the case here on Earth.

In What Forms Can We Incarnate?

Just as we can incarnate on other planets and planes, we can also take on forms that are distinctly different from the human body. Typically, the lifetimes we experience during regression are those in which we had bodies that we would recognize. However, the possibilities are infinite.

We can incarnate into bodies in shapes and materials that we could not even imagine from our present perspective. It is sometimes difficult even to get our minds around the outrageous appearance of some Earth species! Science documentaries have filmed physical forms that would be inconceivable had we not viewed them on the television screen. Seeing these bizarre creatures on our own planet helps us stretch our imaginations to conceive of what might exist on other planes.

In fact, what we see in science fiction may come directly from the artists' subconscious memories of previous life forms, and of phenomena and events in other planes and places. What types of physical forms do you imagine might be encountered in other worlds? What do you imagine a life in those types of bodies would be like? How difficult do you think it might be to remember a lifetime in a form so different from your own?

Can We Incarnate As Animals?

Most of the lifetimes on Earth that we will remember involve inhabiting a human body. For most purposes that a soul might have here, a human body is a good vehicle.

We might choose the body of an animal to serve other purposes, but there would be limitations. Animals have *perceptual* consciousness. They see and react to stimuli. They can learn responses, as was demonstrated by the research of Pavlov and others. They have a basic intelligence that allows them to recognize people and places, to be trained, and to know what to do to survive. However, they do not demonstrate the ability to understand concepts such as peace or objectivity. They do not appear to worry about death, or other future eventualities. Typically, animals simply perceive and respond.

Humans, on the other hand, have *conceptual* consciousness. We can imagine things that we have never seen, create art for its aesthetic value, worry, and have regrets. We not only perceive, as animals do; we conceive.

There is great controversy surrounding the possibility of incarnating as animals, and of animals progressing to incarnate as humans. One theory postulates that a spirit can evolve through incarnations in animal bodies of higher and higher intelligence—and eventually move from the primate or dolphin to the human consciousness. Perhaps spirits making this leap from animal to human consciousness have the appearance of being mentally challenged, naïve, or disabled. Perhaps this difficult lifetime is their first venture into human form. Instead of grieving the challenge, it may be more appropriate to celebrate the accomplishment! However, this is pure speculation.

Memories that appear to be incarnations as animals may come from other sources. These may include astral or mental projection, and totems.

Totems and Familiars

People are fully capable of astrally or mentally projecting into, and even possessing, the body of an animal. This technique was used frequently by practitioners of Earth magic who used "familiars," typically a cat or a bird. By mentally stepping into the body of the animal, the practitioner would gain the use of the animal's senses. Then, as the familiar moved about, the practitioner could view places or events that were not available to his physical body, and gather information that was useful to him.

The use of totems is somewhat different from the use of familiars, in that the practitioner may not actually become, or possess, the animal. In indigenous traditions, people may be connected to a specific animal, which becomes their totem. If their totem is a bear, for instance, they study the bear very closely. They learn and mimic the bear's style of walking, hunting, fighting, eating, and sleeping. They may adopt the bear's attitudes and habits. They may even shroud themselves in the skins, claws, and teeth of their totem animal. They will "be" the bear throughout their lifetime.

Imagine how easy it would be to misinterpret this information, lifetimes later, during a regression. The memories might be faded and vague after crossing the threshold of death and birth, perhaps more than once. We might believe we actually were the bear, when it had merely been our totem.

During a past life regression, I saw myself on a hillside with a falcon on my arm. My companion and I were training the falcon. The regressionist asked me about my surroundings, and I saw a village several miles across the meadow and down the hill. When asked what I knew about the village, I wasn't sure. I then decided to project mentally into the body of the falcon and let it fly to the village to get a closer look. This was very effective. Immediately, I saw the buildings, the cobbled streets, and the people. After that, I was able to recall experiences I had had in that village while in my human body, and the regression proceeded.

Had I regressed directly to that image of flying over the hill and into the village, I might have concluded that I was, at one time, a bird of prey. I know how it feels to fly like that—the sharpness of the vision, and the slight adjustment of the feathers to make turns and change elevation. However, in understanding the full context of the vision, I also know that I was not actually that bird.

Planet of the....

We cannot dismiss the possibility that there are locations off this planet where life forms similar to our animals evolved to become an intellectually advanced species. If spirits who are human here had incarnations in such a place, they might well recall being a tiger or a bird, and still be fully capable of developing technology, industry, and advanced civilizations.

My client Jim, who experienced deep trances and clear psychic vision, recalled lifetimes before coming to the Earth plane. He remembered being on a planet that was dry and hot, like a desert. There was technology so highly advanced that they were capable of building space ships that brought them to the Milky Way Galaxy. In those memories, Jim described himself as having scales like a reptile in place of human skin.

An interesting side note is that he is greatly interested in technology as well as astronomy.

The universe is vast, and there is much more to learn. Carla's past life regression gives us a sense of what it is like to incarnate into a body that is not a typical human.

CASE STUDY

CARLA

Carla had done numerous regressions that were frequently filled with rich textures, colors, and images. This regression allows us to peer into a world that is distinct from the one we normally experience. She also experienced a body that was not a typical human one.

C: I am in an opening between two rocks. I seem to be in a cave. It's damp. It smells earthy, like wet ground. It feels good to breathe it in. It looks like an eco-system of some sort. Perhaps in the roots. There is an opening under the roots. I see the crevices. I must be small. I have a lot of stringy things coming off of my body. They are like clothes, but not. It's tangible, like tangled hair. It's for protection. I can make them spread out. I can use them to comfort, or to spread over my body.

ML: What else do you notice there?

C: There are other faeries there. It's nighttime. I have a job. I'm exiting this place. It feels good to be outside. I fly around, playing. Now I'm near to a woman who was sleeping. I woke her up. She's larger; a human. We are preparing her for something. We are doing something to her hair. We're rolling something over her body. It's not anything physical; more like pixie dust. We are peeling away layers. And as I roll them down, a golden glow appears around her. Another faerie is doing the same.

ML: Then what do you notice?

C: It looks like we have picked her up by the shoulders. We are carrying her to a place in the woods, physically. It seems we fly away with her. It's not to the woods; it's to the edge of a cliff. I see the ocean, and the moon is full. We have placed her at the edge of the cliff. Her spirit just left her body, and her body crumbled to the ground like a dress that falls off. She flies off. She has dissipated into the night sky. It's probably an out-of-body experience. We guard her body to make sure its there when she comes back.

ML: What do you notice next?

C: I stepped into her body. I have to pretend to be her until she gets back. I'm greeting someone. I kiss them on both cheeks. Maybe it is her lover. We're making love now. It's fun. It's interesting how easy it is to go from so small to filling up an entire large body. I'm in her body, and she's returning. Another faerie has to guide her as her lover is still there. She comes in and I exit. We do some grooming. We really love this woman. We are petting her hair and kissing her on the head. Then we leave.

ML: What else do you know about this woman?

C: She has pale skin and curly hair. She's delicate. That was our job for the evening. She had left her body to go home to our world.

ML: What else do you know about your world?

C: I fly and dance about with another faerie. A female. We have a small group of six or seven who live in that root place. We meet and discuss what we have to do. We are peer-oriented. No one person is leading the group. Our group may be part of a larger group. Our whole group is assigned to that woman. It's necessary for people like her to keep the connection open and the communications between our people and the humans. She seems to have some significant position in our world. She seems familiar, I wonder if

I've seen her before.

This information not only tells us about other worlds, but also gives us a glimpse of the spiritual help that we may receive from beings from other realms.

Part Two

Exploring Your Past Lives

Part Two of this book is a guide to exploring your past lives. You will receive tools, learn what to expect, see how an actual past life regression unfolds, and be shown how to verify the memories you have during your regression.

9

Your Tool For Discovery

"Perception is the way we look at things.
Processing is what we do with that perception. Excellence in processing
does not make up for inadequacies of perception."
—Edward de Bono

How do you go about the business of exploring your past lives? Before you undertake any journey, especially a hero's journey, it is wise to learn all you can about the path ahead and to gather tools that will help you along the way.

The next four chapters give you tools and information to conduct your own past life regression—or to seek out a regressionist who can help.

The tools presented in this chapter are varied, and you will resonate with some of them more than others. Choose the ones that work best for you. The more you practice, the more skillful you will become and the richer your regressions will be.

Strategies To Exercise And Expand The Imagination

Expanding your imaginative capacities is one of the best investments you can make in discovering your past lives. There are many ways to empower your imagination. Here are a few:

1. *Practice creative visualization.*

   Listen to guided visualization tapes and CDs, even those that do not directly address past life regression. Encourage your mind to embellish whatever journey or tape you have chosen, adding details and emotions. Let your curiosity take you where you may not have been before, and embrace any surprises you encounter.

   Visualization tapes and CDs are widely available from your favorite book and music sources. Many libraries have them as well.

2. *Make up stories.*

   Practice writing fictional stories with outlandish characters and environments. Don't try to "write well" or tie together all the loose ends. Just write. Let the story go beyond all reason or reality. The wilder your stories get, the better. Don't allow any limitations on, or judgments about, your style. If it helps, promise yourself that nobody else will ever see what you write.

   Volunteer to tell stories to your children, nieces and nephews, or grandchildren. You may even have to borrow a child from one of your friends! It can be great fun, and you may become the children's hero for delighting them with your flights of fancy. Naturally, you will keep your stories age—appropriate.

3. *Read fantasy fiction.*

   Reading science fiction, fantasy fiction, or "speculative fiction" requires a fertile imagination. This genre of stories often embraces characters, landscapes, vehicles, machinery, and adventures that have rarely, if ever, been seen or experienced in this world.

   This kind of reading is one of the easiest, most pleasant, and most powerful tools for expanding your imagination.

Metaphors

A metaphor is a symbolic image meant to suggest, or to substitute for, something else.

When we are dealing in the realm of imagination and intuition, metaphors can help us reach information and experiences that our rational, literal minds cannot quite grasp. When you give yourself permission to describe what you see in a regression in terms of metaphors, you open up an entirely new channel of information and gain access to experiences that the rational mind might block.

For example, suppose that during a regression you are feeling tight, constrained, and closed in—but your conscious, rational mind stops the action because it can't describe what is happening in concrete terms. You might ask yourself, "What was it like?" This question gives you permission to move into the realm of metaphor. You might say, "It was like being inside a bell," or "I felt like I was underwater, with the ocean pressing in on all sides."

As you allow yourself to go with that experience, several things happen. First, you continue the flow of imagination and intuition. That is essential in order to get the benefit of past life regression. When you allow yourself to go forward, one thing leads to another.

Second, you may have stumbled across something that illuminates the past life. That bell may actually have played a key role in that life. Or you may be able to extrapolate from the image of the bell. Ask, "What does the bell mean to me?" It might mean freedom, or celebration, or a death knoll, or something entirely different. Whatever it means to you may be the very clue that takes your regression to the next level and gives you valuable information.

Don't hesitate to run with your metaphors, or to hone your skill with them by using them in everyday conversation. They can dramatically enhance your ability to delve deeply into past lives and to bring back the rewards.

Past Life Guided Visualizations

Many tapes and CDs are produced specifically to guide you through the process of discovering your past lives. These are most effective when you are receptive to the experience and able to relax into receiving the thoughts, visions, feelings, and experiences that such tapes may evoke.

Tapes and CDs are particularly beneficial when you have already experienced at least one regression "in person" under the guidance of a facilitator who can help you get accustomed to the way you receive and process this kind of information.

Meditation And Self-Hypnosis

Meditation and self-hypnosis are similar, and extremely powerful tools. Both may require more practice than other tools do, but you will succeed if you are willing.

The challenges people report in using these methods to discover past lives are the same challenges that generally confront people who are first learning to meditate. They may have trouble staying focused. Their minds may run in many directions at once. Other people cannot stay awake, and even fall asleep before they complete the regression.

Practice is the key to using self-hypnosis and meditation to explore your past lives.

Astral Projection

Astral projection is the ability to move or project your astral body through the astral plane consciously and intentionally, free of the physical body.

As you become adept at astral projection, you develop the ability to direct your experience to particular lifetimes. By remaining alert as you leave the body, you may be able to travel backward or forward in time, and to visit various locations on Earth. With diligent practice, and increased awareness of other dimensions, traveling to other planes of existence becomes possible as well.

During astral adventures to alternative lifetimes, you may observe yourself from a third party perspective, or you may "possess" your body from that time. These are known as, respectively, "dissociated" and "associated" experiences. In an associated experience, it feels as if you are actually in that body, looking out through those eyes. You are walking and talking in that environment. It may seem very real, and yet surreal, at the same time.

Dreams

We often astral project spontaneously when we dream, so dreams are an excellent way to visit other lifetimes. Some people remember their dreams easily. With practice, most people can learn to remember—and use these memories to learn about past lives.

Many people report dreams in which they are playing a part in scenes from another era. They are in period clothing and have distinct occupations and relationships with people in that other time. Frequently, these are actually experiences of astral projection during sleep. They travel through time and space, and discover that they are visiting a previous lifetime.

Dreams involving past lives have a distinct quality that sets them apart from other dreams. That quality is awareness. This is a form of lucid dreaming, so you are conscious or "awake" during the experience and can manipulate your reactions. In addition, dreams about past lives often feel more real, or more tangible, than other dreams.

If you want to experience this kind of lucid dreaming, you can program your mind with specific objectives as you are falling asleep—whether at night or during a daytime nap. Direct your mind to visit a particular lifetime about which you are curious, or a lifetime when you had a relationship with a particular person, or had a specific occupation, or had mastered a certain body of knowledge.

While concentrating on that directive, also program your mind to remember the information when you awaken. To do this, imagine bringing your energy into the center of your forehead, and staying aware of your experience as you fall asleep. It is as if your body sleeps, but your mind remains vigilant, observing the process and the experience. As you awaken, stay focused on what you were just dreaming. At first, you may only remember the emotions, feelings, or moods. With practice, you may remember objects, colors, people, or situations.

Even daydreams may spark memories that you can confirm later are from past lives. Allow your fantasy world to be fertile, conjuring up possibilities and probabilities. Then, follow up with diligent research and regressions to sort out fact from fantasy.

Simple Recall

Sometimes we just spontaneously remember a past life, or some aspect of a past life. The information might pop up in casual, off-hand remarks about the possibility of having been some particular person in another era, or having known someone in a past life.

Later, through more formal regression methods, you can confirm whether these comments have any merit. The spark of a past life memory may be right on target—or it may be close, but not entirely accurate. Memories of things we did even five years ago can become faded or distorted. It is reasonable to expect that memories from five hundred years ago might be a little off target as well. The more we practice, and the more we investigate that particular life, the more accurate we become.

Familiar Locations

Have you ever visited somewhere new, and suddenly remembered an odd detail about the place that you didn't think you knew? It might be information about streets in a strange town, hidden rooms in a cathedral, the location of a cave in a mountainside, or the cemetery in the country.

When this happens, you may have lived in or near that place during a past life. Your subconscious mind recognizes the scene, even if your conscious mind does not. When you have this sensation of familiarity, take a moment to relax. Allow your imagination to conjure pictures, ideas, and possibilities about lives you may have lived there.

Art

Many people report seeing a piece of art or a movie, and having a flood of memories—often even a hint of déjà vu. These can be distinct markers of a past life memory.

The next time you visit an art museum, notice which paintings call to you. Where are you drawn? Relax into the experience and notice whether any memories or feelings surface. Do the paintings that attract you depict scenes of a certain era? Do you recognize an activity or a location? Do the paintings elicit emotions and memories that don't seem to be related to events in this lifetime?

Aesthetics are the concretization of our concepts and values. Perhaps a painting or sculpture elicits emotions, feelings, and memories that you experienced in other lifetimes. Even when the artwork does not depict an exact past life event, it may draw a reaction that is associated with an actual memory.

Childhood Games

What were your favorite childhood games and roles? Did you like playing teacher, artist, musician, witch-doctor, doctor, or nurse? Fireman, shaman, mommy, superhero, or cowboy? Royalty, pirate, spy, shoemaker, dancer, or cook?

These can be clear indications of past life experiences. Children are innocent and open about their purpose in life and their past lives. They naturally gravitate to roles with which they are comfortable or familiar.

Many parents say that their children tell stories about locations, events, or occupations that they claim to remember, but with which they have no experience in this life. It is highly possible these stories are past life memories. Encourage your children's stories and role-playing to enhance their connections to this knowledge. Recalling what your own stories, games, and roles were can point you in the direction of your own past lives.

Channeling

When a person channels, it means that they are willing and able to allow a spirit to enter their body and temporarily animate it. This ability is also referred to as mediumship. When the spirit enters the channel's body, it is able to speak, move around, and partake in normal human functions.

Typically, a person channels a spirit in order to get information and wisdom from the spiritual world. It is also possible to connect with your past life counterparts by channeling their consciousness, but this is more unusual.

I have a friend who is a very talented channel. For several years, he has been able to channel the consciousnesses of his own past lives. My friend's present consciousness steps aside, and the consciousness from another time becomes alive in his physical body. When I speak with him at these times, I am dealing directly with the past life aspect who is animating his body.

When these aspects first arrive, they are usually quite disoriented. In most cases, the past life person was asleep or unconscious in their own era. They often thought that my world was a part of their dream. Many of them found our modern lifestyle astonishing. I taught a man from the 1500's to drive a car and took him on a flight to Los Angeles. I had to win the trust of a man who came through the channel after having been seriously wounded during the Inquisition. He was extremely paranoid, and would not relax until I handed him a sword. Then he began to feel he could trust me.

One man visited me frequently, through the channel, from his life around 500 A.D. I had been his lover when I was alive at that time. We had long talks about our lives together, both in that lifetime and in this one. After a while, he became quite familiar with the present day surroundings and with me. It was common for him to remember the previous times he had visited me.

Once he came to visit, and didn't remember coming here before. While we talked, I realized that he was now younger than he had been during his previous visits. In his reality, he had not yet had the other experiences of coming to visit me! At first, he asked me if I was an angel. When I told him who I was, he didn't recognize my name or my energy. He was so young, about ten years old, that we had not yet met in his lifetime. He explained that he had fallen asleep and was dreaming. I let him believe I was an angel, and guided him back to his dreams and out of the channel's body. After that, he always came to visit as an adult.

Most of the aspects who came into my friend's body would fumble with English for some minutes, and then slowly relax into letting the brain of the channel's body provide the language. They may have spoken with a thick accent, but they were able to communicate in English. However, I once spoke with an Egyptian who never figured out how to speak in English. We spent about an hour drawing pictures and playing charades.

I've included this information to demonstrate the idea that all time is occurring now. Those other aspects of us are "out there" in suspended animation, just waiting for our consciousness to observe them.

Psychic Readings

Many people claim to be able to tell you who you were in a former lifetime, but this is not always the best way to discover such information.

Since it is difficult to research information that a psychic gives you, you may never really know whether or not what they say is accurate. Another disadvantage is that if someone has already told you about a past life, it may prejudice what you see when you do your own past life regressions.

Clients sometimes say that a psychic has already told them about one or more of their past lives. When this is the case, they often have difficulty staying away from the "memories" that have been conjured by the psychic, and looking clearly at what they see for themselves. They can also have a hard time knowing whether what they see is accurate, or whether it comes from what they heard from the psychic.

Some psychics are very accurate in their readings of past lives. However, it pays to do your homework and choose someone who is reputable and talented. In my early twenties, before I started doing this work myself, I went to a psychic and asked for information about my past lives. He told me that I had been a male camel driver in a desert area. He also told me that I had been a female school teacher in America's Wild West—and that I had defended the children against raiding Native Americans, killing off the attackers and saving all my students.

Fifteen years later, when I was fully underway with my spiritual growth, a dear friend of mine experienced a past life. He said that he was a Native American who was riding toward a prairie school house with two companions. They were simply curious and meant no harm. Suddenly, the school teacher shot them all dead with a shotgun. He identified me as the school teacher.

That confirmed the psychic's talent, but I was sad to realize that I had reacted with such fear that I killed three men who meant no harm. It showed me how important perspective is in this endeavor. When I first heard the story from the psychic, I was proud to have been so brave and fended off our attackers. When I learned the truth about this episode, I was filled with shame that I had killed three people who would be my friends in other lifetimes and under difference circumstances.

Hypnotherapy

Unquestionably, formal hypnosis is the most reliable technique for accessing past life memories.

A qualified hypnotherapist guides you into a deep trance and then through the process of discovery, allowing you to explore your memories in a safe and supportive environment. He or she can help you be aware of and remember information and metaphors that emerge as you remember your past lives. If any difficult memories arise, or if issues that continue to create dysfunction come to the surface, your facilitator should be equipped with techniques to resolve and heal them quickly.

Occasionally, a client enters a past life spontaneously during a hypnosis session. If their belief system does not include the concept of reincarnation, they may interpret these visions as a metaphor, or simply as a figment of their fertile imagination. Either interpretation is valuable, and a good hypnotherapist can guide them to its best use. A metaphor derived from the experience can be just as useful as a consciously remembered past life. Each contains lessons that can be applied to the present life.

Although it is entirely possible to explore past lives on your own, Ellen's case shows the advantage of guidance from a hypnotherapist.

CASE STUDY

ELLEN

Ellen's marriage had gone flat and she was attracted to a man she with whom she worked. She wanted to experience a past life that would clarify her relationship dilemma. Because two men are involved, I suggested that we address the issue by going to lifetimes that involve her husband, and then to other lifetimes that involve the second man.

ML: Asking the subconscious to take you to a lifetime that will help you to understand your relationship with your husband, where do you find yourself?

E: I am in a tent. It is an Egyptian setting. I'm in the desert. I believe it is Saudi Arabia or Egypt or India.

ML: What else do you notice?

E: We are at war. I am there with another man. We are good friends and brothers.

ML: Do you recognize the other man as someone you know in this lifetime?

E: Yes, it's my husband now. We are comrades engaged in a battle. We are scared, talking, and trying to be brave. Then my friend went out from where we were sheltered, and he was shot. I crawled out and pulled him back. He died in my arms. Now, I see a cloud of dust going over us. Some of us are waking up. We're in a tent. It's quiet. The battle is over. I am tired, and it is time to go back home. Everyone in our group is either dead or wounded. I'm wounded.

ML: How old are you when you die?

E: I'm sixty-seven. I die of cancer.

ML: I would like to ask the subconscious to take you to yet another lifetime with your husband. Visualize that hallway once again. As I count from three to one, finding yet another door. Three, two, one.

E: It's a homemade door, made of wood.

ML: And as the door opens and you step though, what do you notice?

E: I'm outside this time. It is green and beautiful. There is a hillside, with an ocean in the distance. I see green flowing grass. I have walked out of the house, which is built into the hillside. It's made of sod. It's dark and dank.

ML: What do you notice about yourself?

E: I'm an old grandma. I have a large family. We all live together in this awful place. There is a wood table with a bench. Everything is rustic. My grandson is there. He is my husband in this lifetime. He is so cute, so full of life. He's smiling and laughing. He's always in a good mood. His mother died. I have cared for him like a son. He is the joy of my life.

ML: In what way is he similar to your husband now?

E: They have a similar disposition. He has a positive attitude and a joy of life. It reminds me of how much fun children can be. It's neat to see the generations, and to observe how life begins and ends. It allows me to be aware of the cycles.

ML: Asking the subconscious to take you to yet another lifetime, this time with your other friend, going down that hall once more... Three, two, one...and what does this door look like?

E: It's rattan. As I go through the door, I am outside. The sun is brilliant. I'm on a beach. It's sandy and the ocean crashes against the sand.

ML: What do you notice about yourself?

E: I'm Polynesian. I have long black hair. Maybe Hawaiian or Indonesian. I have dark skin. I am laughing and I'm young.

ML: What do you notice going on?

E: There is a get-together. There is a pig roasting. I see my friend. He's handsome, with a sparkle in his eye. We know each other. We are drawn to each other and we flirt.

ML: As time passes, what do you notice?

E: We fall in love. There is a ceremony.

ML: What else do you notice?

E: Now I see myself crying. I'm scared. I'm scared of dying. There is a fire. I can smell it. The wind is blowing. There is a volcano erupting nearby. We couldn't get to the boat. We couldn't get away. The village is destroyed. It's terrible. We were incinerated alive.

ML: What can you do to comfort that aspect of you in that lifetime?

E: I tell her to let go. There are better things that come later. Let go of what you're clinging to.

ML: What is she clinging to?

E: My friend.

ML: Does she listen to you?

E: Yes, she let's go. There is a peace after that. It's just that I sense the heat, and the screaming. It's terrible. She's so scared of it. Now she lets go, and she's peaceful. It's better now. She's sad, but there is no pain.

ML: And now going to another lifetime with your friend, going down the hallway, three, two, one...and what do you notice?

E: It's an igloo! How funny to be so cold after being burned! We are Eskimos. We have great dogs. Maybe we are scientists. It seems we are conducting experiments. We are going somewhere to get supplies. It's so cold.

ML: What do you notice about yourself?

E: I'm female. My friend is male. It's funny. We are like nerd brainiacs. We love what we do. It's exciting.

ML: What is the relationship between you?

E: We are lovers. We weren't married in that life, but it felt to me as though we were committed.

ML: What do you notice next?

E: We are back home now. I discover that he was cheating on me. He left me. My heart is broken. I had lived my life with a sense of the Pollyanna, and this was a blow to my reality. I am learning that things don't work out as planned. I'm so embarrassed. We have a mutual clique of friends. It's awkward. The other woman was blonde, funny, and gregarious. I was nerdy, and plainer. I didn't want to be a part of that group anymore. I'm embarrassed, hurt, and angry with him.

ML: What have you learned from seeing these lifetimes?

E: How you handle disappointment makes you what you are. Challenges are what make you stronger.

ML: If that aspect of you in that lifetime had advice for you, what would it be?

E: When one door closes, another opens.

ML: Do you see a theme through these lifetimes that can help you in this lifetime?

E: The tragedies and disappointments in life build character. I may have enjoyed those lifetimes that came with a golden spoon, but they are not as enriching as those that require one to crawl through the foxholes of life.

Ellen received enough information to make clearer, more educated, decisions concerning her marriage and friendships. She is now able to see the deeper aspects of her relationships with these two men.

10

What To Expect

"The beginning of knowledge is the discovery of something we do not understand."
—Frank Herbert

What should you expect when you begin to explore your past lives? The ways your past lives unfold for you will depend on your own attitudes, personality, beliefs, circumstances, and willingness to be open to whatever surfaces.

There are no set answers that work for everyone. There are, however, some elements shared in most past life regressions. This chapter gives you a general overview of what to expect.

How Past Lives Unfold

Some people experience a regression almost like a movie, while others report catching glimpses of still pictures, or simply a sense of "knowing," without actually seeing anything in particular. When the imagination is fertile and the mind is open to being creative, the experience of past lives may have more intensity in color, visions, feelings, emotions, and details.

People usually report emotions attached to the thoughts or visions that emerge during a regression. This is a good indication that the memory is valid, or at least that it is significant as a metaphor. In either case, it can reveal issues that are worth examining and understanding.

A Subtle, Filmy World

People often come to past life regression expecting a bold, technicolor, surround-sound experience. In our current life on Earth, we are constantly inundated with loud noises, strong smells, bright colors, and other vivid physical sensations.

During a regression, the experience is usually more like recalling a dream. Some people describe it as subtle and filmy.

Most likely, you will be fully aware that you are here, in this world, in this life during the regression. Yet at the same time, you will be aware of another story line, and of emotions that are not related to your present day experience. You will have a sense that the information you are receiving belongs to another time and another life experience.

If you are working with a facilitator, the experience may be similar to describing a dream to someone. You will be fully capable of speaking and narrating the story, but you will also be experiencing a somewhat dream-like state.

Visual, Auditory, or Kinesthetic Experience

We are most likely to recall events that strongly impact our physical senses, and that have a high emotional impact. Because sensation is so crucial to memory, it is important to understand our own personal style of sensing and remembering events. Each of us is different, but we all have three primary ways to acquire, store, and recall information. They are: visual, auditory, and kinesthetic.

Most of us have a primary mode, and a secondary mode. For instance, we may see events from a past life, and then start picking up the secondary mode of sound, or of sensing in our bodies what is happening. Or we might begin by hearing something, and then move on to sensing or seeing.

As you read about how each sensory mode works, think about what your primary and secondary modes are.

Visual

People who are visually oriented recall their memories with pictures. They find it easy to create pictures in their head. As psychics, they tend to be clairvoyant ("clear seeing"). Even their language is based on vision. They may use phrases such as:

- I *see* what you mean.
- Let's take a *look* at that.
- My *view* of this subject is...

Auditory

Other people access their memories through hearing. They may be sensitive to voices, remember events by the music that was played, learn by hearing someone lecture, or use words that refer to hearing. They often say things like:

- That *sounds* good to me.
- I *hear* what you are saying.
- *Listen* to this plan.

Kinesthetic

Kinesthetic people are "feelers." They have gut feelings about people and events, and tend to be empathetic and compassionate. They use sensory words, and speak in terms of:

- That story didn't *feel* right.
- I'm *feeling touchy* today.
- I was *moved* by their generosity.

Experiment to discover your best modes for accessing memories. Think of the words you use. Ask yourself if you prefer to learn by doing, hearing or seeing. How do you remember your dreams? Are they visually detailed? Are they in color? Do you remember more about the conversations than about people's appearance? Are the emotions more memorable than the way things looked?

Try to avoid the pitfall of basing your expectations on stories you have heard from other people about their regressions. Trying desperately to "see" your past lives, as your friend might have done, will be frustrating if you are actually a kinesthetic or auditory person.

As you practice regressions, you will find that memories flow more easily, and that you begin to develop stronger images and sensations. It is as though each journey into a past life cuts a groove in the pathway between the subconscious memory bank and the conscious mind's ability to access it.

Master Your Style

As you do more regressions, you will learn to master your own personal style of retrieving information. You will also learn a great deal about how your mind works, and this information can be valuable in all aspects of your life. The more you know about how you think and feel, the more self-mastery you gain—and the better able you are not only to access past lives, but to enjoy and succeed in your present life.

Imagine what you might learn about yourself if you notice, during sessions, that:

- Your mind races and won't quiet down.
- You shy away from any painful situation.
- Your mental screen goes blank and you can't decide where to go next.
- You notice, and embellish, minute details.
- You get to a certain point and "get stuck."
- You view the process from a dissociated (third person) perspective.

- You see the broad scope of the lifetime, and are uninterested in the details.
- You find yourself controlling the session, rather than allowing it to flow to you.
- You analyze the information even before the ideas are fully developed.
- You don't believe any information that shows you were more powerful than you have previously imagined yourself to be.

How we observe can be as interesting and revealing as what we observe. Understanding how we process information, and where our blocks are, can be enormously helpful. If your body won't relax when your mind is busy, or your mind won't relax while your body is busy, you can learn techniques to overcome that difficulty. If the analytical part of your mind keeps trying to take over the controls, you can train it to let go and give your intuition a chance to shine. You can even make some of these conditions work for you, rather than against you.

If you are having difficulty, find a qualified facilitator who can help. Often, one session with a past life therapist will help you understand the process and trust your experiences more fully. After that, you can begin to remember past lives on your own.

Pay Attention To All Responses

During one of my early experiences of being regressed, I found it difficult to get any visions. Nothing was coming for me. My first regression had been powerful and quite positive, so I was mystified—until I realized that I had very high expectations and that I was trying too hard.

After a few minutes of frustration, I began to notice a tension leading from my collarbone all the way down my left arm to my wrist. I thought it was peculiar, but it kept growing stronger. Finally, I began paying attention to it. I realized that I was experiencing a past life memory in which I was drawing an arrow on a longbow. The tension was the sensation of pulling the bowstring. As soon as I recognized that image, a whole scene developed in my mind's eye, and I was able to move easily through that life. I was a female in that scene, engaged in a battle with swords, bows, and arrows. In the next scene in that regression, I noticed that I was sad and frightened. Focusing on those emotions, I realized that I had received a message that my father was in danger.

This story demonstrates the value of paying attention to all physical and emotional responses, even when the point of it is not clear in your mind—and even when you were expecting something different. In this case, I was leading with kinesthetic sensations, followed by the visual confirmations. It all became clear after I let go of the expectation, based on the past, that I would have the "visions" first.

Pain And Dying

Some people are afraid to experience pain or death in a past life regression, for fear that it may bring on the same physical symptoms in this life—and may even cause them to die. In all the time that people have been exploring past lives, and despite the vast number of people who have participated, I have never heard of anyone who died in the process! You can fully experience all the sensations you had in a past life, including death, without any danger to your body in this life.

Occasionally, when the past life memory involves pain, some people do report discomfort. If this happens, simply move past that event to a time when you had regained comfort. The sensations will go away immediately. If you experience discomfort while recalling your death in a past life, simply move past that event and release from the body. As you do so, you will no longer feel the painful physical sensations. From your new perspective outside the body, you can then look back over the experience and recall those events as memories.

My client Mike was nineteen years old. His mother had given him a past life regression as a gift, and she was present in the room during his experience. As he went into trance and began the regression, Mike's first words were that he had excruciating pain in his abdomen. As the scene opened, he became aware that he was a Native American female, squatting in her teepee, giving birth to her child. He went on to experience the birth, and then returned to calm comfort.

At the end of the session, we discussed how grateful his future wife would be, because he could be truly sympathetic when she went through pregnancy and childbirth. Very few men can relate to childbirth as directly and personally as he now can!

Beyond The Threshold

In most regressions, I take clients through the death experience of the particular life we are exploring. Again, there is nothing to fear. Once the soul lifts off from the physical body, we do not feel pain or even discomfort. In fact, clients report just the opposite. Death is usually a welcome relief once the dying process is over. Most clients express relaxation and calmness once they have actually left the physical body during regressions.

Often, the cause of death is more traumatic than the death itself, especially if it involves violence or a painful illness. As Isaac Asimov said, "Life is pleasant. Death is peaceful. It's the transition that's troublesome."

Most people describe floating, relaxing, and enjoying the sensation of being out of the physical body. Some stay around and observe the deathbed scene with loved ones gathered around. Others turn their attention rather quickly to their new environment, ready to explore and discover who and what can be found in this new realm. Still others describe meeting loved ones or spirit guides who are waiting for them. Most people feel supported, loved, safe, and happy.

Occasionally, a client will report distress. This is usually associated with some regret from the lifetime they are leaving. Perhaps they died prematurely because of an accident or illness. Perhaps they experience tremendous grief at leaving their young children, or their mate. They may regret something they did, or did not do, during the lifetime. Most problems of this sort can be avoided by remembering, during the physical lifetime, to make ethical choices, express feelings to loved ones, and live life to the fullest.

When my favorite uncle died, I hypnotized my cousin so that he could communicate with his father. He wanted to have a final conversation to put closure on their relationship, and also to ask his father what should be done with all the tools he had left in the basement.

My cousin had never done anything like this before, and he was rather surprised when his father actually appeared! He also found it curious that his father showed up as a young man—vital, energetic, and excited. His father really didn't care at all about the tools, or anything he had left behind. My cousin said, "It's like he is tapping his foot, anxious and impatient." When we asked my uncle about this, he said he realized after dying that there was so much more to the universe than he ever imagined. He was anxious to move on, explore, and have some adventures.

The two of them had their conversation, and my uncle was off to enjoy his new existence. My cousin felt good about putting positive closure on their relationship, and he was able to give away his father's material goods without remorse or guilt.

Which Lifetime Will You Experience?

During your regression, you can deliberately visit a particular lifetime that interests you, or you can simply allow the subconscious mind to choose a lifetime that would be valuable for you to observe. You can also direct your subconscious to bring up a lifetime that gives you information about a particular subject, that involves a specific person, or that deals with any other interest you may have.

For example, you might want to see a life that can inform choices you are making now about relationships, finances, or parenting. You may experience a lifetime in which you faced similar choices, and see the consequences of various actions in an objective manner. You can ask to visit lifetimes when you were with certain people whom you know now, when you were engaged in a similar occupation, or when you had a specific talent or acquired a particular phobia. Or you may want to visit a lifetime that demonstrates the root cause of an illness.

The subconscious is a powerful tool. It contains knowledge and wisdom far beyond what we know with our conscious minds—and its capacities may even be infinite. Trust it, and let it work for you.

Visiting The Future

We have seen that, on some level, all time is now. That means that the "future" is available for us to visit and observe whenever we wish. That said, it is important to remember that there are infinite versions of the future—and that we select only one of them to experience. The future we visit may, or may not, be the same one that we eventually live.

The future that actually unfolds for us depends on many factors, including how much we change. Those changes can be positive or negative, and can involve behaviors, actions, emotions, speech, beliefs, karma, and a host of other considerations.

If we have a psychic reading and do not like the future that is revealed, we have the option to make those changes and, in turn, change our future. The reading may have been accurate, given where we were when it was done, but that particular future may not come to pass if we deliberately choose another path.

Visiting future lives is called progression, rather than regression. Progressions can be informative and useful, but I offer a word of caution. Instruct your subconscious not to reveal information about this lifetime that would be harmful to you or others. For example, if you progress ten years into the future and notice that you are in another body, living in another location, you can assume that your present life will be terminated in less than ten years. That knowledge may affect how you behave, and be more harmful than helpful to you. This is not always the case, but it is a possibility.

Some people are able to handle this type of information in a balanced way, while others may have a difficult time with it. The bottom line is: Think carefully before attempting short-term progressions.

Future Life Progression

On the other hand, you can freely move ahead 100 years or more without worries about significantly altering your path in this lifetime. The benefit of a progression is that you may see what the world is like in the future, and how you are dealing with it. This may inspire you to learn more, or to actualize your life purpose, so that you can be more prepared for the future. You may want to become more active politically or ecologically, or to seek more personal and spiritual growth.

Just keep in mind, as you explore, that the future you see may not be the exact future that you will experience. You have infinite choices and decisions to make between now and then.

In my early years as a regressionist, I had a client who spontaneously progressed during a session. She described the United States in the aftermath of a polar shift. There was mass destruction that included flooding, loss of electricity, and many other hardships. One day I received a phone call from a colleague who lived about an hour away, and whom I had never met in person. During our discussion, she referred to a client of hers who had described exactly the same scenes. Our two clients lived two states away from one another and were not acquainted.

The Future—Then And Now

As you think about what to expect in past life regressions, remember that our infinite possibilities and infinite potential all exist in the pervasive "nowness" of time.

The following story is a great illustration of these principles. In the 1980's, my client Jill asked to be hypnotized in order to explore some time periods that were missing in her personal chronology during this lifetime. The missing times began occurring when she was a child, and continued into adulthood.

She went into a very deep trance, and saw herself on another planet being trained as a guide for humans who were being relocated there. When asked about the year, she replied that was in the early 2000's. I was a bit concerned that this date might indicate to her that she would have an early death in this lifetime. I asked the year of her birth, and she gave a date in the 1950's. Then I understood that she was progressing to later in the present lifetime.

The session went on for about an hour, with detailed information about her off-planet experience, her role in the relocation plans, and what she was doing during the time that had been lost to her. When she emerged from trance, she did not remember anything about the experience or anything she had said to me. As it turned out, her childhood imaginary friends were actually alien entities who would visit her and escort her during journeys to another planet.

Although such stories are rare, dozens of my clients have recounted abduction experiences while in trance. People generally have not sought out these memories. They have simply emerged while exploring other subjects and issues. These experiences may be out of the ordinary, but they are not out of the question.

Donna's regression demonstrates one common element of past life exploration that people don't always expect—the capacity to shift easily among various past lives.

Case Study

Donna

The striking aspect of this regression is that it demonstrates how the memory of one past life can lead into another. Donna said that she had felt alone and disconnected throughout her life, and wanted to remember a past life that might hold clues to why she felt that way.

D: I'm outside. It's sandy. Not much vegetation. It appears to be all dried up. It's not exactly a desert, maybe Italy or something. It's not flat; there are hills and trees. I don't see anyone. It's definitely a different time and place.

ML: What you doing there?

D: I have sandals on, and a sack cloth outfit. I'm walking down a dirt road, looking for something. There is some sort of civilization that I come upon. It's an adobe dwelling. Things are made of sand and earth. It looks like biblical times now. There are not many people. I walk through the village. People are walking along side me. I see children, and people taking care of animals. I don't know anyone. I feel comfortable because no one is paying any attention to me.

ML: What happens next?

D: I come to a temple. There is a round fountain with water spouting up. There is no one at the door. It seems I'm supposed to figure out what to do. I enjoy watching the fountain. I'm curious enough. So, I go in. It has easy access. There are candles burning. I feel I am in a predicament. Why am I here?

ML: What do you know about that?

D: I see a bench and go sit down. I am looking around. It's pretty basic. I lie down on the bench to rest. I try to relax. The candles get bigger and brighter. There is no one there. I'm alone. I think I should fall asleep and get my message from my dreams. I feel secure there, so I eventually do fall asleep.

ML: Then what happens?

D: Spirits come in my dreams. They are floating around the temple. I'm supposed to be at peace, they tell me. I am not supposed to question so much. Just be at peace with it. What is to come will be revealed in the future. They tell me to not worry. To go with the flow. I see the spirits floating, and looking over me. Still I feel alone. There is a feeling of peace that is imparted. Then the visions evaporate. I wake up and am peaceful and at ease.

ML: Then what do you notice?

D: I'm still not sure why I am here and who they were, but I feel rested. I walk out of the church. The town is pretty deserted. I keep feeling like I'm asking myself, "Why am I here?"

ML: About what year is it?

D: It's around 200 A.D. I'm near Jerusalem. In a smaller town.

ML: What happens next?

D: I look at the fountain. I go back the way that I came into town. I still don't understand why I am here, but I am more at peace. I'm not hungry, even though I don't know where I came from or where I am going.

ML: As you continue to travel, where do you go next?

D: The path turns from sandy to a mountain road. There are trees lining the road. Now I'm a woman. The road leads to a plantation home in the southern part of the US. I'm a woman and I'm still alone.

ML: Can you get a sense of the era?

D: It's the early 1800's. I don't see any animals or people. Why am I here?

ML: What do you experience next?

D: I go up the steps to the house. I don't ring the bell, yet the door opens. A big black lady asks, "Can I help you?" I don't know who I am here to see. So I just wait. The lady of the house comes down the stairs. She is not upset that I am here. I don't know her (though she is my mother in this lifetime). She is pleasant enough. I don't know what I need. I have been traveling by foot, but I don't know how far I have come. The black lady takes me to the kitchen and feeds me.

ML: What else do you know about yourself?

D: I'm white, more or less twenty years old. I have come a distance. I seem to live fairly far from here. Yet I don't feel I traveled a long time. This home is pleasant. It seems I just wanted to get away from where I was. I wanted to be on my own. I was wandering so I could figure out what to do. They tell me if I wish to stay, I'm welcome. It's a lonely place; just the two women and myself so far. It seems to be well kept. The woman must be wealthy. Yet, still I am alone. They tell me I need to ask if I need something. Still there is a distance between us. They do not open up to me. It's nice to stay awhile, but we are not connecting.

ML: Do you ever feel disconnected in this life?

D: Yes, my whole life I have felt disconnected, alone, and as though I didn't know why I was here.

We ended the session, and continued with a discussion and healing around the feelings of being disconnected. This regression demonstrates several points. First, it shows us that a similar scene, coupled with a similar message, can allow us to move directly from one past life to another. Second, we see that the message in the past life is a clear reflection of what she is facing today. And third, even though there were many details left unknown, Donna was still able to recall meaningful experiences and memories.

11

Your Past Life Regression

"I went to the woods because I wished to live deliberately, to front only essential facts of life, and see if I could not learn what it had to teach, and not, when I came to die, discover that I had not lived."
—Henry David Thoreau

Congratulations! You have taken the time and energy to prepare yourself for the best possible experience of past life regression. There are many ways to bring your past lives into consciousness. This chapter serves as a guide, offers suggestions, and will help ground you in the experience—whether you work with a facilitator or on your own.

Working With A Facilitator

The most qualified person to facilitate a past life regression is someone who has experienced a number of past life regressions themselves. These people will have the best understanding of the process, and be most familiar with what you may experience so they can support you.

Many therapists offer regressions to their clients, yet in private claim they don't believe in past lives and have never recalled such memories themselves. A session with this kind of therapist may be successful—but if you have a choice, a well-seasoned regressionist who has a broad knowledge of past lives provides a better environment in which to explore your memories.

If you have friends who have had good results with regressions, ask for their recommendations. Ask for references from the practitioner if you wish, as you might do with any professional you are considering. It is common to request an interview with the practitioner before you commit to the session. This is a good chance for you and the regressionist to see if you are well matched to work together.

The Advantages

There are several advantages to working with a facilitator. You are supported by someone who has training and knowledge about the work you are doing, and is in a position to move your process forward. A facilitator may be able to ease your way, allow you to go deeper, assist you in sorting out what the information means and how it can help you, and be there in case you experience anything fearful or upsetting.

It can be difficult to move through painful memories on your own, let alone extract the lessons and value from them. It can be done, but we all have a tendency to stop when we encounter something very unpleasant or painful—especially if we are shielding something from our conscious awareness. A facilitator can help you keep moving through these experiences to the other side of them, where you reap the rewards.

Choosing Your Regressionist

Before the initial interview, prepare a list of questions for the regressionist. Consider asking the following questions, along with anything else that piques your curiosity:

- Have you personally experienced a past life regression?
- How many regressions have you performed on others?
- How frequently are your clients successful in achieving past life

memories?

- Where were you trained?
- What books do you recommend on the subject?
- Is therapy offered along with the regression?
- Is there anything that I should do to prepare for the session?

A professional regressionist maintains an objective stance and keeps the work free from interpretation, judgment, or assumptions. Should he or she fail to do so, understand that it is your right to terminate the session.

Your facilitator should use non-leading language during the session, so that you are free to go in any direction the information takes you—and not where he or she wants you to go. Some examples of non-leading questions are:

- What do you notice? What do you observe?
- What happens next? And then what?
- What do you know about that?
- Where are you? What is the date?

Some leading questions, ones your facilitator should avoid, are:

- Is he your father?
- Is that celebration for your birthday?
- Are you angry about that?
- Do you think you were the President?

These questions suggest specific answers, and push you in particular directions—rather than keeping you free to explore any possibility that arises.

Working On Your Own

If you choose to remember your past lives on your own, there are many ways to do so. The only disadvantage of working alone is that any information that you are hiding from yourself—through shame, fear, or other blocks—will remain hidden. There is no one to prompt you to go a little deeper for your answers, so your own filters and perspectives will color your experience to some extent.

Here are some specific tools to enhance your experience:

Creating the Environment

When you are ready to begin your regression, find a space where you will be free from distractions. Tell any friends, children, pets, or significant others who are in the house that you are going to be engaged in a mediation and need time to be quiet and alone.

Create an atmosphere in the room that will help you go within, find your treasures, and bring them to the surface. What will deepen your experience, or inspire your intuition? Music, incense, candles, crystals, and objects from the location of the lifetime you wish to remember may all be valuable. Use whatever you think will get you in the right frame of mind for your expedition.

I personally have a strong affinity with lifetimes spent in Atlantis. Years ago when I decided to make a solitary excursion there, without the help of a facilitator, I wanted to maximize my chances of success. I created an altar with crystals, candles, a goblet of water, and other items that were sacred to me. I played meditation music that resonated with my ideas of Atlantis. I danced and moved my body in a trancelike fashion to raise my energy and enhance my mood.

When I sat down, I took in my hand a crystal specimen called larimar, from the Dominican Republic in the Caribbean, and which reputedly has connections to the lost shores of Atlantis. I focused on the aqua blue color of the stone, which I personally associate with my concept of Atlantis. While sitting in front of my altar, concentrating only on the blue stone, a picture opened up in my mind's eye that changed to a moving image. I saw myself on a beautiful beach, wearing a gauzy shift. The water was to my left as I walked along the beach, with trees lining the beach nearby. I turned to the right and walked inland for perhaps five or ten minutes.

I then came to a building that I knew to be a temple. There were stairs leading to the entrance. The building was made of a sand-colored stone. I sensed myself as a female in my mid-twenties. I was a young priestess or devotee. I felt carefree, so it didn't feel as if I had yet gained the level of authority or responsibility for which I was in training. Life was simple and spiritual, and I was happy.

Although these ritualistic steps to prepare myself for the experience—the candles, goblet, and stone on my altar—were not necessary, they provided atmosphere and gave me permission to accomplish my goal.

Meditation

Many methods of meditation will give you access to your subconscious, your creative imagination, and memories of past lives. Experiment with various techniques and see which best enhances your recall. Here are a few that my clients have found particularly helpful:

- Visualize going down a hall. Choose a door to enter. As you walk through that door, the past life regression begins.
- Choose an era or a location, and make up a story about it until the details begin to indicate that you are remembering an actual past life.
- Imagine yourself in a fog. As the fog lifts, discover yourself in a scene from another lifetime.

Remember to give yourself permission to have this quiet time, to be open to the experience, and to enjoy the adventure regardless of whether you come away with an accurate past life experience or a meaningful metaphor.

Journaling

Keeping a journal of your regressions will help you remember, notice, and use the details you discover. Take time after each regression to make thorough notes. Writing will help you connect more deeply with the events, visions, and emotions of your memories, and also help clarify the experience.

You may discover that you remember even more than you thought you did when you take the time to write down everything that occurred during your regression.

Guided Meditations

Many audiotapes and CD's are available that provide guided visualizations for recalling past lives. Many are available at: *www.AwarenessEngineering.com*.

You may also make your own audiotapes by recording an induction, along with a guided session for experiencing a past life. If you would like to do so, the following script will give you some ideas. You are welcome to record this meditation directly for your own purposes—but not for sale, as this material is copyrighted. When recording, speak slowly and be sure to pause after each question.

A Script For Your Past Life Regression

Closing your eyes, take a deep breath. As you release your breath, release the tension in your muscles. With each breath in, draw in energy from the universal source. With each exhale, release tension and any concerns for the activities of the day. Turn your attention inward. Relaxing, deeper and deeper.

I wonder if you can imagine locating that still point within you. That place within you where you are at peace. Connecting fully with that still point within you, allow yourself to relax as deeply as you are comfortable doing, knowing only you can allow yourself to go deeper and deeper.

And now, I wonder if you can imagine your favorite safe space. This space can be a place where you have been, or it can be completely derived from your imagination. And, as you imagine this safe space, you begin to look around and explore your surroundings. What do you notice here at this time?

As you continue to explore your surroundings, you discover a special place where it would be so comfortable to sit down and relax. As you settle into this comfortable place, you realize that this place has special energy. In this place, you are connected to vast wisdom and knowledge. In this place, you are fully aware of how to go into the deepest trance state of meditation that you have ever experienced, knowing only you can make that happen. Going there now. Deeper and deeper, down, down, down.

As your body relaxes and your mind continues to go deeper, begin to envision a hallway stretching out before you. And, as you begin to move down along that hall, you begin to notice the texture of the floor covering beneath your feet, and the color of the walls. And there are doorways along this hall, each one leading to past life experiences that will be so helpful for you at this time. As I count from three to one, you will find yourself in front of one of those doors. Three, two, one. And how would you describe the door that you are standing in front of?

When you are ready to step through that door, it opens and you move through the threshold. As you do so, do you find yourself indoors or outdoors? Describe the environment. As you explore this place, what else do you notice?

Allow your imagination to guide you through the regression. You can add other questions of your own to assist you in staying focused and moving through the memories. They may be questions about your clothing, location, the date, your age, gender, activities, whether you are married or have children, how old you are when you die, and so forth. As you continue through the regression, encourage yourself to be curious and inquisitive. Read the case studies in Part 3 of this book to get ideas for further questions, to see what kind of information others have uncovered, and to learn more about the process.

Kendra's regression demonstrates many techniques that you can use, even when working on your own.

Case Study

Kendra

Kendra came in with weight issues, a desire to know about her life purpose, and an intention to bolster her self-esteem. Due to various stresses, she had gained about forty pounds over the past several months. She had been extremely successful in her career, and wanted to leave her position to begin her own business.

We began by talking about Kendra's issues, and this led naturally into exploring her past lives. Because these issues were all tied together, and because the session illustrates several techniques that you can use, I am presenting the entire transcript here. We start by addressing the presenting problem, the weight issue.

ML: Taking a breath and closing your eyes, begin to imagine that you are in a pool of still water. Any ripples you may notice in the pool are in response to your thought patterns and energy. As you continue to observe the pool, relaxing deeper and deeper, you will notice the ripples become calmer and less frequent. As a part of your mind continues to observe the pool, relaxing, I would like to ask another part of your mind to answer four questions. Remaining this relaxed, and yet able to speak, please tell me what carrying the extra weight allows you to do.

K: Hide. It allows me to not have to do things that are risky.

ML: What does carrying the extra weight prevent you from doing?

K: It prevents me from doing risky things. Even things that I am capable of and that are good for me.

ML: If you did not carry the extra weight around, what would that allow you to do?

K: I'd feel more confident about being in the public eye. I would stand up and be heard. I would move out of my comfort zone.

ML: What would not carrying the extra weight prevent you from doing?

K: I can't think of anything.

ML: Is it true that there is a part of you that wants to lose the extra weight, and another part of you that for whatever reason resists that?

K: Definitely.

ML: Imagine separating those two parts distinctly, so that the part of you that wants to lose weight is on one hand and the part that resists that is on the other hand. Which hand wants to lose the weight?

K: The right hand.

ML: And the left had resists that?

K: Yes.

ML: Allow your focus to move into the right hand, the hand that wants to lose the weight. If it had a soap box to stand on so that it could tell me whatever it wanted to convince me that its desires are right, what would it tell me?

K: It could tell you a bunch of things. I could be an active participant and a leader in various issues. I would have a voice, and be listened to. People would feel differently afterwards. I would coach people about their potential. Give them positive self-belief. I would have a life and reach my potential. I could make a big difference. This is good—and fun! I feel fabulous, and can do anything at all!

ML: Come out of the right hand and over to the left hand. What would it have to say?

K: Why would you want to do that? It could be embarrassing. Who would listen to you? What makes you think you have anything to say? What makes you so special? Don't draw attention to yourself. It's better to take the tried and true path. It's clear and dependable. You can count on it. There is no need to rock the boat. Life is already really good now.

ML: How would the right hand respond to that?

K: Life is short. Let's have some fun. Let's stir things up a bit. The only way to get your confidence up is to do it.

ML: How does the left hand respond to that?

K: Life as you know it will be very different. Are you sure you want to take that risk? Look at all you might lose.

ML: How does the right hand respond?

K: It banged the left over the head! It says look how much I have to gain. I have never been frightened before.

ML: How does the left hand respond?

K: It's your call.

ML: And the right?

K: It's quiet. Yep. Life's too short for regret.

ML: And the left's response?

K: It shrugged. Okay, it's your call.

ML: How does the right respond?

K: Watch me fly!

ML: Does the left hand want to support the right, or just get out of the way?

K: It wants to hang around and check that I don't hurt myself. It doesn't want me to fly too far too fast. It wants to watch from the side-lines.

ML: In holding back and watching, what is the goal of the left hand?

K: (Burst of tears and emotion.) It wants me to succeed!

ML: If you could succeed, fully and completely as it imagines it now, then what would you have that is even more important?

K: I'd be doing good things and making a difference for a lot of people.

ML: If you could make a difference for a lot of people, fully and completely as it imagines it now, then what would you have that is even more important?

K: I'd be really proud.

ML: If you could be really proud, fully and completely as it imagines it now, then what would you have that is even more important?

K: I would have the freedom to do what I want, when and where I want it.

ML: If you had the freedom to do what you want, fully and completely as it imagines it now, then what would you have that is even more important?

K: I'd have time to spend with people I love, room for more people, time for my garden, and playing, and being with children.

ML: If you had time to spend with others, fully and completely as it imagines it now, then what would you have that is even more important?

K: I'd have a sense of peace and contentment. It's warm, cozy, and calm.

ML: As you experience that sensation of peace and contentment, allow it to intensify. I would like to ask the subconscious mind to produce a symbol for you that represents this feeling. What is that symbol?

K: A star.

ML: If you were to carry that star and this feeling of peace and contentment with you into each and every moment of the future, how would that change your experience of having time to spend with others?

K: It would remind me that that is what is important. I would be very clear that I would want more of that kind of time.

ML: If you were to carry that star and this feeling of peace and contentment with you into each and every moment of the future, how would that change your experience of the freedom to do what you want?

K: I would have a wee secret that I could cuddle close. It would remind me and restore me. It would let me know that what I am doing is absolutely the best thing, that it is right.

ML: If you were to carry that star and this feeling of peace and contentment with you into each and every moment of the future, how would that change your experience of being proud?

K: I would be able to be openly proud rather than privately. I wouldn't brush off compliments.

ML: If you were to carry that star and this feeling of peace and contentment with you into each and every moment of the future, how would that change your experience of doing good things?

K: I would be more comfortable and confident when sticking my neck out and getting involved. It would polish the star.

ML: If you were to carry that star and this feeling of peace and contentment with you into each and every moment of the future, how would that change your experience of succeeding?

K: I would take more risks.

ML: If you were to carry that star and this feeling of peace and contentment with you into each and every moment of the future, how would that change your experience of carrying the extra weight?

K: I can get rid of it. It slows me down. It holds me back.

ML: What does the left hand have to say now?

K: It's sad. It wants to hang around me.

ML: What can you do about that?

K: It can be in the audience cheering. It would say, "I knew her when…" and "Didn't she do well?" It would have a front row seat.

ML: How is the right hand feeling now?

K: Responsible. It has to be vigilant and really deliver. It feels liberated as well.

ML: Is there any part of you that would resist losing the weight now?

K: No.

ML: Imagine drawing the energy of the right side over to the left side, balancing the energies across your body. How does that feel?

K: Tired, calm, and yet bubbly and fizzy.

ML: I would like to ask the subconscious mind to now provide past life experiences that will help you to understand more fully your life purpose. Imagine a hallway stretching out before you. As you move down along the hall, you begin to notice the texture of the floor covering beneath your feet, and the color of the walls. There are doorways along this hall, each one leading to past lives, memories, which will help you understand your life purpose. As I count from three to one, you will find yourself in front of one of these doors. Three, two, one. How would you describe the door you are standing in front of now?

K: It is a white cottage door with glass squares and a brass knob.

ML: As the door opens and you move through, where do you find yourself?

K: It's bright. I feel uplifted.

ML: As your eyes become adjusted to the brightness, you begin to discern shapes and colors. What do you begin to notice?

K: Oh! I think I am in heaven. I see light. It's bright. It's so pure and enveloping. It's drawing me in. I see someone above me. Is it God? He's sending light down. I see his face above me in the light. I'm not frightened. He makes me into an angel. He puts light around me, and turns me around. He is sending me back. He waves as I go. He is smiling and encouraging. I feel sad about leaving. I am walking away from the light. I see myself looking back over my shoulder at the face. He is urging me on with the light, saying, "Okay, it's okay. This will be good." I get to the door and open it. I'm back in the hall. I'm going down the hall to another door.

ML: What do you notice about this one?

K: It's green, wooden, and paneled. I don't feel good about it. I look back over my shoulder. I see the white and glass door with the light. I know that I have to go through this other door. So I do.

ML: What do you notice?

K: It's dark, and feels cold. There are people with palm fronds urging me forward. I walk into golden sunshine and light. I think I'm a queen or something. I'm wearing…the light is amazing. It's so golden. My hair is black with bangs like Cleopatra. The people are all bowing and falling down. I walk, and then sit. As I turn, I have a train of material behind me. It swishes to the side. I sit and smile at all the people bent down before me. The palm fronds are still waving. It must be warm. I say, "Arise." The people sit up. Everyone is smiling. The people are happy and content. We are a prosperous nation. People come out of the crowd to ask me things. I lean forward and they ask me for advice. I am able to answer them. They smile and go away. I think I am wise. I am wise, very wise. And nice. I get up and walk down the carpet. They all bow again. I come up to big wooden double doors that form an arch. The people are happy. That disappears. I'm feeling better.

ML: Then what happens?

K: The doors get opened for me. When I go in, I'm in a suit. No more black hair anymore. I go into a business meeting. There is an oval table. I'm in a straight tweed skirt. I have skinny calves, black shoes, heels, and a boxy jacket. I look like Margaret Thatcher. I sit at the head of the table. I'm making decisions. There are papers, and men in dark gray suits. They are old and pompous. They don't think I should be there. I'm quite abrupt with them. Some shift in their seats. They are uncomfortable. I say, "If you don't like it, feel free to leave." I'm firm. A few smile and nod encouragingly. Then they go. They file out with their papers. I sit on a chair and draw a deep breath. I tell myself, "Well, you did that." I want to sit awhile. Someone comes in and I have to go. I draw a big sigh. I pick up my briefcase, which doesn't match my suit or shoes. That bothers me. I go back to the door that I came in, which is behind the head of the table.

ML: What happens next?

K: As I go through it, there is bamboo everywhere. And tortoise shell. It is very quiet. I see water and butterflies. It is a garden, like at a Japanese teahouse. It is open on one side. I'm standing under the cover of the bamboo trees. I'm looking at some rough stepping-stones. I am wearing a kimono, and funny little white sox with sandals. I am deciding whether I want to walk on the stepping-stones. And there is a bridge farther down. It would be nice to sit on the other side and look at the water. I look to see if anyone will see me go. I pick up my skirts and fly over the stones and bridge. I sit and listen if anyone calls for me. It is peaceful. I'm grabbing a few minutes of solitude before I have to go back and do something. The water quietly goes over the stones and moss. I feel sad. My time is not my own. The people count on me to go back and do something. I am public property. It's unusual for a woman to be listened to. I have to be wise with my words. It is a heavy burden, being wise. The people—the men—wait for me to do the wrong thing. But I'm very good friends with the emperor. Because I am good friends with him, they watch me closely. They think that I haven't earned my right to have the people listen to me. I know that what I am doing is important in its own right.

ML: Then what do you notice?

K: I bow at the people, and they bow at me. I go off to the doorway. There is no door. It is a wooden frame.

ML: As you move through it, where do you find yourself?

K: I'm in a concert hall. It is softly dark. It is full of people. I am sitting in the front row near the maestro. I'm wearing a green velvet dress. The men are in tuxedos. I have long hair swept up, and I am wearing jewels. My eyes glisten. The music is beautiful and I am swept away, transported, moved. I am so happy. My man is very good looking. My skirt is like a meringue. I'm tall and elegant. The man gets our coats and then puts on his top hat and coat. We sweep down wide stone stairs into a horse and carriage. My skirt is too puffy, and we are trying to get it into the carriage. We are laughing and laughing. He tells me, "It came out of the carriage so it must go back into the carriage." We have a driver. We go to a restaurant. There are candles and it is beautiful. I believe we are in England. We sweep in. There is a big dance floor. I know people here. I tip my head to them and smile sweetly. We are a golden couple. The people like to talk about us. We are so happy. It is all shiny, glittery, with white table clothes. Just lovely. I wear long gloves past my elbows. Our table is near the dance floor.

ML: What else is going on?

K: I wonder why the people know us. They are friendly yet aloof. Very British. We dance, and are so happy. I feel like a princess.

ML: What year is it?

K: 1868.

ML: What is your name?

K: Princess Leonora

ML: What is your man's name?

K: Michael. We are from Sweden. We are visiting England. This is a reception. We are the guests of honor. Oh, that's why we were in the front row at the concert. It was put on for us. Michael is not royal, it is my family that is. He's very kind. He does good things. He has a good heart. We have lots of fun at home, behind the gate, so to speak. We laugh, not like the rest of the family who are starchy. I have to make a lot of decisions. Now, I see myself in a room behind a desk with a big seal and wax. I am not so happy.

ML: Why are you not happy?

K: Michael is not there. He left me. It was too complicated. He needed more for himself. He went riding and never came back. He wore a red sash over one shoulder. For a while people thought he was dead. Eventually, he was, but not straight away. He had a horse riding accident. I didn't get to see him. My last memory of him was when he was getting on the horse with his red sash. I had to be very strong. I didn't laugh so much. But I still had that green dress. Sometimes I would go and snuggle into it. I would hold it and cry.

ML: What have you learned from these lifetimes?

K: I am wise. I have the ability to be very, very happy and to make others happy. I am strong and can be tough when I need to be. I need to have time for me, too, to play. The wisdom and decision-making can weigh heavily on me. I am absolutely meant to do something with this wisdom. I have lots of it and to not use it is to not do what God wanted me to do. I'm alone a lot. In the making of my decisions, I affect a lot of people. I feel alone.

ML: How will these lifetimes affect your present life?

K: It gives me confidence and courage in a way that my present path should be comfortable for me. It is okay to do this. I almost couldn't not do it. I need to be mindful of keeping something for me. I need to save quiet time for friends, and to keep my balance.

When I spoke with Kendra some days later, she shared that she was surprised when she was tempted to eat some doughnuts and easily passed them up. She heard a strong voice within her that said that eating them was not a part of her new path.

It is somewhat unusual to have a client go from door to door in their visualization, finding a new lifetime through each one. In Kendra's case, it was extremely effective.

12

Verify Memories

"We live in a world whose realities are defined by science, which tells us how things work. And yet there are some things which don't seem to work that way at all. Our science tells us that these things are impossible and don't exist, yet they stubbornly refuse to go away. They are often elusive and hard to control, but they are there for anyone to see. They exist."
—Lyall Watson, Beyond Supernature

After your first few regressions, you may wonder whether your visions, sensations, and experiences were actually memories, or simply stories conjured by an imaginative mind.

This reaction is normal and understandable. Whether you work alone or with a regressionist, it is important to investigate your memories for accuracy. As you do this, you can examine them for further details and for any messages they may hold for you in this lifetime. Keep working on them over time to fill in information and unearth subtle messages.

Don't take everything at face value—but don't dismiss your memories simply because you don't find any "proof" in the form of birth records, gravestones, and so forth. There may be no way to prove scientifically that your memories are accurate, but there are ways to verify them and anchor them in reality.

This chapter gives you ways to check the accuracy of your memories, gain certainty about specific lifetimes, and accept the wisdom that those memories offer.

The Nature of Memory

We have all had moments when we realized our memories were not completely reliable—whether we were trying to recall events from childhood, or just find the car keys.

Where memory is concerned, we always have to leave room for error. Can you describe, without a doubt, in completely accurate detail, everything you did two weeks ago last Thursday? Include chronological accuracy, and details about the people you saw, the places you went, and the conversations you had—as well as all the emotions associated with what happened. Almost no one among us can do that, except perhaps if there had been some catastrophic event that made us hyper-alert and vigilant that day. Most people recall only vague data, general patterns, and special occasions.

Some of my clients have remarkable recall, and can vividly describe minute details of their past lives. Most people can retrieve a general understanding of their occupation, marriage, and number of children, plus the location and a sense of the era. A facilitator can help flesh out these memories, and also point to life lessons and correlations between that life and this one.

The point here is to be gentle with yourself. Give yourself some latitude in remembering events, occupations, and relationships that occurred 100, 500, 1,000 or more years ago. You may be separated from these events not only by vast spans of time, but by many deaths and births.

Are Your Memories Real?

How do we know that our past life memories are real? We cannot be completely, 100% sure of these memories, because all memory is subjective.

Most of what we call our memories are actually just our *perceptions* of, and *reactions* to, events—even when we are simply talking about what happened last week.

With past lives, the "reality" of our memories gets a bit more complicated. If you remember the strategies of a battle in a past life, for example, don't jump to the conclusion that you were the general. You may have been his right hand man. If you see yourself as royalty, you could have been the queen—or you could have been the queen's cousin, who was included in all the activities. Or the sister, who fantasized that *she* was queen.

One female friend remembered being on the Isle of Avalon during the Camelot years. She recalled the ceremonies, the politics, and the lifestyle. She also remembered being in love with Lancelot and practicing magical rites. Her conclusion was that she was Morgan LeFey. This made perfect sense, and she had a great deal of information to support the claim. However, upon further regressions to that lifetime, she realized that she had actually been one of Morgan's several sisters.

This confusion is understandable. They shared the same parents and family structure, they were raised along side one another, and they grew to have similar interests and activities. They lived in the same place, and perhaps had the same hopes and dreams.

My friend discovered the initial error and was able to correct it because she was willing to return to that lifetime many times for verification. She was able to get various perspectives on the situation, and more exposure to the information. (Returning again and again to one life is always a good idea, not only for the purposes of verification but also because it lets us flesh out such details as customs, geography, styles, and battles, which can later be researched at the library or online.)

The reason we need to be cautious about our memories, and do whatever we can to verify them, is that what we recall is processed through our personal filters—the vast array of beliefs, emotions, and ideas about reality through which we take in information.

OUR "REALITY FILTERS"

We have seen that we all filter our reality and our memories—whether from this life, or from past lives. Our personal filters consist of the entirety of our emotions, wishes, desires, dreams, fears, beliefs, judgments, and false ego.

All of these things can all cause our memories to be less than accurate. We see what we want to see, or what we are afraid we will see, or what we believe we will see—sometimes at the expense of what is actually *there.* For example, it may be difficult to see the good in a person whom we detest. Or we may refuse to accept negative information about people whom we love and trust. Our filters latch onto facts that support our views, and reject any information that isn't consistent with our perspective.

As we set out to verify our past life memories, we need to be aware of our personal filters and how they work. We need to know what kind of information we are likely to seek out, and what kind of information we are likely to avoid. Only then can we begin to approach our memories objectively.

Why Do We Filter Information?

Each day, each hour, we are inundated with massive amounts of information. We need some way to sort through it all, to figure out what is useful and what is desirable—and what is not.

Our brains have created a system that accommodates this need and makes it possible for us to operate in the physical world. That system only allows information to reach our conscious minds when it is either *necessary* or *desired.* Our personal filtering system sorts out all the incoming information, and brings to our conscious mind only the data that seems necessary or desirable.

Over the course of many lifetimes, we have adjusted our filters to accommodate various cultural and social needs, practical needs, and basic survival. Our filters typically represent a means of *protection* and *survival.*

How Do Filters Block Reality?

We are often unaware that we are filtering reality—until we discover that we are blocking something that we actually want or need. This information may include past life memories, sensing auras and spirit guides, knowing the truth about ourselves and our nature, or even becoming aware of memories from this life that we have blocked.

Jennifer is a college student who wanted to resolve some negative emotions she had toward her father. Her father had divorced her mother when Jennifer was eleven, and she felt certain that he did not love her. The divorce proved it! She was crushed by this "fact," which had affected many areas of her life, including her romantic relationships.

During our session, Jennifer regressed back to the time when she was in the womb. She then moved forward in time to her present age, recalling details of her father's affection for her mother and herself, including his excitement about the pregnancy and her birth. She traced his involvement with her from conception to adolescence, and was able to see the emotional and financial support that he had always given her.

By the end of the session, she saw clearly that she had misinterpreted the divorce, due to her immaturity and confusion at the time. She realized that her father had loved her all along, and continued to do so. It was her *interpretation* of the divorce that had tainted her perception of her father and his feelings toward her. Her filters had defined the events and emotions around the divorce, and had veiled her ability to see the reality of the situation.

She felt full of energy and joy after the regression, and was excited about contacting her father and reestablishing her relationship with him.

How may your personal filters have distorted your view of reality?

Unhooking Our Filters

Most spiritual quests involve identifying our filters, and then adjusting or removing them to allow a clearer view of reality. As we become aware of our filters—and recognize them as filters, not as reality—we can alter our perceptions of the past, and thereby change how it affects our present and our future. When we understand how our own personal filters work and start to dismantle them, we can also gain more access to information in other planes of reality. Here is how it works.

We have seen that in the astral, our minds impose interpretations on the energy patterns we encounter—translating that information into pictures, objects, and events so that we have language to interpret the experience, and can derive meaning from it. When we encounter our spirit guides, for example, they are not really in the form in which we "see" them, since there is nothing physical in the astral plane. Our minds interpret the aura and energy pattern that we see into facial features, clothing, and physique. These "physical" traits may be projected into our minds from the guides themselves, or they can be our own interpretations—pictures that our minds draw from the raw data to create an image that we can recognize and understand.

All of this interpretation is a function of our filters. If our favorite color is blue, for instance, we might picture our spirit guide wearing blue. That, of course, is a harmless interpretation. But allowing filters to dictate what we see, and don't see, can become extremely limiting. We close ourselves off from vital data not only in the astral, but in our everyday lives.

We can shift our filters, and even let them go entirely, as we become ready. But in order to do that, we need to know what they are. There is no reason to fear the process of identifying our filters. We will not suddenly be unprotected, laid bare, or exposed to all of reality, without any way to guard ourselves or interpret what we experience. Typically, nothing will be revealed to us that we are unwilling or unable to grasp. If we are blocking any information, we will gain access to it only when we are ready to let it in.

Understanding that we have had certain filters, and that we are shifting them and allowing new information to be revealed, is a marker along our hero's journey toward self-realization. When we start receiving more information about ourselves and are willing to experience and process the emotions that may come with it, we have proof of our spiritual growth. Only our filters keep us from seeing reality and experiencing truth. As we clear them, we move closer to self-actualization and enlightenment.

Deep Memories From The Subconscious

As we move through life—experiencing images, feelings, sounds, smells, and so forth—the subconscious searches its memory banks for information that matches what we are perceiving in the present. Some of that information is stored in ancient memory "files" from long-ago lifetimes. We may have a sense that we recognize a certain smell—the scent of a particular incense, for instance—but not be able to "remember" anything specific about it. When that happens, we can simply dismiss it—or we can become curious and investigate further.

It takes some practice to allow these memories to bubble up from the deeper regions of the subconscious mind, but it gets easier with practice. We learn to pay attention to the signals, and to decipher their meaning. The more frequently we attend to these deeper memories, the more easily we access them and the more readily we recall other memories associated with them.

For instance, a person may not speak fluent French after one regression to a French lifetime—but that language may start to sound more familiar and become easier to learn. I have had clients emerge from past life regressions with information about herbs, healing, customs, and other skills that they had not previously known.

Memory Versus Fantasy

Remembering a past life does not feel the same as remembering something that occurred in this life. Nor does it feel the same as relating a fantasy or making up a tale. During past life regressions, we seem to activate a different part of the brain than we use to create fantasies. Even the sensory qualities of the memories are distinct from what we experience during storytelling.

Stop reading for a moment, and think of a memory from this lifetime—perhaps a childhood event. As you continue to move through that memory, notice if there is a part of your brain that seems to be active. Do you feel the frontal lobe, or the sides of your head? With your eyes closed, make a mental image of where, spatially, you seem to have stored the information about that earlier event.

Now, switch modes and concentrate on making up a story—perhaps a bedtime story you might tell a child. While creating that story, again locate the part of your brain that feels active. Once again, make a mental image of the location where you have come up with that story.

This kind of exercise helps you become sensitive to how it feels when you are remembering an actual event, as opposed to how it feels when you are creating stories. That is an invaluable tool for discerning whether you are experiencing true past life memories or fabricating them.

Eye Movement

Eye movements are also a clue to whether you are remembering or fantasizing. Enlist a friend to help you in this process.

Place two chairs directly across from one another, separated by a few feet. Your friend will watch the movements of your eyes while you relate a story about something that actually happened. It might be something that you did just that morning. Then, have your friend watch your eyes as you tell a fictional story from the first person perspective.

Give each story about five minutes, so that your friend has plenty of time to become familiar with the movement of your eyes and your expressions as you talk about facts, and when you describe a fantasy. Ask your friend to pay special attention to:

- Frequency of blinking
- Whether you look more to the right or left, or upward or downward
- Whether or not you fidget
- The brightness in your eyes
- The tension in your face

There should be a noticeable difference between your mannerisms when you are relating an actual experience, and when you are making up a story. This is a fascinating exercise that can help you distinguish between memory and fantasy as you explore past lives, and also give you subtle clues to when you may not be telling the whole truth in your daily interactions with people.

Use Your Intuition

You will often have an intuitive "knowing" about whether information from a regression is actual memory, or fantasy. It will either ring true to you, or not. This can be a bit tricky, however, because even intuition comes through our filters. The more you test your intuition, the more you will trust it.

Try not to let your emotions sway you when it comes to investigating your memories. Whether or not you *want* to believe the information has nothing to do with its accuracy. If you let the information settle over a few days before you examine it closely, you can get some perspective and your intuition can work more independently from emotions and filters.

Allow your intuition to guide you, then follow up that guidance with successive regressions and any other research that can help verify your experience.

Historical Records

A few lucky people access information that is sufficiently lucid and detailed that they can check it against historical records, court documents, hospital records, cemeteries, maps, and other hard evidence.

When regressing to past lives, always ask for the date and the location. Search for details of clothing, uniforms of war, insignias, flags, coats of arms, and the names of people and streets. Be particularly watchful for information that you would not have known otherwise.

Identifying these details prepares you to investigate further. Much of your research can be done on the Internet. In addition, you can use encyclopedias, newspapers, historical societies, and many other resources. One of my clients was able to get past life information that contained a name, date of death, and the location of the tombstone. He drove across the country and found the grave site!

Another client was so lucid during a regression that she acquired the street address of her home, along with her own name in that life and the names of her husband, children, and grandchildren. That lifetime took place during the twentieth century, so she was able to investigate the information fairly easily. In fact, the events in her regression took place only an hour's drive from her present life home. She was able to meet her past life children, who were still alive!

Subtle Clues

You can substantiate your memories in subtle ways, as well as with hard research. For instance, ask yourself whether or not the details of your story are surprising to you. Were you amazed to learn how many children you had, or the nature of your occupation? Would you have made up that story? *Could* you have made it up?

Generally, the stories I hear during regressions concern the events and details of everyday life, sprinkled with some romance or adventure. Occasionally, they contain elements of tragedy. Most people agree that if they were to make up a story, it would contain more chivalry or adventure. It would be devoid of any embarrassing or shameful elements, and would have a successful conclusion. But most people are not royalty, and do not belong to a privileged or esoteric class. Most of us do not make a profound mark on the world. And at some point in our lives, most of us experience emotional or physical pain, and at least some embarrassment.

One clue that your memories are accurate is that they concern everyday events, or have something embarrassing attached to them. If your story is fantastical, extremely romantic, or about some well known historical figure, it bears more scrutiny.

Another subtle clue that your memory is accurate is *emotion*. An emotional reaction to the information is an indication that it may be correct. My clients occasionally cry, become frightened, laugh, or feel deep shame or regret in response to the experiences and information they receive in regressions.

During one session, my client Aaron recalled a past life in which he was a small child and his mother died. My first reaction was compassion for him, and it was tempting to give my condolences. Instead, thankfully, I simply asked him how he was feeling. He said he was relieved, because she had been abusive and negligent. Her passing meant that he would be raised by his grandmother, who was sweet and nurturing.

The surprising nature of his response led us both to believe that the memories of that lifetime were fairly accurate. (This story also demonstrates that it is wise to resist assuming, or second-guessing, the internal experiences of other people—or to ask leading questions or make comments that point people in a particular direction.)

FALSE MEMORY

How can we tell when memories are false? From a certain perspective, all memory is false memory. Because of our filters, all we can really know are our perceptions. It is well documented that when three parties witness the same automobile accident, there will be three differing accounts of what happened.

In an effort to be as accurate as possible when experiencing past life regressions, practice being honest with yourself in all the situations that life presents to you—and remain aware of your filters. Remember, too, that being overly conservative in describing your reality is just as false as exaggerating it.

Facilitators can help you avoid false memory by using only non-leading language we discussed in the last chapter. If your facilitator or hypnotherapist consistently uses leading language and questions, consider working with someone else, or on your own.

SO, WHAT IS REAL?

With all the pitfalls of filters and false memories, how do we know what to trust? The best strategy is simply to relax into the experience, remember that the information may be filtered, and create value from whatever we receive. We are always receiving many layers of information, and we can learn from whatever we perceive—regardless of whether or not it is specifically connected to events that actually occurred in an earlier physical reality.

Even when memories are not fully accurate—and even if they do not actually represent a past life at all—they can still offer valuable information about how we perceive ourselves and the world. If we simply treat the information as metaphor, we will always find something that helps us grow in our present life. Perhaps we are facing the same type of moral dilemma, relationship issue, or personality dysfunction as is experienced during a regression. If we view it as a metaphor, it doesn't matter whether it came from a past life or from our own internal subconscious wisdom.

Our motto should be: *Use whatever we are given to grow and evolve.* Quite often, the metaphor not only brings valuable information, but also provides inspiration and support for our current dreams and goals.

Whether we know for certain that the information is accurate, or whether we view it as a metaphor—we can always extract a meaningful message.

Was Everybody Famous?

Most of us did not incarnate as Napoleon or Joan of Arc. As we have noted, the vast majority of past life memories involve everyday life experiences. Once in a while, extraordinary feats do show up—but these are almost always of a personal nature. Rarely do people remember life experiences that had a major impact on a country or the planet.

That said, famous people get to incarnate, too. All of the presidents, rock stars, martyrs, and heroes have an opportunity to come back into physical form and continue their journey.

If you recall a lifetime as a well-known personality, be careful to discern whether you are dealing with an actual memory, or with fantasy or simply admiration for that person. This can be confusing. It is easy to move from actual memories of a past life, into other "memories" that may actually be scenes from a recent movie or book. You might begin a regression with accurate memories of a sailor's life, for instance—and suddenly, you are a character in "Pirates of the Caribbean!"

It is also easy to assume that if you see images of a particular event, you were at the center of that event. For example, imagine that you were the personal aide to Napoleon. You would understand the details of his battle strategies. You might remember his daily rhythm and personal habits. Perhaps you were a bit envious of him and, in your fantasies, would pretend to be him. During a regression to that period, it might feel as if you understood all of his emotions, and were intimately aware of his relationships and the reasoning behind his decisions. It would be easy to assume that you were, in fact, Napoleon. With further investigation and inquiry, and some objectivity, you might later discover that you were actually his aide. This type of confusion occurs fairly frequently.

It takes diligence to discern whether you were the famous person, or someone closely related to him or her. In your present life, is there anyone with whom you identify so closely that you might be confused if you were to regress from a future life back to this one?

Do You Feel Famous?

We carry certain patterns with us as we move from one life to the next. We may find ourselves in leadership roles, or in the spotlight, lifetime after lifetime. Or we may be used to being helpers, people who are more comfortable in a supportive role, affecting the world from behind the scenes. Some souls gravitate to roles of saintly virtue, while others may cycle in roles of a darker nature.

What role do you think Albert Einstein would choose if he were to reincarnate today? Do you envision him as a movie star, teacher, mother, assembly line worker, criminal, musician, or farmer? Would it seem likely that he would be very bright, or not? What is it about his character that leads you to have that opinion?

When examining your own energy, preferences, and comfort zones, ask yourself whether it would be natural for you to be a leader, taking risks—or more in the shadows, behind the scenes, as a helper. Although we all have a variety of roles and experiences, and may switch from being a leader to being a supporter from life to life, we usually have a tendency in one direction or the other.

Pamela was adept at retrieving past life memories. Her regression demonstrates a wonderful capacity to capture detail.

Case Study

Pamela

Pamela had been working steadily on her life journey and had recognized some inner subconscious blocks that were causing her trouble. Her goal in reviewing her past lives was to get a better understanding of her own nature and character, and to remove any barriers that might prevent her from moving forward to attain her life goals.

ML: What do you notice about the door?

P: It is a rich wood, textured, with squares. There is a knob in the center of each square. It's natural wood, with no varnish. It has been hand rubbed. There is a brass handle, ornate, and molding carved with oak leaves, acorns, and flowers. It's rich. It's heavy and it gleams. There are candles in the hall. They flicker. The walls are satiny and smooth.

ML: As the door opens and you move through the threshold, what do you notice?

P: I'm indoors. There is a man sitting at a small wooden table. It looks like a desk. There is a card table with a candlestick, made of glass with a finger loop. It has a beeswax candle. The man is writing on parchment with inkwells and rocks holding the edges. There is a quill, a knife, and a pewter cup. And there are more goose feathers.

ML: What else do you notice?

P: It's a bedchamber. There is a four-poster bed. There are curtains, which are pulled tight at night. The walls have red silk and wainscoting. There is an Indian rug. This man is intense at his work. He is older. With gray-white hair, a Vandyke beard. He is my father.

ML: What do you know about yourself?

P: I'm female, about nine years old.

ML: As I count from three to one, you will know where in the world you are. Three, two, one…where are you?

P: We are in London.

ML: As I count from three to one, you will know what the date is. Three, two, one…what is the date?

P: 1420.

ML: What else do you notice about this scene?

P: I wish he would pay more attention to me. However, he is doing something very important. It seems to be political. Finally, he reaches a hand out to me. I walk to him. He puts his arm around me. He holds me, but he is still writing. He knows that I was there. Now I feel better. He looks like William Shakespeare.

ML: Do you recognize him as anyone you know in this lifetime?

P: Maybe he is my father this life. It feels like the same connection. It's deep. There is a thread between us.

ML: What do you notice about that thread?

P: It is gold, with colors. It is thin, ephemeral. It appears to be just a filament. it stretches to my dad in this life, too, even though he is now deceased.

ML: What else do you notice?

P: Now we are outside. My father is giving a speech. He is on a wooden platform. People don't agree with him and they say awful things. I'm on a wooden stairs or ladder of sorts. I understand how important his message is. I'm sixteen now. I should be doing that too. He's telling people about tyranny and the yoke of oppression. They don't have to believe him. They have only to change their minds and be free. They don't want to believe that it is that simple. There are spies in the audience. He will get hurt. I think that if I wasn't a female, I could help him. Even so, I could help. It won't be easy. I'm frustrated that I'm a female. It's not the right time for his message. They will hang him for sedition if he doesn't get away. But, he gets away. What a relief! I see torches. It's night. I feel the heat on my face. But, I know he got away. I'll be taken care of. I'm not bothered, but I should be scared. It's as though they can't see me. I'm invisible to them. It doesn't occur to them that I could be a problem, since I'm a female. My mind is working, though.

ML: What do you notice next?

P: Now I'm in America. I'm frustrated again. I'm really angry. It's a different life, this is 1764, and I'm fifteen years old. I'm with my father. He's in a blue suit with a white shirt and collar. He's a lawyer. He tells me I can do anything I want. Then my mother comes in. He believes in me. She tells him not to put thoughts into my head. She thinks I should learn to be a good wife. She's in a fancy dress. She's a vacuous woman. He acquiesces. I have to go to the dance. I'm expected to flutter my eyelashes and act stupid. I don't like it at all. I figure out who to listen to, who to trust. No wonder I feel so strongly now. I can't sell myself short. It matters to me what happens. I'm tired of wasting time and energy.

ML: What else do you notice?

P: I end up getting married to a cruel man. He does ugly things in bed. I bear his children. I pine for myself and then die of a broken heart.

ML: Moving to another life that will give us additional information, where do you find yourself next?

P: It is the 1920's and 1930's. It's during the Depression. I have a hard time breathing. I'm in a shaft. There is no air. There has been an explosion. It's hot, wet, dirty, and we're running out of air. They are all clawing at something. We're dead already, so there is no point.

ML: What do you know about this event?

P: We—these men and I—supported the union. They set us up. And now we're dead. I'm a man. I'll never see my family again. I have a baby I won't see grow up. Everyone settles down. They're exhausted. The candle is flickering. And then, it all goes black.

ML: What else do you know about yourself?

P: I'm about twenty-five years old. I was just married. My wife asked me not to go to the meeting. I knew my child would spend his life starving if we didn't do something about the situation. I had to do it. Now nobody is even talking. It's quiet. It smells like cordite, gunpowder. The sons o' bitches. Nine of us die! Not all of us were at the meeting. Some are here just doing their shift. I feel so guilty that they got hurt. They'll be dead now because they were in the wrong place with the wrong people. All of us knew there was a risk. We saw people being beaten up. The word came down the line, but we didn't believe it. We shouldn't have let them come. We shouldn't have been so damn naïve.

ML: What else do you experience there?

P: It is so dark. I shouldn't have shot my mouth off. Now guys are dying.

ML: If that aspect of you there could give you his wisdom, what would he tell you?

P: It's not the way to do things. It was irresponsible. It's not the way to go about a change. Offer it as a gift, a possibility. Don't try to change things in big chunks all at once. It's easy to whip up a crowd. But then people get hurt. There is a better way.

ML: If you could offer him your advice, what would you tell him?

P: It wasn't his fault. His passion was great, and his purpose was noble. If he knew another way, he would have done it. He left a legacy of commitment to his children. They'd know him as a courageous man. That makes it easier for them. He goes on through them. He feels better now. There is some joy in his heart. He was stuck on that. I'd also tell him to be thoughtful. You don't have to dive into a vacuum.

ML: What have you learned from this that will help you in your life here?

P: There are all sorts of ways of doing things. I can trust my native intelligence. I don't have to be the leader. I can be a member of a group.

ML: Moving on to the next life that will give you greater insights into yourself. Three, two one…what do you see now?

P: I'm in a big room. It's comfortable and I'm happy. There are big windows open, and doors that are windows, like they have in France. I'm at a desk, writing. I'm female. I've put purposelessness away. I do what I need to do for myself and for my own knowledge. I have a sense that what I write will be universal. It's about humanity—essential humanity. About connecting, kindness, and inclusion. They are stories. I left politics behind. This is not hard-edged stuff. There is more connection to the feminine and the gentle side of life.

ML: What else do you notice?

P: I'm wearing a soft gown. It's easy to wear. It is something like Josephine might have worn. It is empire style. It's 1894. I'm in France. I'm outside Paris in the Bois du Boulogne. I'm in a cottage. There are pine trees. It's nice being a woman. (She laughs.) I am married to an army captain. When I am with him, I feel safe. I can write when I want to write. Oh, he's my next-door neighbor in this lifetime. And now he's a US Air Force Captain. Interesting!

ML: What else do you notice?

P: This life is so much easier. There is much less pain. I write from happiness. Could that happen? (Chuckles) We're just happy. What a novel idea! I finish writing. I put the pen down. Now I feel I've done something good.

ML: What have you learned from reviewing this lifetime?

P: I want no more fighting. There will be no more raging against the gods. It's too hard. It leads to disaster. I have to embrace the feminine. I'm a woman. I have to further understand what I've been seeing. I can relax and feel protected. I say things that are hopeful,

> attractive, and magnetic. I offer the carrot, but it's deeper. I can put a positive spin on things. I can examine what to do with the problem to make the outcome positive for everyone involved. I can understand it if I think of it like a garden. I make a decision and then perpetuate it.

Pamela's perceptions, imagination, and memories are articulated in wonderful detail. She is an easy subject and moves smoothly from lifetime to lifetime. She has gained information that will help her with her life work, her personality, her courage, and her sensuality.

PART THREE

REAPING THE REWARDS: CASE STUDIES

This part of the book is devoted to case studies,
actual sessions that have been performed over the years in my office.

These case studies are grouped into broad subjects like relationships and physical healing, but each one covers several topics—and also demonstrates powerful techniques for accessing these memories, the general wisdom to be gained from regressions, the way our subconscious minds work as they access this information, and how best to pursue and use that wisdom. You will get a feel for how past life information surfaces that will be enormously helpful when you do your own regressions.

Parts of some of these case studies have appeared in other chapters. Here, you can see that information in a larger context. Each case is unique, and I have attempted to include a range of regressions that will help and encourage you in your own quest to discover your previous lifetimes.

13

Understanding and Enhancing Relationships

"Wherever you go, there you are."
—Buckaroo Bonzai, the movie

Many people seek out their past life memories in order to learn more about their relationships with others—family, friends, mates, children, colleagues, and acquaintances. This is one of the richest aspects of past life regressions. It is fascinating to see who we have been to the people in our lives, and who they have been to us.

This chapter contains three case studies that touch on the subject of relationships. They contain other material as well, but relationships are their focus.

Kathy's regression represents a true healing, and demonstrates the potent technique of the "empowerment symbol" that allows her to access a feeling of elation whenever she wants to do so.

Lori learned why she feared her mother's death so much, and used a desensitization technique to mitigate that fear. She met her grandfather, whom she had never met in this life, and clarified her relationship with her boyfriend. She also came to a new realization of the fact that everything would work out in her life.

Alice gained invaluable insights into her relationship with Tom, from whom she was getting a divorce. Her regression also demonstrates a "retrieval" technique using symbols to represent the feeling she wanted to retrieve.

Case Study

Kathy

Kathy wanted to clarify several issues, including her "bad luck" in relationships. She loved intensely and wanted to have a soul mate, but so far felt she had been a "bum magnet." She had not been in a relationship for several years. Kathy said that she had not been abused in this lifetime, but suspected that she might have been in a previous one.

As she went into trance, she began to describe the scene unfolding in her mind's eye.

K: I find myself in a garden. There is a little path, like a sidewalk, only not made of cement. It curves to the left, where I see lots of flowers everywhere. It is a peaceful day.

ML: What do you notice happening around you?

K: Someone is walking toward me, but maybe they don't see me. They look like they are out of place.

ML: What else do you notice about this person?

K: It is a man, in his twenties or thirties. He looks rather Amish, with a white shirt, black vest and pants, and a hat that makes him look like a farmer.

ML: What do you know about yourself?

K: I'm female, in my teens or early twenties. I am wearing a dress or skirt with an apron. Alternatively, is it a pinafore? I seem to be wearing a bonnet, also.

ML: As the man approaches, what else can you discern about him?

K: I am curious about him, and interested. I don't have any fear. I know who he is, but I don't know him. He comes closer. I'm not walking forward. He looks at the garden.

ML: What happens next?

K: I'm a bit nervous. It's the anticipation, or the fear, of the unknown. I am wondering about him. He looks at me and says "hello." He reaches for my hand in greeting. I'm not used to it. I'm quite shy. He tells me his name.

ML: What is his name?

K: I don't know. Maybe I'm too nervous to remember it. He is very polite. He kisses my hand, and it makes me laugh. He is someone I have admired, but I don't understand why he would pay attention to me.

ML: What else do you know about this scene?

K: It feels like this is my relative's garden. I am feeling embarrassed and shy. I have a crush on him. I can't even speak, I'm so nervous. He seems so comfortable. I wonder what he is doing here. There must be something going on at the house. I came to the garden to be comfortable and alone. And now he is here.

ML: As you look at him there, do you recognize him as anyone you know in this lifetime?

K: He has blue eyes. I don't seem to recognize him right now. He seems so comfortable with me. I don't know if I have ever met him here in this lifetime.

ML: What happens next?

K: He asks me why I am here and not at the party. Evidently, the party was for me. It is a type of debutante event. He offers to go back to the party with me, and to be with me. I realize now that has never let go of my hand. He leads me down the path to the party. He is so nice. He is so gentle and yet so male. I am starting to feel more comfortable. I'm more at ease. The initial embarrassment is gone. I see the house now, across the lawn. There are people, all laughing and talking. It's a sunny day. They don't seem to notice us. Most of the people are close to our age, and some are parents. Now they see us. I see some of the girls there, and they are not my friends. Their mouths are open. I realize now that they are the reason that I left the party. Now I feel better. He's holding my hand and they can see that.

ML: What do you notice next?

K: I don't know where his hat went, but it is off his head now. My mom has a silly grin on her face.

ML: Do you recognize your mom as someone you know in this lifetime?

K: She looks like my present mom.

ML: Some time passes, and what do you notice next?

K: I notice that other things are happening around me. I am now completely immersed in the feelings I have about this man. I know now that his name is John. He has been so kind in the face of the others. I think the other girls are much prettier than I am. I don't understand why he is with me. I notice the music playing. Maybe it's coming from inside me. I am so elated!

I wanted Kathy to be able to access that feeling of elation any time in the future, and so I offer her an anchoring technique I call the empowerment symbol.

ML: As you feel that elation, how would you describe the sensations that you are experiencing?

K: I feel whole, complete. It doesn't feel like a crush anymore. It feels so nice.

ML: As you continue to feel that elation, that wholeness, allow it to be fully expressed in your body. You may even imagine turning up the volume on that sensation so that it is even more powerful. As you do so, I would like to ask your subconscious mind to provide for you a symbol, which you can imagine holding in your hand, that represents this good feeling of elation. So as I count from three to one, that symbol will appear. Three, two, one. What do you notice?

K: It's a key. A short skeleton key, about two and a half inches long. It is smooth, has a round end, and it's silver. It fits so well in my hand.

ML: Any time in the future when you would like to experience this sensation of elation and wholeness, you can simply visualize holding that key, and remember that you already contain those feelings within you. What do you notice next about that lifetime?

K: We are still at the party. John goes to get a drink. I look around and wonder if this will last. It is so unusual. From what I know about me there, maybe my doubts come from my dad. He is nice to my mom, but then he looks at other women. As I notice John getting my drink, I see him looking around. I expect him to look at the other girls, but he looks at me. He is smiling. The other girls go over to him and flirt with him. He is polite, and then excuses himself and comes back to me. I can't believe it!

ML: More time passes and what do you notice next?

K: After a while, everyone leaves. There is another man still there who is watching us. He is older. He seems to be a leader. Perhaps he is a spiritual leader, although not religious. He seems to be more connected to John than to me. He slowly takes his leave. He was so kind to me when we met. I had known of him, but we just met at the party. This man held my hand with both of his, and said that he had wanted to meet me for a long time. I couldn't imagine that. What could John have said to him, since I didn't really know John until today? I think that this man is John's father or stepfather. He leaves. Now my mother is there, all bubbly, and full of chitchat. She has to go now, too. I'm starting to get nervous because now it will be just John and me. We have been standing all day. I am very nervous. It has been such a different day for me. We decide to sit on the bench.

ML: Then what happens?

K: John is apologizing for not introducing himself to me earlier. He had not wanted to make me nervous, but he had been paying attention to me for some time. He knows how shy I am. It is so different to see someone so polite. Yet, I am like that too. It is a different way of acting. He tells me that he wants to come to see me more often. He asks me if that would be all right.

ML: How do you respond?

K: I can't quite spit the words out. I am baffled and excited. He is comforting me, and yet I am afraid. And I am happy. It's nice because I don't feel pushed. I have been pushed in the past, and maybe that is why these situations make me uncomfortable. John is different. We are both getting tired. He says he had better go. I don't want him to. I was only uncomfortable about everyone leaving and having to be in the house alone. I am afraid about something in my house. I have never been happy there.

ML: When you experience those feelings, what do you know about them?

K: I am not sure. My mom is okay. She is kind, but always busy. I feel like I go unnoticed a lot. That is why I found it surprising that John noticed me.

ML: What happens next?

K: John leaves. He asks if he can come by tomorrow. It is fine. It is more than fine! When he leaves, I feel he has taken a piece of me with him. I am so happy knowing that he will be back. I go to my room. I know that life will be different now.

ML: Moving ahead in time, what is the next relevant event that you notice?

K: We got married. I can't believe it!

ML: What do you remember about the wedding?

K: It is a great day. I can't even speak. It is odd to be so overcome at your wedding. It is something that I have never felt. There are so many people there. I don't really know most of them well. John only has one or two people in his family.

ML: Moving ahead again, what is the next significant event that you notice?

K: I see us in a church. We go to church, because of the community, but that is not really who I am. Now I see that I am having a baby. I see our house. Something is wrong. I don't know if it is me or the baby, or the childbirth.

ML: What do you notice about the childbirth?

K: There is a midwife.

ML: As I count from three to one, you will know what year it is. Three, two, one. What year does this birth occur?

K: 1756.

ML: As I count from three to one, you will know where in the world you are. Three, two, one. Where are you?

K: Tennessee.

ML: What do you notice about this childbirth?

K: I die during the childbirth. It is worth it. I feel bad for John, though. I always felt that I would die young. I knew that I would have a hard time. I was quite petite.

ML: What lesson were you to learn in that lifetime?

K: I had to learn to let go. Let go of everything. I had only a short time. I could be loved for who I was, not for who I was supposed to be.

ML: Do you notice any correlations between that lifetime and this one?

K: I need to let go of a lot of stuff here as well. I haven't believed that I could be loved.

ML: What will be different in your life now that you have experienced that past life?

K: I will know that I should give myself a break. I have a little faith and a little hope, but they are hard to hold onto. I had a hard childbirth in this lifetime also. It was the same child, the same baby. It makes me think that maybe I could attract John back to me again.

ML: Anything else?

K: Although I am shy, I have an open mind. Like her, I don't have any

> malice. We both have a sense of humor, though it is a little bit different.

Our session continued with specific techniques concerning Kathy's lack of belief in her own lovability. In subsequent talks, she said she later figured out who John is in this lifetime. They have not been able to reestablish a romantic relationship, due to other commitments they each have.

Case Study

Lori

Lori had several concerns about relationships that she felt could be resolved through past life regression. She wondered about the nature of her relationship with her boyfriend, James, since they didn't appear to be on the same spiritual path. She was very close with her mother, and was experiencing fear about her mother getting hurt or dying. She was also curious about her relationship with her father, since they had never been close.

Guiding her into a trance and asking her to visualize a hallway, I asked her to describe the door she has chosen.

L: It's a white door with a silver knob. There are three separate pieces of wood in it. It is not really distinct, but the white paint is chipped and the knob is shiny.

ML: How do you feel when you stand in front of that door?

L: I'm feeling calm.

ML: As the door opens, and you move through it, what do you begin to notice?

L: I see a tree, and a swing, and children playing. The swing is a piece of wood with two ropes, and it's hanging from the tree. There is a girl on the swing. She has dark hair and dark eyes. She is between five and seven years old. I think that is me. I'm happy. I'm wearing a white dress.

ML: What else do you notice about this scene?

L: There is the presence of a man. Is it my father? I'm not sure, but it feels that way.

ML: What else do you notice about him?

L: He has the face of my grandpa (in this life) whom I never met. He died before I was born. I feel respect for this man, and I'm not scared. I also feel the presence of a woman. She is wearing an apron. She came out of the house. I can't see her, but I feel no connection to her. I think that man is my grandpa from this life. That's odd, as I never think of him. I see his face and I feel the respect.

ML: What else do you notice?

L: I see the image of my mother. I see her face. I feel the love I have for her and I cry. It makes me sad to feel how much love I have for her. And it makes me happy too.

ML: Where do you feel that sadness on your body?

L: It's in my throat and chest.

ML: As you focus on that area of your body, what else do you know about those feelings?

L: Now it is not so much like sadness. I wanted to touch her. But she is gone.

ML: What do you know about the circumstances around her leaving?

L: We are outdoors. It is daytime and we are near the water. It is the ocean and we are on the beach. We are holding hands and walking. We notice the indent of our footprints in the sand. And then the waves cover our footprints, and the sand is all smooth again. I feel a shaking in my head. And then it stops. It's the sadness. It feels like my baby is gone. Something happened.

ML: What do you know about what happened?

L: My child drowned. She was my daughter. She was two years old. I was about twenty or thirty years old. I let her go, and she drowned in the water.

ML: Go back to the beginning of that episode, and tell me what you remember about the events leading up to her drowning.

L: I notice horses. Many of them galloping through the trees. I am watching the people riding them. Now I see the baby sitting in the sand. She is my mother in this lifetime. There is that feeling of sadness. I let it happen. I lost her. Now I just see the sun and I feel light.

ML: What have you learned from observing that lifetime?

L: I understand now why I fear losing her so much in this lifetime. And then there is the responsibility of the loss.

ML: Asking your subconscious to take us to another lifetime that will help us to understand more about the other relationships in your life, where are you now? Three, two, one.

L: I'm in a field. I feel like I am about ten years old. I'm with a little boy. He's really cute. I see flowers, white dandelions. My hands feel hot. We're playing and he's watching me. Now my feet feel cold.

ML: Do you recognize that little boy as anyone you know in this lifetime?

L: It seems like James. We're happy and he watches me. I'm running and playing. Now he is hurt or he's gone.

ML: What do you know about that?

L: It seems like someone takes him or hurts him. There was a wagon with no top. It was pulled by horses. Before, we were playing, and afterwards I'm scared and he's gone. I'm so sad.

ML: There is a part of your subconscious mind that knows full well what happened to him. As I count from three to one, that information can be revealed to your conscious mind. Three, two, one.

L: Those people killed him. It was a battle. We were seven or eight years old. Now I see that same little boy, but he is a man now. I see us with our baby, who is wrapped up in a blanket. We have other children also. We're very happy and calm. I can feel the love. My hand twitches. It has to do with the baby.

ML: What do you know about that?

L: I see myself standing on dirt. I'm feeling old. I'm with the same man. We have had a happy life. It feels like the man was James. I also feel the energy of my father. It is good energy, but I don't really see him. Maybe he was the baby.

ML: What do you notice next?

L: I see myself walking down the hall again, but it is as though I am an angel. It's airy. It doesn't seem to be light or dark, but I see lights outside the hall. It's very flowing. I see images of people and faces. They feel familiar. Now I notice a valley, mountains, a river and lake, but no people. I feel calm. I feel like it is okay to be alone.

ML: What do you notice next?

L: I see myself outdoors. I'm walking through a field. The field has corn that is no taller than I am. I am walking home. I go in my house and up the stairway. It is dark, and feels mysterious. I'm scared. I hide. I am afraid of something or someone. There is a man that scares me. He seems like a bad person. I hide behind the chair. I can see him, but not his face. I feel like a teenager.

ML: What do you know about your relationship with this man?

L: He is an intruder; at least he intrudes in my life. Actually, he lives in this house too. It's his home, but I move freely in it. Maybe I'm a maid or something. I think that he will hurt me, but I don't know that he will. Maybe I think he will beat me.

ML: What do you notice next?

L: He gets old and something happens to him. The fear I have of him is gone. I'm still there in the house. I see myself folding clothes. It's a flowing, pretty cloth or sheet. I feel happiness. I feel young again, like a teen.

ML: Do you recognize that man as anyone you have known in this lifetime?

L: I don't think so.

ML: What have you learned from observing that lifetime?

L: I hear the words, "Don't be afraid, it will go away." In this life, I have been afraid. Afraid of losing my mother, and now the experience of that little boy. I see him lying there. I feel scared.

ML: Where do you notice those scared feelings on your body?

L: In my stomach and chest.

ML: When you look into that area, what do you notice?

L: The little boy still watches me. I'm sad and he is comforting me. He gives me energy and protects me. He says that it's okay and I understand. I also see the ocean and the little girl. She is watching me too. She wants to be back there with me. She feels sorry for me. She loves me and wants to help. I understand that if I lose my mom, she is not really gone. I will see her again, even in this body. She is offended that I cannot accept the thought that she would still be around after her death. I am not ready for her to be gone.

At this point in the session, I facilitate desensitization techniques that allow her to become more comfortable with the possibility of eventually losing her mother. At the end of that exercise she continues:

L: Now it seems fictitious, more distant. Losing her is not so present, not here in the now. When she leaves me, I see that she comes to talk with me. She is guiding me. She is there. I know now that it is easier for her to communicate with me if I relax and feel her. If I make it harder, she can't get through to me.

ML: Let's visit one more lifetime that will help us to understand your relationships. What do you notice this time? Three, two, one.

L: As the door slides open, I walk through into something goopy and muddy. It is night and it is raining. I'm a girl. My little sister holds my right hand. There is a boy, too, who is about two or three years old. We also have another sister who is older, but she is not there right now. We are in the house, sitting around the table eating. There is a terrible storm outside. It begins to tear down our home. It is so dark. We are so scared. Now I see us running. We're lost and scared. We are walking through that goop. It was a tornado. Now we sit in the dark, scared. I don't see our parents. Maybe they are dead. I am comforting my siblings.

ML: What do you notice about your connections to any of your siblings.

L: The little boy seems to be my boyfriend, James, in this lifetime. The girl is my girlfriend here.

ML: What else do you notice about this lifetime?

L: We were happy before the tornado, and we are happy afterwards. As we get older, the three of us are still together. We are in another house, which is near the river. We work together to make our lives happy. It feels inspired. We learned to overcome our hardships and stay happy.

ML: How do you think knowing about this experience will help you in this lifetime?

L: I don't have to fear that bad things may happen. It will be okay. It will work out. It will all come together, and we will all keep coming back together.

Experiences from a variety of lifetimes contributed to Lori's unconscious fear response. After understanding the roots of her fears about her mother's death, she has been able to resolve those fears with very little therapeutic intervention.

Case Study

Alice

Alice was going through a divorce with her husband, who had been unfaithful to her. We will call him Tom. She wanted to gain a deeper understanding of her relationship with him.

A: I'm in the library or office of an older home. I notice desks, books and something that is red, that seems important.

ML: What else do you notice about that?

A: It's a testament. There's gold writing. It appears to be a Bible. It has those thin pages. It is a gift. I open it and there are Proverbs. This is Tom's library. I have a sad feeling. He's gone.

ML: What do you know about him?

A: We were in love, but we weren't married. He's older in that life, and more caring. Maybe he's my father…maybe not.

ML: What do you know about yourself there?

A: I'm a twenty-five year old female. I live there. I have forever, since my birth.

ML: What do you remember about growing up there?

A: I see myself at about fifteen years old. I'm outside. I play, do laundry. It's grassy there. I have a younger sibling. When I'm twenty I see myself helping to run the household. It's a big house. I see people cooking. I'm in charge. I carry the responsibility.

ML: Are you the mistress of the house or are you hired to do that?

A: I'm hired. And I'm happy. I'm comfortable here.

ML: What do you know about the owners of the house?

A: I see a female with light hair. She's pretty, in a blue dress. And Tom is her husband. He's a colonel.

ML: What do you know about their relationship?

A: It's a nice marriage, but they are not connecting. It looks okay, but I know they are not happy. I am in love with him. She's in the back of my thoughts and he is in the front of my thoughts. He's powerful. I don't have any family; this is it. I was brought into this family. I don't have any connections except for this. He wears a uniform.

ML: What do you know about your relationship with him?

A: It doesn't feel warm or loving to me. He wants me, but I don't think it's right. In a way it's scary. He has raped me. That's when our relationship changed. I fell in love with him after that.

ML: What else do you remember?

A: He gets killed in battle. I'm sad. Or maybe he is just gone, and I miss him. This is when I am twenty-five years old.

ML: Where, in the world, are you, and what is the date?

A: We're in England and it's 1803, I think.

ML: What do you remember about the circumstances surrounding your separation from him?

A: I am happy to see him, but it is always a secret. I recognize his wife, now. She has the same demeanor as a friend of mine. Then, I'm sad. He tells me I have to go.

ML: What do you notice next?

A: I'm in a city. I see brick. I have an apartment. It's in Paris. There is a saloon or bar. I live above it. I'm a bartender there. I have a good family now. My family is now the regulars who come into the bar. They love me. And I love them. I'm older now.

ML: Do you remember anything more about your relationship with Tom?

A: My heart races when I am thinking about that original home. There is fear, adrenalin. I am afraid of getting caught. I remember him pushing himself on me. I was scared…and not. The first time we had sex it was in the bedroom. I was a virgin. I was 17 and scared. But I liked it too. I don't like the fact that I like it. I have self-disgust and guilt.

ML: Where do you feel that on your body?

A: In my chest. It is heavy. There is a hole being burned into my chest. (Interestingly this client has had a mastectomy due to cancer.) It's a big black hole.

ML: What purpose does it serve for you?

A: It protects me from other people's opinions. And from harm. It's uncomfortable. It doesn't work, but it is a part of me now.

ML: What would happen if it were gone?

A: I would be lighter, freer, unburdened, unchained.

ML: If you could give the you in that other life some of your wisdom, what would you tell her?

A: Stand up for yourself. Take control of yourself. Be proud. Stand and be firm. Believe in yourself. Don't be afraid of rejection. It doesn't matter.

ML: Does she hear you?

A: Yes, she listens to me. Her back gets straighter and stronger. She feels enlightened.

ML: Would it be possible to let go of that hole in your chest?

A: Yes. I can fill it with self-love. It's red now and filled with love.

ML: What else do you notice?

A: I see the Bible again. It was given to me by him. It reminds me that we used to share the Bible. He taught me from it—about Christianity and religion. He read to me. We spent a lot of time with the book. That was secret too.

ML: What was secret about it?

A: Our relationship grew when we shared the book. We set aside time every week. The hidden feeling is the shame feeling. I was hiding it from me because I feel so bad. I had lost my innocence and freedom. I felt trapped and controlled.

ML: If your innocence and freedom had a shape and color what would it be?

A: A yellow ball.

ML: If you could go back there and retrieve it, where would you find it?

A: Under the bed. I take it and I can carry it with me now.

ML: How does that feel?

A: I'm at the bar now. I am happy, content, warm, proud, and smart. I needed the wisdom of that experience to survive in the bar and in the city. I learned a lot, and I grew from it. But I don't have to carry it around.

ML: What do you notice about your chest?

A: It's not so heavy. I can breathe now.

ML: Move ahead to the end of that lifetime. What do you notice?

A: I'm about fifty years old at the end. I'm at the bar. I own the bar by then. I'm sick in bed.

ML: What did you gain in that lifetime?

A: I learned that I could go from knowing no one, to being proud of building up something at the original house, being pushed out, and then building it all up again. I had a full life. I am proud of my accomplishments. I had no blood family there.

ML: What correlations do you notice between that life and this one?

A: The starting over. Having new beginnings. How many lifetimes are in one life. Now knowing that it is good. That's reassuring. You don't have to have just one experience per lifetime.

In the past life, Alice had been this man's mistress. In this life, she was the wife and the man had a mistress. Their roles had changed a bit, but the man's character had remained the same.

14

HEALING AND VITALITY

"Life can only understood backwards; but it must be lived forwards."
—Soren Kierkegarrd

Many physical dis-eases and unwanted emotional conditions have their roots in past lives. When we understand and experience those roots, we can often dissolve the difficulty. This chapter contains five examples of clients who used past life regression to heal physical or emotional difficulties and renew their vitality.

Marta was given wisdom about healing and forgiveness, and a level of compassion that helped alleviate her physical symptoms.

Barbara saw the roots of her ankle pain, and her panic when she got hungry.

Kim found an image from a past life that helped her heal back and shoulder pain, and learned a lesson about a suicide.

Lisa saw that a negative attitude, and clinging to the past, were keeping her from releasing the pain of her multiple sclerosis. She received an image that let her float free.

Ted learned to manage his pain by balancing duty with freedom and self expression, and independence with valuing companionship.

Case Study

Marta

Marta came to the office with a long list of issues. She had had a tumor in her ear several years earlier and said that the operation "took my smile away." She complained of headaches and dizziness, and sensed a blockage in her first and second chakras (energy centers relating to the tailbone and genital areas). She said, "I'm holding onto something."

Two weeks before our session, she experienced her colon spasms worsening and said, "Nothing moves through me." She has had a history of eating disorders. Because she was experiencing a headache at the time of our session, we began with a technique called Object Imagery.

This and other hypnosis techniques are fully explained in my book Hypnotherapy: *A Client-Centered Approach* (Pelican Publishing, 2003). With this technique, we can often bypass the need for a long visualization induction leading to the hypnotic trance state. It is one of many techniques that encourage people to go to a deeper state naturally, while engaged in a productive therapeutic exercise. Although the visualization began as a metaphor, it quickly became apparent that it was a past life regression.

ML: Focus on the pain of your headache. If those sensations had a shape and color, what would they look like?

M: It looks like a green bubble. Like a solid ball with a rope tied tightly around the middle of it. And it's pulling to the left.

ML: If you could telepathically communicate with it, what would it tell you that it is doing there?

M: It has something to do with the physical, and something to do with the emotions.

ML: What would you like to do with it?

M: I want to relax it. But I can't seem to do that.

ML: I would like to ask the subconscious mind to provide your conscious mind with a metaphor, a story, which will give us information and insight about the origins and purpose of this green bubble. As I count from three to one, you may begin telling me the story. Three, two, one. Does your story begin indoors or outdoors?

M: Indoors.

ML: What else do you notice about your surroundings?

M: It is nighttime. It's a dark place. Confining. A dungeon. It is cold and damp.

ML: If you were in the story, would you be a man or a woman?

M: I'm a man.

ML: And how old do you feel?

M: Twenty-five.

ML: What else do you know about your situation?

M: I'm being punished for stealing. I had very abusive parents so I ran away. I had to steal to survive. There was no work for me. My little sister was with me, too.

ML: When you look at your little sister, and feel her energy, do you recognize her as anyone you know in this lifetime?

M: She is my husband in this lifetime. I'm protecting her. We are so hungry. I have hurt someone. I stabbed them in the side of the head. I didn't kill them, but I left them with a scar on the side of their face. Now I am in prison and my sister has to fend for herself. I feel so much guilt. There is nothing that I can do about it. I have to suffer the consequences. My sister has forgiven me. She understands and manages to get through it. She knew that I took care of her in that lifetime, and has now come back as my husband to take care of me here. I die in jail in that life. I don't live long at all. I die peacefully.

ML: Imagine the man that you stabbed is standing in front of you there. What do you notice about him?

M: He is young and blonde. He is very angry with me. He is rich and spoiled. He doesn't want to share anything. He owns a bakery. I was not asking for food, just the scraps. But he won't give me anything at all. It angers me so because we are both the same age, yet I'm deprived of his lifestyle. I go crazy. I slash at his face. He buckles up and curses me. I run and hide, but they find me. I have taken away some of his perfect life, and now he won't forgive me.

ML: Look even deeper at him. What does he really want?

M: In his soul, he wants to be forgiven by me. He asks me to forgive him for not giving us any food. I forgive him and tell him that I am sorry. He forgives me, although begrudgingly. I find it difficult to accept apologies.

ML: What did this episode allow him to learn in that lifetime?

M: He learned that he shouldn't judge people by their appearances. He needed to extend himself, and not be so self-centered. He needed to understand that we are all brothers. He says that he's learning that lesson in another lifetime. He tells me that my actions moved him along faster. He learned from the disfiguring that people looked at him differently. They now go beyond his beauty. He has become a more caring person. He is not as attractive in this lifetime, and he finds that to be okay. He is learning. Now he is forgiving me. I am relaxing more. My body is more relaxed.

ML: Picture the twenty-five year old that was you in that lifetime. What do you know about him now?

M: What he did was not good, but what he did for his sister was good. He protected her and provided for her unselfishly. He was being so selfless and had gotten frustrated. His intention was the right thing, but he needed to let go of the anger at the other person. He has been storing it, and carrying it around. He was unhappy at that time and felt that life was unjust. He was creating more tension, and therefore, creating the circumstances. He knows it's true. He had to learn his lessons, so he chose that experience.

ML: Did he learn what he needed to?

M: He learned a lot of lessons, but not the one about letting go of the resentment and anger. He needs to forgive his parents from that lifetime, also. And he needs to thank them.

ML: Why would he thank them?

M: Because those circumstances allowed him to learn independence and love. When he lashed out, he severed his spiritual contact. He had to learn that life is not a punishment. I need to forgive him.

ML: Can you do that?

M: I have forgiven him now. It makes me feel light.

ML: What are you noticing now?

M: I see a rainbow and clouds. I'm a light being. I see that my work on Earth is to bring joy. Life is colorful. My spirit guides and angels are always there, streaking across the sky, and making halos. The signs will be there. I, too, can streak across the sky and be as colorful as can be. I can keep my eyes wide open. I don't have to be so harsh on myself and others. I can be in the moment, in joy and peace.

ML: Is there anything else?

M: I will recognize when others have pain because I have been there. I can help them recognize their pain. I don't have to change myself or anyone else. I can accept them. I can love them. I can start with myself. I have such gratitude for this day. It has been an epiphany for me. If I sense the tension, I can just breathe in the rainbow.

Marta experienced relief from her physical symptoms right away, and she received a visual anchor that will allow her to achieve similar desired states of mind in the future.

Case Study

Barbara

Barbara said that she frequently injured her feet and ankles, and that she often felt a sense of panic when she was hungry. She sensed that there might be some past life connection to these issues.

We began our session with a visualization that eventually took us down a hall. When I asked her to choose a door, she said that it kept changing, and that she was not sure which one to choose. I told her that she could choose one and we would return to explore a different one later. She chose the black door with the brass knocker.

ML: As the door opens and you move through the threshold, where do you find yourself?

B: I notice an oriental rug in front of me. I'm indoors, and there is a banister to the left. I could go up the stairs or down the hall. I choose to go up the stairs. It is dark up here. I am holding a candle. I'm afraid of something. There is someone in armor, holding an ax. He comes after me and injures my foot with an ax. I am lying in bed with my foot propped up. It is gashed, but still connected. I'm very sick.

ML: What do you know about his motivation to do that?

B: I owed him money. I didn't pay my taxes.

ML: What do you know about yourself in that lifetime?

B: I'm a man. Someone comes with the money to help me out. They give the money to me. Later, I recover from the injury. I see myself hobbling around on a stick. Years later I am having trouble with that foot. I also see a warm and joyous scene with my family there. I am about sixty when I die.

ML: What have you learned from observing that lifetime?

B: I was selfish about money in that lifetime. I think maybe I was even unethical and unfair.

ML: What wisdom have you gained from that experience?

B: I learned to be generous. It is not right to prosper at someone else's loss. I have to deal fairly. Love the people you are with. Don't cheat.

ML: Is there anything else that you have learned from that lifetime?

B: I don't want to make decisions or take a course of action based solely on monetary issues. I want to go after things because I love it. And I want to be generous.

ML: Let's go back to the hallway and choose another door. As you do so, what do you notice about this door?

B: This one is an archway made of stone, with a wooden door.

ML: As the door opens and you move through, what do you begin to notice?

B: It is an open, spacious room with hay on the floor. There is a table there. There are many of us. I am a child, a boy. There is not enough food. We work on a farm. It's hard work. I get drafted into the army. I'm forced to go. I say goodbye to my family. I am miserable.

ML: What do you notice next?

B: I'm in the mud. It's cold and wet. I'm hungry and tired. I see the battlefield. A cannon ball hits me in the chest. Or maybe I'm carrying it. I'm a prisoner of war, I think. I am emaciated. My blanket is threadbare. I have wooden shoes. I die in the camp, on the cold earth.

ML: What have you learned from observing that lifetime?

B: I never want to go to war again. I wouldn't want to be in that position again. There is too little for the people. It is easy here in this life, with the women's control of pregnancy. Then, it was difficult. Back then, the families were so big, and there was no food. Although there was a lot of love. I didn't have the courage not to go to the army. I didn't question authority then. Now I'd question it, or I would find a different solution. I learned that you have to fight for what you believe in. And I learned that I have to make the most of myself.

ML: Do you see any correlations between that life and this one now?

B: There was not enough love from my parents to go around. Actually, there was plenty, but they just couldn't give us their undivided attention. I mistook attention for love.

From this point, I took Barbara through various hypnotherapy and neuro-linguistic techniques that allowed her to heal some of the wounds from her childhood in this life. Then we completed our session.

ML: What do you notice about your ankle now?

B: It feels like it is shackled.

ML: Tell me the story about how those shackles got there and why.

B: I am imprisoned. I have been dragged by a chain attached to my foot. It is really painful. I'm a slave and I have been disobedient. I have a lot of courage and pride. They didn't like that. I was born into slavery.

ML: What else do you recall about that lifetime?

B: I am a man and I live to be old. I am free by then. My foot never healed completely.

ML: What wisdom did you learn in that lifetime?

B: He was foolish. He didn't fight the right battles. I need to think about what I say and do beforehand. I have to not be so single-minded.

ML: Do you recognize any correlations between that lifetime and this one?

B: I have not always heeded that. I have not always been smart in my battles. In this life, I am pretty good about it. I am more attentive. Yet, I still need to think before I act or speak.

This session revealed how present day physical pains can have roots in past life experiences. We continued our sessions with other techniques that furthered the healing of these and other issues.

Case Study

Kim

Kim complained of a pain in her shoulders and back. She was already in trance, as we had been working on other issues, so we moved seamlessly into a past life regression.

ML: If you were to look internally at the pain in your back and shoulders, and if the pain had a shape and a color, what would it look like?

K: It looks like a rod or a spear.

ML: Tell me a story about how that came to be there.

K: I am a man. I am at war with my enemy. I am outside, in the woods. I am wearing head armor and a brown cloak. My enemy is there, but I don't know that he is behind me.

ML: What are you doing?

K: I am moving toward my group. I am a blacksmith. And I have children.

ML: What is the date?

K: 1584.

ML: Where in the world are you?

K: I'm in Europe somewhere.

ML: What else do you notice happening there?

K: I just fall to the ground and he leaves. I lay there, prepared to get hit again. But it doesn't come. So I get up and start walking. A friend on a horse comes by. I get on the horse with him. He takes me to a doctor. They pull the spear out from my back. The doctor bandages me, feeds me something, and then I leave.

ML: What do you notice next?

K: I see myself on horseback. I am the commander of an army, or the second in command. We are going to battle. It is in an open area. There is a lot of tension. Our side gets slaughtered. I take a knife to my chest. It is gory and sad. We have shame about this. There was no need for the loss.

ML: What did you learn in that lifetime?

K: I learned to be a man.

ML: Do you see any correlation between that lifetime and this one?

K: My sense of honor.

ML: What would you like to do to heal from these wounds?

K: I would like to pull the knife out and heal.

ML: Do that and tell me when it is complete.

K: Okay. It's done.

ML: If that man who you were in that lifetime could share his wisdom with you, what would he tell you?

K: He would tell me to be strong. To live life heartily. Such things matter not.

ML: How do you feel now?

K: Fine, but sometimes I feel a tightness in my belly. It makes me just want to stab it myself. It feels like a hard ball of human organs.

ML: If you could see it, internally, what shape and color would it have?

K: It is brown, dark, and is shaped like a cylinder. But it is kind of non-specific.

ML: What else can you tell me about that?

K: It is like a little knife. There is a hand that holds it there. It feels like I committed suicide.

ML: Tell me what you remember.

K: I am a female. I am wearing a red dress. I have long brown hair. I am terribly distraught. It is about something that I can't have. I am about twenty-one years old, and I speak Spanish.

ML: What is the year?

K: 1204.

ML: Go back in time about a month. What do you notice at that time?

K: I am happy. I am outside my home on a beautiful night. I am getting married soon. I am sleeping when I get awakened. I am told that the man I am to marry is dead. He has been murdered. It was senseless.

ML: Go back to an earlier time. What do you remember about the events leading up to this?

K: I am in a barn. I am going riding with my brother and some friends. After a while, the group is further away from me. I'm alone and someone on a horse rides up to me and gives me a ring. It is ruby and gold. It symbolizes him. I am so happy. He escorts me back to the group.

ML: Now going back to the image of the knife. What do you remember now about that event?

K: I am alone. He is gone. I hold my heart, and a knife. It is a turning point. I didn't want to live alone, so I killed myself.

ML: As you are dying, what are you experiencing?

K: I regretted it immediately. I didn't think that I had a choice. It was rash.

ML: If the aspect of you in that life could give advice to you, what would she tell you?

K: She would advise me to give myself time before making big decisions. Love with all of your heart, and don't be afraid.

Suicide is rarely advisable. As is demonstrated in this case study, dying will not take us away from pain. It only prevents us from learning the lessons presented at that time. If the lessons are not completed, they will surely be presented again at a future time.

When my clients appear to be avoiding an opportunity to learn an important lesson, I ask them, "How bad does it have to get before you will be forced to face this lesson?" If the subconscious mind feels ignored, it will make us increasingly uncomfortable until we listen. I urge my clients to learn each lesson as soon as it is presented.

Case Study

Lisa

Lisa had been diagnosed with multiple sclerosis, and was looking for some answers. She had experienced a past life regression with another therapist years earlier, and felt this had had a strong impact on her. Yet, she still wasn't clear why it was relevant to her situation. We decided to explore that same lifetime once again.

ML: Tell me about that regression.

L: I had a husband who didn't come back from war. I took that message to mean that I wasn't good enough to return to.

ML: Go back to that time, and tell me what you experience when he left.

L: When he left, I couldn't maintain the house. It was the central home for the community. It fell into ruin. In the later years, life was never the same again. I became a recluse. I couldn't cope. My children had moved on, and I was left alone.

ML: Move toward the end of that lifetime. What do you notice then?

L: I am on the property. I live in a log cabin. It was the servants' quarters. It is rough. I'm inside, and my daughter is next to me. She is my daughter in this life, too.

ML: What else do you notice about that scene?

L: I am very sad. And I'm bewildered. I wonder why.

ML: If you could have a conversation with the woman you were in that lifetime, what would you tell her?

L: You didn't do it right. You didn't go on with life. Be happy.

ML: What else do you notice?

L: It fades away. I am in the present, with the music. I see the horizon. The sun is coming up. I see the first light. I am hopeful. This is a new day, even though it hasn't fully emerged.

ML: What have you learned from this?

L: It is all right to let go. I don't have to hold on to the pain. Just because there was disappointment doesn't mean I am not worthy.

ML: Is there anything else you would do for her?

L: I would tell her to go in peace. She did the best she could. She is a loving person. It is okay to love. She has courage and strength. It is okay to let go. To move on. It is time to do it. I still want to understand where the MS comes from.

ML: I would like to ask the subconscious mind to present another image, or experience, that will help us to understand the cause of the MS, and steps to take to heal from it.

L: I see myself outdoors. There is a tent, long and flowing. I go into it. It is the top only. The wind blows around and through it. The tent is just floating in it. It is a bright white light.

ML: What else do you notice about that experience?

L: It is just before this lifetime. I have a big present, wrapped in white paper with gold and blue. There is a ribbon on the left side.

ML: What do you know about that?

L: I can move through and beyond it. It goes into the sky. I am finishing something and releasing. I do it. Now I am above. I am lighter. I didn't have to go and examine it. I can go right through. I'm light. It's lovely.

ML: How does that correlate to you now, and the MS?

L: I don't need to examine the details of the pain. I can just release and

> move past it. It's a gift. To learn more about myself. And remind me to release.

Lisa learned a great deal about her physical and emotional condition in this life, and received a metaphor at the end of the regression that gave her additional information and inspiration for her healing.

CASE STUDY

TED

Ted and I had been exploring the trauma and physical pain he was experiencing, and he wanted to see if there were any past life connections to his condition.

T: I seem to be in a black abyss. There is no floor. It is empty space. I'm floating down. I land and I notice lots of pillows. I'm laying on my side, propped up by my elbows. I see a lot of red colors. The area is plush, like a lounge, with deep burgundies. It's relaxing. It appears to be in an Aladdin style. I'm a man, about thirty years old.

ML: What else do you notice?

T: I'm alone. I'm a young prince. I'm not really happy. Mostly bored. I like my life, but I don't get to do anything that is terribly fun. There are a lot of expectations of me. There are so many complications. I feel the stress in my hips. It comes from a deep seated suppression.

ML: What else are you experiencing?

T: It is a sad life. Unfulfilled. I don't want to disappoint anyone. I am supposed to feel happy, feel like royalty, with the prestige. I don't want to be there. If I had the choice, I wouldn't be.

ML: If you had a conversation with this young prince, what would he say that he needs?

T: He needs things to be different. He would like to be able to split down the middle so that he could fulfill his obligations and not disappoint his family, and yet shed himself of the obligations and move out to experience the world. He wants to explore, learn and be free. That is what he wishes he could do.

ML: What lessons are there for him to learn in that lifetime?

T: He learns selflessness, duty, patience. He has to exercise these, even with a total range of choices, so that he won't disappointment the family. He must carry on the bloodline, lead the people, and be a symbol of royalty.

ML: What else do you notice about that lifetime?

T: He has several wives and plenty of children. He is a good leader. He is a good man in general.

ML: What correlations do you notice between that life and this one?

T: In some ways, I am shedding any obligations I can shed. I am resisting commitment and obligation wherever possible. I try to allow myself all possible freedoms. I'm living the life that this man wishes he could have lived. I am feeling his tension, his pain, that he had throughout his life.

ML: What wisdom can you gain from observing his lifetime?

T: The message is to follow your heart, if you can. If life doesn't obligate a person from birth, then explore and go out into the world. Do what your heart desires. Be free. I want to sit and feel his energy for a bit.

ML: Take your time and let me know when you are ready to continue.

T: Okay. I was able to tell him that he can have the best of both worlds. He is me. He will have the opportunities he desires eventually. The right thing to do is to stay where he is and do his best. That message makes him feel better.

ML: Associate yourself with his body, viewing the world through his eyes. Now allow your memories to take you back in time to his childhood, to the infant stage, and now to the time prior to attaching to that body. You are in the astral, making decisions about coming into that body. What do you notice about that time?

T: I knew what I would experience. I am calm and peaceful.

ML: Did you have assistance with your decision?

T: There are other presences. They have a different form of communication. It is telepathic. They help me to understand that this is a good thing to do.

ML: Do they reveal their reasoning?

T: I need to have that experience. I need to grow in this area.

ML: For what purpose?

T: To learn selflessness, patience, and a sense of duty. I needed the full gamut of experience, to learn about relationships early in my existence. This experience was one of many to come. I needed to learn to appreciate freedom and freedom of choice. It was also important to understand dependability, along with the importance of doing what you want to do, within the context of being true to yourself. He and I are sharing our energies, bringing our experiences together. We have more energy work to do, but that can be in the future. For now, I am ready to say goodbye to him.

ML: What are you experiencing in your hips?

T: When we started his hips felt really tense. It's still there. As I left him, it was very much dissipated, reduced. The sensation was a lot more dull. Mine feel the same.

ML: Is there another past life correlation? Another cause? Go back into the hallway, and choose another door. What do you notice?

T: Dark wood, grainy, with a white frame. There is a bright light. It's a laboratory with big windows on one side. The sun is coming in. It's fairly modern.

ML: What else do you know about this place?

T: It's at a college or university. It's modern. There are numbers on the walls and doors. I'm not sure I am a person. I'm watching the scene. I see a balding man, with a beard, glasses, and a white jacket. The lights are off, and the sun is coming in through the windows.

ML: What else can you notice about him?

T: He's in charge of the lab. There are no students there now. I can't sense whether he is happy or not. He seems somewhat content. He is thinking about a woman. A few years ago…oh, he has regrets. He is focused on his work because now that is all he has. He doesn't know where she is anymore. He just has a vision of her face. And a dull regret. It is not disempowering or a handicap. It is a background awareness. He wished he had done things differently. I don't feel he is me, although I feel his feelings.

ML: What else do you notice?

T: He slumps over on a sink, and his eyes are rolling back in his head. I don't know whether it is real or not.

ML: Your subconscious knows exactly what is going on here, and as I count from three to one it can reveal that information to you. Three, two, one. What do you know about what is going on here?

T: It's the path I am on. It is where I will be. Not the exact environment, but…I never really loved anyone deeply. That's all. It's a warning. A mirror.

ML: Now that you are aware, what would you like to do?

T: The opposite is to love someone deeply. The common denominator is regret. My path is about focusing on selfish things I enjoy. My attitude is about not sacrificing my time.

ML: Is it a sacrifice to invest in not having regret?

T: There is something in me that doesn't want to be involved in a relationship.

ML: Why don't you have a conversation with this man, and find out what he has learned about this?

T: He feels alone. He is detached from anyone else. He is wondering if he made the right choice and whether he had a choice. He needs someone to hug him.

ML: You may go ahead and do that.

T: It is really helping him to heal. Just someone else being there with him feels good.

ML: Do you have someone?

T: I have someone, but I don't trust her. She is deceptive.

ML: Could you attract someone else?

T: It is possible. I would have to learn to relax a little. I would have to believe that is what I wanted.

ML: How would that have made a difference in that man's life?

T: The presence of another human being would have created an energy exchange. Even another man, a friend, would have been beneficial.

ML: What can you learn from his experiences?

T: I learned what I need to do differently in my life. I've become aware of the value of companionship. It is a point of reference of where I would rather not be.

ML: How does this knowledge relate to your issues with your hips?

T: I don't know whether one is causal of the other or not, but it seems like it would be very difficult to have a relationship or co-exist with another person while having all this tension in my hips.

ML: What would happen if you chose to release it?

T: If I could, I imagine I would be more relaxed in general, less uptight, more even keeled.

ML: If that were to happen, what would that allow you to do?

T: I would have more comfort in living with someone else, having a loving partner. I would be happier in many ways—in the presence of others, with myself, and in being able to focus better.

ML: If you were to relax the tension, what might it prevent you from doing?

T: It would prevent me from living the dysfunctional way that I do. It may or may not slow me down in my career, but I would be happier and perhaps more efficient.

The session continued with other therapy techniques designed to resolve the inner conflict that had been revealed by this past life.

15

Finding Your Life Purpose

"Learn to get in touch with the silence within yourself and know that everything in this life has a purpose."
—Elizabeth Kubler-Ross

Past life regressions can give us powerful tools for finding our true purpose in life. The seven regressions in this chapter demonstrate how our earlier lives almost always hold clues for our direction in this life.

Jayne saw what it took to be contented with herself, regardless of circumstances.

Melanie began her regression with the intention to heal childhood abuse, and learned that she must first love and honor herself.

Jean saw that life is simpler than we think, and that happiness stems from finding people to love—and learning to enjoy life. She realized that her purpose in this life was to help people, and experienced one past life in which she did not take a human form.

Pat confirmed that being a writer was on her path, and Sam confirmed his life as an artist.

Sally saw the joys of a simple, spiritual, communal life. Anne found that her purpose was to learn not to care what people thought of her, and simply to let herself be happy.

Case Study

Jayne

Jayne's regression demonstrates the wisdom that can be gained about life purpose, and how we can switch between being male or female in different lifetimes.

J: I'm in a desert. There's not much vegetation. It looks like the Southwest. I see myself at work there. I'm a potter. I'm in the marketplace. It seems like it is early A.D.

ML: What else do you know about yourself?

J: I'm a male, maybe twenty-five to thirty years old, but I look like I'm fifty. Maybe I'm not in the best of health, or I don't feed myself properly. I'm intent on the potter's wheel. People ask me what I sell. I make house wares. If I sell them, okay. If I don't, it's okay. I don't have as many customers as the people who sell vegetables or cloth.

ML: What else do you notice?

J: I'm intent on the potter's wheel. My hands are dry from the clay. I'm a loner, but I am able to communicate easily. I'm just not one for small talk. I don't seem to live long. When I die, the people miss me, but my passing also hasn't made a great dent in their lives. I simply served a purpose, filled a need.

ML: What wisdom did you gain from viewing that past life?

J: That you can be content with life. You can be internally happy. He didn't care what people thought. He didn't have to impress anyone except with knowledge and skill. He had all that he needed. He was willing to die, and he died quietly.

ML: How might that wisdom change what you do with the rest of your life here?

J: It could actually make me more of a loner. I realize now that my interests are sufficient. I don't need to look elsewhere for approval. I can do as I like. Life is too short to be upset about everything. Who knows how long or short it will be.

ML: To understand more of the message and its significance to you, I would like to ask the subconscious mind to take you to yet another lifetime. What do you notice?

J: I'm in a hospital. It feels comfortable and familiar, but I don't work there. I see an x-ray machine. I'm getting a treatment. Is it for cancer? I'm not happy but I'm not scared either. I seem to have to do this frequently.

ML: What else do you notice about this?

J: I make the most of every day. I don't know how long I will be on Earth. I don't have all the time in the world to be content. I have to find it now.

ML: If the aspect of you in that lifetime could give the aspect of you here some advice, what would that be?

J: Don't worry about the future. Enjoy each day, without looking to the future. There might not be one. I will try to be happier like I used to be. She took life too seriously. The negativity got to her. She internalized too much.

ML: Based on her advice, what will you be willing to do differently?

J: I'll stop the negative thoughts. I'll be more positive. I'll let things bounce off me.

This session produces two different lifetimes that brought Jayne the same message. Her soul had obviously been trying to learn the lesson of being content in the here and now, and making the most of life no matter what the circumstances.

Case Study

Melanie

Melanie was working on healing childhood abuse issues. We had successfully used other techniques, and decided to complete our third session with a past life regression. She received a valuable insight from her past life counterpart that spoke to her purpose as well as to healing.

M: I'm outdoors. It is daytime and I'm in the country. I see trees, a farm, horses, crops, plows, and dirt. I am just observing it.

ML: What do you notice?

M: We are working. There are many of us. We're plowing. I feel old.

ML: What else do you know about that scene?

M: I'm a woman. I live on the farm. I have a big family consisting of a husband and ten children. We all work together on the farm as a family. I died in my nineties.

ML: If you could speak with her, what advice would she give you?

M: Life is simple. You make it harder than it has to be. We worked hard, and had a lot of love in the family. We each gave a lot. We worked together to make it, to have food to eat. It was hard work, but it was okay. We all worked together.

ML: What correlations do you see between that lifetime and this one?

M: I need to find people that know how to love. I want to work with people who will work with me. It doesn't have to be difficult. So many people go through life and don't do it right. They do someone else's thing, and not their own. They follow other people's dreams, and miss their own.

ML: What have you learned from this?

M: I need to believe in myself. I need to love myself. The rest will come.

It is a powerful lesson to respect our own path and follow our own destiny—especially when we are taught that other people come first, and that what others say is more important than our own knowledge. Being true to yourself, and then finding others who find delight in supporting you on that path, makes life happier and more fulfilling.

Case Study

Jean

Jean wanted information about her career path and her purpose. Impatience, shortness of temper, and experiences of frustration at work were starting to bother her. She also wanted to learn more about her relationship with her significant other, Tim. She was curious about why they were together and whether they were soul mates.

At first, Jean experienced difficulty knowing where she was. She described her visualized location as being in the air, with fumes around her. It was not light or dark, and she was just observing. She decided to "go find out" more about her surroundings, and took a step to discover what was behind the thick air. Then she went through it and found herself alone. This is where the session picks up…

ML: What else do you notice?

J: There is an opening. I see blue sky, with clouds.

ML: What do you notice about yourself?

J: I am a male, about thirty years old.

ML: Do you notice anything else about your surroundings?

J: I am indoors. It is a closed space, much like a museum. I am looking at statues and art. I am calm and relaxed. I am walking through the museum, observing the sculptures. Then I leave and am outside of a major museum. It seems to be Europe. Perhaps it is Italy or London. I am at the top of some stairs. I come down them into an alley. The streets are beautiful and I don't see many people. In fact, I don't see anyone. It appears now to be a stone city. I wander around with no particular goal. In front of me, I see a huge rock, as though the earth was split here. It appears to be an abyss. I am on a cliff, and I see waves below. There is a storm now. Still there is no one around. The ocean looks viscous. I jump off the cliff onto the beach. I begin to walk along the beach. Now it appears to be Kauai, with twenty-two miles of sand and beach. I see local kids. They push me to hurry. They want me to see. There is a fire. It is a local ritual with music, many sounds, and a Hawaiian pig roasting. I wait my turn to enjoy the pig meat.

ML: Then what do you do?

J: I am just observing and participating. I am enjoying myself. There is balance and we all seem to be in tune with each other. It is relaxed. We know how to enjoy ourselves. I am wearing a black suit. It doesn't fit this event. I want to stay and participate. I have to go back to where I came from. I live in the village. So I climb up the cliff. I wonder what I should do next. I fly out of that male body. I just go. I see myself flying up through the clouds, into space. I see the galaxy. It's pretty. I circle around it. I enjoy the flight. There is no agenda. There is no hurry.

ML: Do you notice any correlation between that lifetime and this one?

J: I was carefree there. I had no fear. I could enjoy myself. I was free of obstacles. It feels good. I was in balance and harmony. I could travel the world, not just be in the office. I was independently wealthy. I could help others.

ML: Move through the astral experience, up to the time just before you chose to be in this body. What do you notice about that experience?

J: I have confidence. I am not weak, but rather strong.

ML: What purpose did you have in choosing to come into this lifetime?

J: I wanted to learn to not worry. To be patient and to be self-accepting. I wanted to strengthen my ego. To be aware, loving and kind. To be calm, and to learn to enjoy life.

ML: How will this experience change what you do in the future of this lifetime?

J: I will change careers. Maybe I will win the lottery or get an inheritance. I will go to a different country. I have to come up with an idea for a new business.

ML: Let's continue to explore these issues by asking your subconscious mind to take you to yet another lifetime that will give you even more information. As I count from three to one, you can go to another past life. Three, two, one. Where do you find yourself?

J: I see bright red all around me. The wind is blowing through me.

ML: What else do you notice about that experience?

J: I am wearing a red dress, from about the 18th century. I have beautiful red hair.

ML: What do you notice around you?

J: I am in a bar. I am the owner. It is a joyful atmosphere. I feel the connectedness of everyone. We are in good spirits. It reminds me of a western movie. There are horses and carriages.

ML: Some time passes and what do you notice next?

J: I am in a restaurant. We are attacked and there is a looting. Someone tries to kill me with a knife.

ML: What else do you know about that?

J: We are attacked by robbers. All the patrons in the bar die, including me. I have a knife through my stomach.

ML: What else do you know about that?

J: I didn't like it. It was a good life, but it was so short.

ML: How do you feel about that lifetime?

J: I was fulfilled.

ML: What have you learned from that lifetime that would be of help to you in this life?

J: I need to start a business that is around helping people. In that lifetime, I was single and I wished that I had had a family. I want to live life to the fullest. I want to enjoy every minute with no regrets. I have learned that it is important to live life as though I may die tomorrow.

ML: Asking your subconscious to take you to yet another lifetime, where do you find yourself next?

J: I see black, with fresh paint. It seems to be something new. I am floating, comfortably, higher and higher. I am surrounded by cupids and angels. We all hold hands in a circle. It is like a beautiful painting. One of them looks like my boyfriend, Tim. Here he has big cheeks. It is just the two of us. We are floating and holding hands. We come to a castle. Is it ice or crystal? It's beautiful. Like a palace. I am at the door now. I open it, and walk in. It is like a cathedral. There is a long hallway, perhaps like a large Catholic church. I keep walking. Something jumps out at us. We run to the door. There is a green light that seems to push us onto the central altar. There is a bad man floating around, a creature. It sits and watches. I send healing light to the creature and it goes away. It seems to disintegrate. We run to the door and something stops us. We are pushed to the altar once again. Then we kiss and we get married. There is an older person that does the ceremony.

ML: What do you think that this means to you?

J: I see it as meaning that we have resolved our differences. We have made peace in front of a spiritual authority. He seems very pleased that we made it. We rush toward the door. Then we walk out of it, and begin to fly.

ML: What do you experience next?

J: We are dancing and flying, and we come back to Earth. We have lost our charm and we look like people now. We are in a house, just being people. We dance, and bicker, and fight over little stuff. The male kills the female, but it is hard to tell who is who—whether I am the male or the female. We are just tired and exhausted from the fighting. It is a bad situation. We are constantly arguing.

ML: What have you learned from experiencing this?

J: It is better in this lifetime. We have been given a chance in this lifetime to correct the killing from that lifetime. We have the opportunity to not repeat the same mistakes. We can make it work. We are like one person.

ML: What can you do to make it right in this lifetime?

J: I can listen to him. I can be pleasant and cheerful, and try to get along. It would feel better. He would be pleasant back, and he is mostly. I would get more out of him if I were more pleasant.

ML: And asking the subconscious mind to take you to one last experience that will give you information that will be helpful for you in this matter…three, two, one. What do you notice now?

J: I am a man. I am looking for something. I think I am a soldier or a fire fighter. There is a fire in front of me. I am alone and am putting it out. It's big, across a whole field. I just have to do it. It is an enormous job alone. I am so tired. I wish I had help. There are more fires on this little planet. I am here to protect the planet.

ML: What do you know about yourself?

J: I am a monstrous, powerful non-human creature. Rather than having skin, it is more like thick snake or lizard scales. Nothing gets through it. I am here to protect the planet. It is so tiny that I sit on it and can see the rest of the universe. I am all alone.

ML: What else do you notice?

J: The air is thick with fire and smoke. I am lonely and bored. There is no one else around. I fall off the planet and I am nowhere at all.

ML: What do you notice next?

J: I was powerful, angry, and passionate. I didn't need to eat or drink. I had no feelings. I was huge. I could go from being about six or eight feet tall and stretch myself out to be as big as a dinosaur. Still I had some human features. It seemed I could take on any form and then go back to normal.

ML: What have you learned from that experience?

J: I don't want to be like that anymore. Yet, I want to be more flexible in my relationships. It is important to reach out to others.

It is interesting to note that when our session began, Jean was in thick air. Again, at the very end, she experienced thick smoke and fire in the air. There is no telling whether we had come full circle or if it was a different, yet similar, experience.

In about two hours of regression, Jean was able to capture memories from four lifetimes, gain a greater understanding of what she could do with her life, and receive information that considerably changed her perspectives on her relationship. Do you think that vision of flying with cupids and exchanging vows with her boyfriend was metaphorical, an astral experience, or memories from between lives?

Case Study

Pat

Pat wanted information about her purpose in life. As a hobby in this lifetime, she writes poetry and keeps a journal.

P: As I move through the door I see purple. I am walking straight ahead and there seems to be something that I don't see. There is movement. There is a veil of a curtain, and people moving behind it. I move past the curtain and I can begin to see what is going on. I see several people sitting at high desks. They seem to be scribes. Now they are looking at me, and nodding.

ML: Then what happens?

P: They say, "Welcome. Hello." They are smiling and warm.

ML: What do you know about why you are there?

P: I'm supposed to be there. I go over to the man on my right. I say, "Hello. What do you want me to do?" He gets off his bench. He's smiling. He's so nice. He sets up a table for me to the left. It has a high bench. He places a big book on the table and opens it for me. It is filled with blank pages. He also gives me a pen with feathers. I don't like the big skirt that I'm wearing. It makes it uncomfortable to sit on the bench. I notice that I have black button shoes. I really don't want to be dressed like this. Nevertheless, there I sit in front of the blank pages. They are lined, like a ledger. The cover has a beautiful color. It's purple. The feather is also a light purple.

ML: What else do you notice about this?

P: There is a sense of order. There is a man with a red robe and a big collar. He is at the front of the room. He reminds me of the Hierophant card in the Tarot deck. He says, "Now you can learn." The other man nods at that. His name is Mr. Payton. I am the only woman. Yet, I feel accepted. I wonder why.

ML: What do you know about that?

P: There are two other men who seem to be less important. One of them hands me a scroll. I have the best penmanship. I have to copy the scroll for masses. I say, "I'd be happy to." It feels right that I am there. I love to write.

ML: What happens next?

P: I start writing. I'm very careful. I don't want to make any smudges. I'm not nervous even though they are watching me. I am thinking that the ledger is so big my arm will be tired. But I keep writing.

ML: What else do you notice?

P: They bring me some water. The others move around, talk, and check each other's work. There are many scrolls on the shelf to my right. Also many old books. I'm allowed to take a break to eat. When I do, I go to the books. I love the books. I touch their bindings.

ML: Do you notice anything in particular about the books?

P: I wrote one of them. I see it on the shelf.

ML: What do you know about that book.

P: There is something about a rose in it. I believe it says "Muses" on the cover. It has a red rose, and the binding is black. These are my writings. Now I know that's why I am here. I wrote it. It's a book of poetry.

ML: As you look at the book, can you also read the author's name?

P: The author's name is not on the binding. I pull it off the shelf and look at the book. The name is on the lower right, printed in gold. It is well worn.

ML: As I count from 3 to 1, you will know the name of the author as you see it there on the book.

P: Johanna Smythe. She thinks, "See I am different, I spell my name with a 'y.'"

ML: What else do you know about this experience?

P: I am not being paid for what I do. I see the light through the window by Mr. Payton. He tells me that when the sun starts to set, which will be pretty soon, I can go home.

ML: What happens when the light begins to dim?

P: I wrote fourteen pages on both sides. The man who reminds me of the Hierophant nods at me, and I know I can go home. I leave. Everyone is so very nice to me.

ML: What do you know about your purpose from having experienced this past life?

P: I know that I need to be writing. On every blank page that I see, I need to write. I need to write about the feelings of my heart. Sometimes you only have to touch one person. When I saw that rose, I knew that I had touched some people. Every blank page is a treasure. You have to put it in a chest.

ML: Do you know anything else about that?

P: I need to get a special journal, with fresh blank pages. In special moments I need to do some writing. I can see the journal. I need to write while I'm on my sabbatical. It won't be enough to hear my poems read on the radio, they need a binding. Interestingly, I just bought myself a ring with a rose on it. When I bought it, it symbolized "Continue the Quest". To me that means writing. It doesn't mean that I won't have a life. It is a whole new slate. I feel empowered.

Pat continues to write her poetry and keep her journals—with renewed energy and enthusiasm. She says that she has a greater sense of purpose in writing now. She understands that it is an ancient skill that she had mastered lifetimes ago, and that it is part of her soul journey.

Case Study

Sally

This case study was obtained while attending a Spiritual Counselor Certification Course. One of the participants was experiencing a past life regression while four of us asked her questions and took notes. She graciously granted permission to have her session presented here.

There was no particular purpose for the regression, but it revealed some interesting information. After being led into a gentle trance by our workshop facilitator, Shelley Lessin Stockwell, Sally observed herself outdoors. Since several of us were asking questions, I will designate our part as Q.

S: I'm outdoors. I am rolling down a hill. I had climbed through a window and fell. I am trying to get away from my father. I am afraid I will be found.

Q: How old do you seem to be?

S: Sixteen or seventeen years old.

Q: What do they call you?

S: Mary.

Q: Where are you?

S: Bethlehem.

Q: What is the year?

S: The number fourteen comes to mind.

Q: What are you doing?

S: I have a place to go. Someplace that is safe. There will be people there. I have to get there.

Q: What do you notice next?

S: Someone is there now, with a horse. He let's me ride. We go to a safe place in the city. Everything appears brown and tan. We go downstairs to get to the place. I feel my father getting further behind me. I feel safer.

Q: Where have you gone to?

S: I was in a city, then in the desert, and now I'm in another city. I don't know the name. There is a wall around the city. And a gate. I get off the horse at the entrance to the city. There is someone who will return the horse. I am hurrying. There are many people. I am tired and then I am hungry.

Q: Where are you now?

S: I am taken down a stairway. There is a door. The person I am with knocks. The door opens. There is one person there. A man. I know him. He is a lover of mine. I am not as excited to see him as one would think. This is his parents' house. I don't want to be here, but I have to go here first. It is a place on the way to somewhere else. I have to wait until dark. I don't like him. He is a past lover. He wants to touch me, but I don't want him to. It is dark in this place. His mother comes. She knows where I want to go.

Q: Then what happens?

S: It is dark. The mother bundles me, and takes me to another place in the city. It is a nondescript place. It's big. She knocks. A female voice says something. We indicate that I want to be a student here. The door opens. Inside there is a group of women. They are wise. It is the spiritual path that I am drawn to. Sometimes they take in new people. It feels good to be here. The woman who brought me here leaves. Now another woman comes and feeds me bread and milk. I am hungry.

Q: How long will you stay here?

S: I could stay forever here. It is a way of life. The people live together. It seems to be a Christian and Pagan mix. I finish eating. Then I meet the woman in charge of this group. We call her Kendall. When I see her, my heart leaps. I am drawn to their beliefs. I am not sure she will let me stay. She says that I can stay for thirty days to see how it works out. It is a simple life.

Q: How long do you end up staying?

S: I stay forever. I am there until I die.

Q: What is the happiest event that you experience in that life time?

S: I am worshipping. I feel a connection with that which is beyond knowing, that is the same as us, different yet not. It fills my heart and body. It connects with all beings, including one's family.

Q: How old are you when you die?

S: I'm about forty-five years old. I am sick and am nursed by the women in the group. It is clear that it is terminal. I am surrounded by all who live there. I hear the message that it is "Okay to go." With great ease, I leave my body. It's almost like not leaving. For a while I am still attached. Then I have a stronger pull from... There is an opening. I see other people, images waiting to greet me. It's like being able to touch everyone's heart. I move to the openness. I feel less distinct. There is more spaciousness. A blending. It appears like being individual, but more like formed to help me transition. I ease into a rhythm, like a heart beat. I have a sense of compassion. It's an indescribable sense of love and compassion. I'm not me, just love. It's very good.

Q: What else do you notice about that experience?

S: I am home. There is nothing more to do.

Q: What have you learned from that experience?

S: It is important to do what I am drawn to. Above all the spiritual life was important to me. The connection to God.

Q: How will this experience impact your present life?

S: I will be more quiet. Experience the beingness in the moment.

> Where there is no separation between the Self and God and Consciousness. No past and no future. Purity in the moment. I love God. I would like to stay there. If I can get out of my own way. This aspect of me lives within my cells.

This past life regression developed into a beautiful spiritual experience for Sally. It had a powerful impact on her sense of herself, her connection to God, and her understanding of her desires for her path.

Case Study

Sam

Sam is a white man, an artist and musician. He wanted a better understanding of his connection to the arts. His session also demonstrates that we can carry instructions from one lifetime to another, and that we alternate between races. If we regress enough, we usually discover that we have all been every different race, and have lived in a variety of cultures.

S: I seem to be in an auditorium or a theater. There is no one there. I am standing and looking around. I feel comfortable. It's familiar.

ML: Move ahead in time until something changes.

S: Now there are people in the seats. The lights are brighter. There is a performance.

ML: What do you know about that event?

S: I am either a player or the conductor. I can't tell yet. It seems serious, yet fun. Serious in that it is important. We are all players. We're just doing what we do. It's a big audience. They really like what we are doing.

ML: Then what do you notice?

S: Now I'm in a bed. In the hospital. Friends come to see me. Something happened. I'm coughing sort of. I'm really sick, or it was an accident.

ML: Where does your body hurt?

S: In three places. My left arm, though my hand is okay. I'm not concerned about that. My left leg. It's all bandaged or in a cast. And my right foot. My abdomen is messed up. I have serious problems in the stomach, but I won't acknowledge it. I keep telling them, "There's nothing to it. I'll be fine." We laugh and talk about playing music.

ML: What do you remember about the events leading up to this condition?

S: It was a car accident. It was in the 1930's or 1940's. Maybe the late 1940's. I don't know if I was driving. I think so. I don't know what I hit. I was in a station wagon on my way to…I can't remember where, and I don't remember the accident.

ML: What else do you know about that lifetime?

S: I am a black man, in my early to mid-forties. Or maybe late thirties. I may have vision problems or I'm partially blind. When I was looking around the auditorium I couldn't really see it, but I know that room from the sound and from having been there before. I see my friends. They are all black. It's the 1940's, and we're wearing those suits from that era. There is a woman in a beautiful flowered dress. She has bright red make-up on her cheeks. She is very concerned about me. She won't talk to me, though, because she is mad.

ML: What do you know about her?

S: She's part of the group, and she's in love with me. I apparently was doing stupid things again. She and the others are concerned about my left arm. I think I'm really lucky.

ML: What else do you notice?

S: Either before or after that, I see myself wearing a tuxedo. We're playing music. I'm playing a bass made of dark or black wood. It seems to be later, because it is the early 1950's now. It was an important performance and it was amazing. To do that was the whole point.

ML: What do you notice next?

S: That was my last performance. It was May 14, 1952. Near Chicago. There was a car accident after that. I eventually died in the hospital.

ML: What do you notice about the death experience?

S: I look down at my body. I see the room, better than ever. It's so beautiful. There is color everywhere. When I see my body, I see a black man in his 40's, slightly graying, and a little overweight. I notice broken limbs, and a beat up body. There are flowers everywhere. But no one is there. I'm floating away. It's okay.

ML: What did you learn in that lifetime?

S: I learned expression, tolerance, modesty, and to have fun. I was able to help people. Not just my family, but everyone. The music made them feel better. It was a good life. Fun, but hard.

ML: Move ahead to the time just before coming into this lifetime. What were the considerations at that time?

S: I am supposed to do something. I'm not supposed to forget. Forget what? I need to remember what I know. About what I do. I hear, "Let it flow. Let it go." I'm not going to live forever, no matter what they say. Do what you can and make it good. Do as I say, not as I do. Be careful with your body. Always find that note. Always be there. I don't have to play the scale. Don't do it the way they do it—do it as you do it. You're the only one who can. It helps to learn from others though.

ML: Do you notice anything else?

S: The old man would be happy if he could come back as a white person with great vision. He had a joke. He'd say, "I think I'm going to be an artist. Make paintings because I could never see. He would construct beautiful scenes in his mind. He wanted time for a vacation or break. He wanted to go to Hawaii or California after this. I'm not supposed to forget him. He had terrible grief of being left. All the others in the accident were fine, but he never played again. They were going on without him. He was sad.

ML: What injuries did he sustain?

S: On his left side. His left arm. He had the same pains as mine that I got from a car accident in this life.

We went on to resolve some of the emotions around that lifetime and to release the pains in Sam's left arm. It is interesting to note that he incarnated very soon after the death in that lifetime.

Case Study

Anne

Anne wanted to gain greater understanding about her life's passion so that she could make more sound decisions concerning her path. Notice how the door she sees reflects her subconscious view of how difficult it is to discover answers—rather than the location of her past life.

ML: What do you notice about this door?

A: It is a metal door. It's big and heavy.

ML: As the door opens and you step through, what do you notice?

A: I'm in a cave. It is earthen, rounded. There are tunnels. It is dark and moist. It is raining outside. I'm afraid of predators. I am hungry and I need to fetch berries and water.

ML: Are you alone or with others?

A: I sense someone else in the cave. They need these things too.

ML: What else do you notice?

A: There is a stream nearby. I go and collect water and berries. I also collect leaves. They are for medicine.

ML: What do you sense as your role here?

A: I am a healer.

ML: What else do you notice?

A: I'm tall. I am being careful of bears. I go back into the cave. There is a woman and baby there. They are sick.

ML: As time passes, what do you notice?

A: They get better. I am an accomplished healer. I'm good at it, and I'm right about the treatments.

ML: Imagine going back into the hallway. You discover another door that will lead to yet another lifetime, which will help you in your quest for purpose and passion. Three, two, one...what do you notice about this door?

A: It's a clock. When I go through it, there are gypsies, music, colors, flowing clothes. There is a party, with people drinking. There is a lot of excitement.

ML: What else do you notice?

A: Friendship, lovers, and passion. Everyone is happy. I notice music.

ML: What do you know about yourself?

A: I'm a female. I am wearing a chiffon dress. It's shoulderless, billowy, and I have flowers in my hair. I play the flute, dance, drink, eat, and have fun. There is so much passion! It feels so good to not be weighted down, not be afraid to move on. I can take chances and live life. I don't worry about the future. I go for it!

ML: What advice would she give to you?

A: Don't be afraid of failing. Have fun. Don't care what people think of you.

ML: If you followed her advice, what would be different in your life?

A: I'd shed my obligations. I'd be more mobile, less weighted down by things. I'd help people—children or the elderly. I'd care for the infirm. I'd make a difference in life. I'd be lighter. I'd have a better perspective. I wouldn't take things for granted. I'd enjoy the small things.

ML: And going to yet another lifetime...Three, two, one. Where do you find yourself now?

A: I'm in the light. I'm in the atmosphere. I'm airborne. I see stars. I feel the presence of a higher being. It draws me to it. It says that it gives me strength directly. I feel its energy. It's warm, good, electrical, powerful, elevated.

ML: What else do you notice about this experience?

A: It seems to tell me that I'm wasting my life by…no…I'm not getting it. I see a yellow beam now.

ML: What else do you experience?

A: It's a perspective. I see life as though from a higher consciousness. Humans look like ants running around like idiots. I want to open my arms to those beings. All the children, the infirm, and the animals. I want to open myself up more.

ML: What have you learned from this experience?

A: I've learned to not be afraid of failure. I've learned to not fear love or life. In the big scheme of things, when you see life from a different vantage point, there are many lessons. It is wasting time if you don't love. The purpose is to share it, to give, to nurture. And, to be surrounded only by people who can also feel that way. When you feel that way, you will make a difference.

ML: So what are you to do in your life?

A: Walk the talk. I don't want to have a job for the money, but for the fulfillment. I won't worry about a briefcase and pantyhose, but strive to make a difference. I can make a difference. I need to be happy. I need to smile more, get dirty, wear my hair up, and not worry. It's better to laugh a lot.

ML: What else do you know?

A: I need to start now. Take steps and begin the journey. The end result is what I will look for. I will take the time, do it right, and do it once. If it's not right, I'll keep trying. I won't be afraid of mistakes.

ML: Is there anything else?

A: Less is more. I'll be a better mom when I am happier. I will stop talking and start doing. Look for a job that is fulfilling. Take a chance Not be afraid. It feels selfish, but really good.

ML: Is it okay to make yourself happy?

A: Yes, if everyone did, everyone's quality of life would be better.

Frequently, the wisdom that comes from regressions is universal. What person couldn't benefit from heeding these words?

16

Meeting Challenges

"He hoped and prayed that there wasn't an afterlife. Then he realized there was a contradiction involved here and merely hoped there wasn't an afterlife."
—Douglas Adams

People often come to past life regression in order to meet a challenge, release a block, deal with a fear, or dissolve some unwanted condition. This is a good strategy, since many challenges that we face have their source in a past life. When we know what we are dealing with, we are in a better position to dissolve or release a difficulty—and to rise to any challenge that presents itself. The three regressions in this chapter illustrate various facets of this dynamic.

Faith learned the source of her anger, which had become a kneejerk response and was blocking her experience of life.

Kevin met fears about dying by actually experiencing his own death in several past lives, and coming to peace with the experience.

Bill found the meaning of a nightmare that had haunted him as a child.

CASE STUDY

FAITH

I had been working with Faith frequently over the months on many issues, including fear of flying and anxiety. During one session, she realized that she was using anger to block her progress in several areas. We viewed a past life that gave us more information about the roots of that anger.

F: I am outdoors. I seem to be in an airplane. I can see the Earth below me. I am alone, flying the airplane. This feels so good! I'm happy and I'm tired. I appreciate the view of the Earth and I see its beauty. I think that I am attempting to fly around the world. I'm not sure, but I think I am trying to do this without a break, or something. There seems to be a reason I am doing this.

ML: What else do you know about yourself?

F: I am a man in my thirties. I started this journey in St. Louis, Missouri. I'm flying eastward. Now I'm over New York. Now I'm over the Atlantic. I have a good landing, in some exotic place. It seems like maybe Saudi Arabia or somewhere like that. It is in the desert and the people have colorful clothing. I get a lot of attention from the women. I see them belly dancing. We are at a dinner. Later, I leave and go back to the plane. It won't start. I need fuel. I talk to the people and they all tell me, "Yes, yes," but no one does anything. Nothing happens. I can't believe it and I am so frustrated. I get very angry and I start yelling until someone shoots me. And then I'm dead.

ML: What did you learn from observing that experience?

F: I've learned that in the past my anger has gotten me shot. I need to remember to enjoy the journey. I realize that I had no one in that lifetime who cared that I was gone. I had no wife or children. So, it was okay to learn that lesson then. Of course, I don't want to have to be put in that position again.

ML: Let's move to yet another lifetime that can reveal even more information that will be helpful to you in this regard.

F: Now I am in an adobe hut. There is an arched door. I am looking out. There is a fire burning. I am barefoot. There are seven of us inside. I am the daughter. My mother is cooking. I have two brothers and four sisters. I'm the oldest, and I'm helping my mother. A lot of men come back to the village on horseback. They are barefoot and wear deerskin clothing. We have dark skin. They have brought back food. It is an elk. I have to skin it. That is strange for me since I am a vegetarian and so conscientious about animals in this lifetime. In that life, it is okay. I skin the elk and the tribe utilizes every part of it. There is a use for everything so we have to carefully put the parts in piles. I am flirting with one of the young men. We keep exchanging flirtatious glances. When we finish, we all go to our own huts. There is a sound for dinner. It is a chime of sorts. Everyone in the tribe eats together as a group. There are no fences around our property or ropes for the horses, but I notice that the horses stay around by choice, like pets. During dinner, I am still flirting with the young man. The elders notice this. There is drumming and an announcement that the two of us will be married. The language there involves a lot of hand movements.

ML: Do you know where you are?

F: It seems like the South American highlands. Perhaps Peru. We are plateau people.

ML: Move ahead to the next significant event.

F: I'm an elder now. Everything is still the same. There has been no destruction. My kids have kids, and I am a great great-grandmother. Life hasn't changed at all.

ML: What have you learned from viewing that lifetime?

F: I realize how much I grew as a person even though I never went anywhere different. Everything stayed the same, but we were able to achieve great spiritual depth. There is so much that can be gained from that flowing lifestyle. I learned that it is not boring to just experience life. I think I am just too caught up in the 21st century craziness.

These memories allowed Faith to contrast the problems arising from her angry responses with the benefits of experiencing a calm and consistent life. It was interesting that she was comfortable flying in the previous lifetime, while having to overcome a phobia of flying in this lifetime. She is drawn to intensity of expression and experience, and now understands that she can allow that intensity and depth without getting involved in undesirable conflicts.

Case Study

Kevin

Kevin had a debilitating fear of death and dying. To complicate the matter, he had extremely high blood pressure, and had had heart surgery. We decided to do a series of regressions that would bring forth his memories of the death process in order to desensitize the fear.

K: I'm on a ship. An old ship. I'm in the process of being hung. I am on a pirate ship. I've been captured. I'm sad. My wife and children are witnessing this. Someone else ends up shooting me. Now I am on the deck of the ship, dead.

ML: What do you notice about that experience?

K: It's like a black hole, a tunnel. I come out in a place that is bright. It is not defined, without form. I see blue and wide-open spaces. Nobody else is around. There is white light, like the universal energy, or god. I am bathed in light. And then I am reborn as a baby. It's okay.

ML: Allow your subconscious mind to take you to another past life experience that will demonstrate the death process to you.

K: I am in a farm house. It is old, perhaps the 13th century. I'm sick and dying. I look old. I am full of love. I have had a good life. I have a nice farm, a wife and kids. They are all around the bed. It's very peaceful. There is not a lot of anguish or suffering. My spirit leaves the body. It lifts straight up. I am viewing myself from above. I look back at that past life. It's okay. The process is very natural. There are no doctors. It is not forced. It is the way I would like to go.

ML: Go back to yet another time when you have experienced the death process.

K: I am in a church, a monastery. Someone is praying over me. I'm really old. Actually I am already dead. This is the funeral. There are lots of people. It was several hundreds of years ago. I was a parishioner, and well-respected. They are singing hymns. I am observing. It is so normal. This is what happens. This is a normal passing, without drugs, or other artificial means. This is the kind of awareness I would like to have. The spirit manifested outside the body. It's the way to go.

ML: How are you feeling about the death process now?

K: I am relaxed about dying now. I believe that I have a greater fear of being kept alive unnaturally, by artificial means. I don't want to be drugged and unaware when it is my time to pass on. I am more afraid of being incapacitated than actually dying.

Kevin was able to release his fear of dying, which helped him go forward toward his dreams.

Case Study

Bill

Bill was haunted by memories of a recurring nightmare that he had as a child. He thought he had been about one or two years old when he kept dreaming that he had drowned in the ocean. It was easy to go right into the session by simply asking him to recall the dream.

ML: Close your eyes. Going back in your memories to the dreams that you had as a child, please begin to tell me what you remember of the dreams.

B: I am in darkness. There are waves. They are choppy. I'm drowning.

ML: Can you tell if you are a man or a woman?

B: I am a man.

ML: How old do you feel when this is happening?

B: I feel I am in my twenties or thirties.

ML: Go back to the beginning again. Can you tell me how you got into the ocean?

B: I am on the ocean, in a boat.

ML: What can you tell me about the boat, or why you were sailing?

B: I went out on a fishing trip. We were caught in a storm. The boat capsized.

ML: Were you alone or with others?

B: There were about four or five of us.

ML: Were the others men or women?

B: All men.

ML: Go back to before you boarded the boat. What do you remember of that time?

B: We were getting ready for the trip. We were loading the boat from the dock, putting our equipment on board. It was not a big dock.

ML: Where in the world do you seem to be?

B: Somewhere on the eastern seaboard.

ML: What else do you remember?

B: I have an interesting sensation. An emotion. I think I am getting close to feeling this.

ML: Is that okay?

B: Yes. It's just strange.

ML: What were your feelings that day?

B: It was a wet day. Overcast with occasional sun. This trip was part of my job. It was a sail boat. We were fishing for big fish. Maybe tuna.

ML: What is the year?

B: 1880's or so.

ML: Was it a day trip or would you be gone for some time?

B: We would be gone for a few days. Everything is wooden.

ML: What are your duties?

B: I handle the nets. I'm a laborer. A storm comes up. The rain comes down. And then the ship goes down. I am struggling to keep from drowning. And then there is a peacefulness.

ML: What did you learn from experiencing that past life?

B: Don't go out in the water when it is stormy!

ML: What else?

ML: It was a part of my job. I learned that everything is okay. I don't need to be afraid of death. I also placed responsibility over rationality. It was my work ethic. It is a lot like how I am as a person now.

> I am a risk taker. I could learn that sometimes you pay the price for risks.

In our conversation after the session, Bill told me that he was a scuba diver. He has no fear of water at all in this life. In fact, he has an affinity with it.

17

Deepening Your Spiritual Journey

"To see a world in a Grain of Sand,
And a Heaven in a Wild Flower,
Hold Infinity in the palm of your hand,
And eternity in an hour."
—William Blake

In the end, everything is about our spiritual quest—our hero's journey through life. The three regressions in this chapter brought people back to that realization, and gave them wisdom for following the path.

Tamara met her spirit guide and gained insight into pre-birth decisions that shaped the difficulties she was experiencing in this life.

Terry's regression demonstrates a technique called Core Transformation, which is useful when people become overly analytical during regressions. She also received wise guidance to fulfill her mission here.

Dan experienced a series of adventures that illustrate aspects of our highest adventure, the hero's spiritual journey.

Case Study

Tamara

Tamara is in her teens, and came for a session at the request of her mother. The mother had adopted her at eighteen months, and Tamara was having many behavioral problems. Both of them wanted to find the root cause of these difficulties, and perhaps find a resolution.

We began the session by regressing her back through her present life memories. Starting with deep relaxation techniques, I asked her to go back to her earliest recollections.

T: I'm a child. I feel like I am maybe between seven and eleven months old. My parents are trying to dress me. They couldn't and I am crying. I hear my dad in the back room yelling at my mother. Then he comes into my room and picks me up. He tries to walk out of the house with me. My mom tries to pull me back in. Then he hits her. He takes me for a walk, and tells me it will all be okay. Then he takes me back to the house.

ML: Then what do you notice?

T: My mom lays me on the floor. She lies down with me. After a while, she picks me up and puts me in a chair. Then my grandma comes in. I think it is my grandma. I don't recognize her. She tries to feed me.

I puke. She yells at my mom.

ML: What is she saying?

T: She says that my mom has to take me to the hospital. My mom doesn't believe her and kicks her out of the house.

ML: Then what happens?

T: I don't know. I don't see anyone now. I am just sitting there. My mom is gone too. I see the white wall and a window. Then my mom comes back.

ML: What happens next?

T: We went away. We moved to an old broken down apartment. She puts me in a blanket. I think it is something that she found. She lays me there with some juice. Then she leaves again. When she goes it is sunny out. And it is dark when she returns. I notice that she has a wound on her leg. I look at it. She is in tears. She leaves me and goes to her room. She comes back later and picks me up, saying it will all be okay. I remembered those words from when Dad had said that. Now she tells me that I am staying in this separate room because it wasn't going to be safe for me otherwise. But I didn't know where I was. I hear yelling in the other room. Then the door slams open. A lady picks me up and puts me in a carrier. I cried and cried, because they wouldn't let me say goodbye to my mom. I see my mom trying to get to me. But they put her into a different car. When we get out of the car, the old woman...she has white hair... she picks me up. She tells me I am going to stay with her. She has a nice house and she dresses me and feeds me.

ML: What else do you remember about that?

T: That's all.

ML: I wonder if you can go back to an earlier time, before this event. Perhaps you can go back to the days leading up to this event. What do you remember about that?

T: We are at home. Mom and Dad are doing fine. They are being nice to each other. I remember that Dad leaves. A little while later, maybe five minutes, he comes back and he has a gun. He tells Mom that he has some unfinished business. Mom got really scared and grabbed me. She wondered what he would do. Dad left the house. Mom is scared. She just kept holding me. Then Dad returns. He says that it is done, but we have to go. It seems he tried to kill someone.

ML: What else do you remember about that time?

T: The cops were there, waiting for him. One cop told my mom that he had to be taken to jail for first degree murder charges of my uncle, my mom's brother. My mom tells him that it was an accident. She says that my dad has anger problems and she didn't know why he does things. But the cops want to know more. They let my dad out on bond, and then the cops followed him. When he came to say goodbye to us, he tried to tell my mom about it without getting angry, but he couldn't help it. He got mad and yelled.

ML: I would like to ask your subconscious mind to go back in time to a month before this incident. What do you remember about that time?

T: I see my dad smiling. My mom is gone. Dad just keeps smiling at me. He said that we are going to my grandma's house. That's his mother. While we are driving there, we get into a wreck. I had a bruise on my face. He had a bloody arm from the window breaking. We go to the hospital. My mom came and picked me up. We go to see my dad. He has stitches, but he is still smiling, even while in pain.

ML: What else do you remember about that time?

T: We're happy. Life is good. He kept saying it was. Then my mom found a bag in his pocket. She didn't realize what it was. She opened it and sniffed it. It was a drug. She didn't want him having it around, so she threw it away. He didn't know that she had. When he came home and looked for it, mom said that she had thrown it away. He slapped her. She sat there in tears, with him yelling at her. He just wouldn't stop. He told her to go to work. She would get dressed up every night. When she came back, her eyes were bright red, and she talked funny like she was just learning how to talk. I remember she stood up to dad, and he punched her in the stomach. She acted like she didn't feel anything, so he left. It was a long time before he came back.

ML: What else do you remember?

T: We are at someone's house. A lady's. It is decorated. I see mom and dad and they are happy. They are nice to each other. There are no bruises on them, and nothing seems to be wrong. The lady is my grandma. Everyone is happy and dancing. Dad has a job. He goes to work. He was so proud of me. He would show me off to his friends. He worked at a place with tools. Everyone was happy.

ML: Now allow yourself to go back even further. Go back to before you were born, to the time when you were deciding to choose this lifetime. What do you remember about that?

T: Someone has a hand on my back and they are pointing to two people. He was saying something that I can't understand.

ML: There is a part of you that knows fully what it was that he meant. What do you know about what he was communicating to you?

T: He says if you go down there, you can help them. They have tried before and couldn't conceive. They don't want to adopt. Having me as their baby would be good for them and for me.

ML: Why would it be good for you?

T: Because there is someone waiting for me. It isn't them. Someone else. He says, "These people are to have you." There is some difficulty in life that I needed to fix for them. He tells me, "Don't be scared whatever happens. Always be happy. They may not be perfect, but they need someone in their lives." I regretted it at first. I didn't want to leave where I was. But he told me that I had to go. He said they would bring me something that I needed. I had to be with them. There was a plan for me, something waiting for me. When I asked him about that, he said that there had been a mistake and it needed to be fixed. When I asked what that had to do with me, he told me they are a part of me. They tell me that it will help me in my life. It would help me to be someone who was very different. He said they would help me through it. They know what's going on and what would happen. They say there is a dark force trying to hurt me. They never told me what it was. If I don't do this, I will be here forever. He wants to help these other people so I said I would do it.

ML: Let's talk with your spirit guide. Asking your present guide to come to you now and speak with you, as he joins you there, what do you notice about him or her?

T: He is the same one as before. He says that there is something wrong, but that I am doing good. The darkness that was going to come hasn't yet. I need to stay close to someone who can protect me.

ML: Who would that be?

T: There are different people. My adopted mom and Bill, who she works with. I have known him since I was little. He is like a dad to me.

ML: Ask your guide about the dark force.

T: He says it isn't human. He says that I have to choose who can protect me from it. He says it is alive, but not human. It doesn't breathe. It kills people, like a virus. I need to be strong. I need to stay close to those who love me and give me strength. They will know I need help even before I will. I am to trust them.

ML: What else can he tell you?

T: He says, "There will always be things in the way. Push them away and go on. Don't underestimate anyone. You don't know whether they are a part of your life." He says he is sorry.

ML: What about?

T: Oh, I know what it is about. That he had to take people away from me. Close people. I did the best I could with my parents. It was a good thing. He says, "I kept my word about you being happy. Even though it didn't turn out, we told you before you left that there would be difficulty." He tells me that it was good that I couldn't stay there, that it got interrupted. It is better in my new family. I have another purpose in this family. My (adopted) mom is going through the same thing. She had a relationship with someone who didn't love her. This mom had a gun held to her head. It has been the same, though different. I can learn from her, and then find my own way. I don't have to go on other people's word. I need to take on all the obstacles that come up. And he says that I need to stay away from bikes.

ML: Does he mean bicycles or motorcycles?

T: Motorcycles. Yes. He says they are unsafe for me.

ML: What can you do to stay connected to your spirit guide?

T: He tells me he will see me in my dreams. Also that I will have an instinct.

ML: What can you call him?

T: Joshua.

ML: What have you learned from this?

T: I still feel I am missing something. I am told that it comes from a past life. Even if I feel like something is missing, it will be whole again.

ML: How are you doing?

T: I am doing well.

This young lady had a rough start to life this incarnation. With this deeper understanding of her pre-birth decisions, and of her early childhood experiences, she will have the opportunity to strengthen herself, and to see the bigger picture.

Case Study

Terry

Terry is very analytical. Her hyper-alert mind was interfering with her ability to experience the regression. Using a technique called Core Transformation, she allowed herself to relax and move into the regression effortlessly. This and other techniques are discussed more fully in my book, *Hypnotherapy: A Client Centered Approach* (Pelican Publishing, 2003).

I led her through a short induction, and then the visualization of the hallway.

ML: Describe the door that you are standing in front of.

T: It is a Ritz Carlton style hallway. The floor has red carpet. The hall is long and nice.

ML: What does the door look like?

T: I'm not finding a door. When I look for a door, it kind of fades.

ML: Would you say that it is true that a part of you wants to relax and experience a regression, and another part of you is analytical and prevents you from relaxing?

T: Yes, that's very true.

ML: I would like to ask the analytical part what its goal is for you.

T: To be right.

ML: If you were right, fully and completely like you imagine it, then what would you have that is even more important?

T: I could finish things.

ML: If you could finish things, fully and completely like you imagine it, then what would you have that is even more important?

T: Accomplishment.

ML: If you had accomplishment, fully and completely like you imagine it, then what would you have that is even more important?

T: I could offer help to the world.

ML: If you could offer help to the world, fully and completely like you imagine it, then what would you have that is even more important?

T: I could do anything.

ML: If you could do anything, fully and completely like you imagine it, then what would you have that is even more important?

T: No rushing. I could be relaxed and stress free. No one would be waiting for me.

ML: If you could be relaxed and stress free, fully and completely like you imagine it, then what would you have that is even more important?

T: My body would feel lighter. It would be like floating.

ML: I would like to ask your subconscious mind to produce a symbol that you could imagine holding in your hand that would represent this good feeling. What is that symbol?

T: A lotus with a star, in a bright circle of light.

ML: If you were to carry this lotus star and this light floating feeling with you into each and every moment of the future, how do you think that might change your experience of not rushing?

T: It wouldn't fit me. It would be too non-responsible.

ML: If you were to carry this lotus star and this light floating feeling with you into each and every moment of the future, how do you think that might change your experience of being able to do anything?

T: I just could.

ML: If you were to carry this lotus star and this light floating feeling with you into each and every moment of the future, how do you think that might change your experience of giving help to the world?

T: I would be able to influence my corner of the world.

ML: If you were to carry this lotus star and this light floating feeling with you into each and every moment of the future, how do you think that might change your experience of accomplishment?

T: I would follow through on my projects and work.

ML: With the goal of following through with your desire to experience a past life regression, would your analytical part be willing to allow you to relax and enjoy this adventure, so that it will later have even more information to analyze?

T: Sure.

ML: Going back into that hallway, how would you describe the door?

T: There is a door that is open. As I go through, I am outdoors. It is daytime. I am in the country. I notice grass. It is springtime.

ML: What are you doing there?

T: I am fishing in a pond. It is a simple life. I am a boy, and I'm fishing with another boy. I look like a Huck Finn character.

ML: What else do you notice about that scene?

T: Not much else. That's all.

ML: What have you learned by viewing that lifetime?

T: I like that. It is slower, simpler life. It's more comfortable.

ML: Asking your subconscious mind to take you to another lifetime, what do you notice next?

T: I am in the mountains. It is green. It looks like South America. I'm in a jungle. There are monkeys and vines. I am walking back to the place where we all gather. It's a village. I am barefoot, and I am wearing Indian woven clothes.

ML: What else do you notice about yourself?

T: I'm a teenager, female. I'm daydreaming and relaxing. I live with my parents. My dad is big and round, like my dad now. I like them both. They are the same it seems. We make bread and crackers. It is not clean here. Everything is dirty. The house is small and square. It is made of dried mud and spit. I climb up the stairs to sleep. Everyone sleeps up there.

ML: Move ahead in time. As you get older, what do you notice happening?

T: I don't see me getting old.

ML: What have you learned from this lifetime?

T: I need to go slower. I need to relax.

ML: Asking the subconscious to provide one more lifetime, what do you notice next?

T: I'm in old Boston. It is foggy. It is night and I am walking to the pub. I'm an older man. I smoke a pipe and wear funny socks. I know everyone in the pub. They are all men. I am a lawyer or something. I do a lot of writing and reading. I feel light and big. I see myself getting older. I have children. All girls. We live in the countryside, and I enjoy watching the girls playing.

ML: What advice would that old man give to you, if he could observe your life?

T: He would tell me to enjoy a pint, relax, and not be so serious. He'd say to do what I want to do while I am young. He is a smart old guy.

ML: What would you tell him if you could?

T: I'd tell him that he would enjoy being here with all the new things that have been invented.

ML: What have you learned from viewing these three lifetimes?

T: I have to rely on what I think. And don't think so much about everything. Usually the first thoughts are the right decisions.

Case Study

Dan

Dan was about to travel to foreign countries and was curious about possible past lives in these other places. Through visualization techniques, he moved down the hall and chose a door.

ML: What do you notice?

D: The door is a blue covered wood with a gold handle.

ML: As the door opens and you move through, what do you notice?

D: It is Roman scenery. It actually looks like a scene from the movie, *The Gladiator.* Do you think I might be just making this up?

ML: Allow yourself to make it up for now. Let's see where it goes. If you were there, would you be a man or a woman, and how old would you be?

D: I would be a man, and I would be in my late twenties or early thirties.

ML: So if you were a man, there in Rome, what would you see yourself doing?

D: I see myself on a chariot. I'm going through a parade. I am standing, waving to the crowd. There are lots of people. The women are throwing flowers at me. This has been a military victory. I smile and

I laugh. But, I can also feel my body. I have a cut on my right shoulder.

ML: What do you remember about how that got there?

D: While I was fighting one person, another came from the side and cut me with his sword. I was in such a rage from the cut that I took my sword and chopped the head off the man that I was fighting, and in the same motion, I took out the guy who cut me. Then I just went on to look for the next person to fight.

ML: What do you notice next?

D: I am in an open field. It is all cleared out. Now it is a field of people. Bodies are everywhere. I'm standing at the side, looking at the bodies and at the smoke rising. I'm thinking, "Another day at work. I've accomplished my mission. It's time to go home."

ML: Where is home? And what do you know about it?

D: My home is in Rome. I have an apartment or a house on a hill. But I know that I don't ever really go home. It's just on to the next battle. I'm single and it's an empty house. I have a pet tiger and a lion. I have had the tiger since its birth. It is fairly tame. I can remember picking him up as a cub and putting him on my shoulders.

ML: What else do you remember about your home?

D: The walls are white in a Grecian style. There are vases, and gold and silver ornaments. I see a fireplace. There are marble floors. There are French doors that kick out onto a veranda. I have an Egyptian servant or two. I see a picture of the Emperor.

ML: What would you call him?

D: Sarinius...or Cerenas...or Augustus.

ML: Some time passes by and what do you notice next?

D: I have to walk up a hill to get there. At the bottom, in the lowlands, is the main town. It is dusty and there are street vendors. I notice a snake charmer. There is a one-legged person selling fruit. Children scamper around. It's not the cleanest town. I have another battle to face. It will be in a place with green trees. I smell it in the air. It feels like this will be my last battle. I'm so tired of fighting.

ML: When it is time to go into battle, what do you notice?

D: I don't want to get involved. I direct the battle more than anything else. It is a creepy fight. The enemy is Barbaric. They play by different rules. I see a monkey. I look at him for answers. He indicates whether it is smart to move or to stay put.

ML: How does he communicate that to you?

D: With a smile or a chuckle. If he doesn't show fear, he smiles. When he shows fear, his eyes bulge, he scratches himself, and he becomes quiet. We are successful in this battle. It was not as difficult as we had thought. The enemy was stumped. We killed a lot of them right off the bat, and the rest we took as prisoners.

ML: What happens next?

D: I leave Rome. I go to Greece. I am standing by icy blue water. I am sitting on a ledge, looking at my sandals. In the water's reflection, two angels appear. They don't say much. They tell me my work is done. It is time to move on. Now I am going through a tunnel. This may be the end. I look back at my life. They tell me, "You were not responsible for what you did." My job was to kill. I was following my orders. It is possible that I did die in that battle.

ML: At the end of that battle what do you notice happening?

D: I have a spear through my stomach as I lay on the ground.

ML: What do you notice about that experience?

D: There was a woman that I left behind. She is wearing a white dress. She has beautiful eyes and long dark brown hair. She is not my wife. She is my girlfriend.

ML: When you look at her and sense her energy, do you recognize her as anyone that you know in this lifetime?

D: Possibly. I'm not sure.

ML: What else do you notice?

D: I can hear the wheels turning on the chariot. The horse hoofs are clacking against the cobblestone roads. There is such poverty.

ML: What did you learn from experiencing that lifetime?

D: Despite the killing, nothing changed. There was always just another battle.

ML: Do you recognize any correlations between that lifetime and this one?

D: I have to make sure that I make the most of what I have. The military role is just like a corporate role. You are just a tool for the corporation. You aren't really pursuing what you want to pursue. The pleasure that you receive—like a smile—can be simple. I see the peasants on their knees, thanking me. They are glowing. I feel bad that they 'worship' me, as though I didn't deserve it.

ML: Is there anything else that you notice?

D: There is a statue of me in the middle of town. It is white marble. In the statue, I am standing straight. I am covered with big armor.

ML: Can you read the inscription?

D: Augustus Serenus. Pompeii. XVII.

ML: Moving on to yet another lifetime, as I count from three to one, the scene will open before you. Three, two, one. Where do you find yourself?

D: I'm going back and forth between two images. In the one, I'm in a suit. It is like something that Dick Tracy would wear. I have a slick hat. I'm tall and thin. In the other, I'm an old Jewish jeweler in an old three-piece suit. I hold a pocket watch in my hand, and am wearing horn-rimmed glasses.

ML: Let's start by going into the life of the jeweler. What do you know about him?

D: It's the 1920's and I'm in New York. It is the typical old street scene in New York. There are row houses, with stores along the bottom. There are buggies in the street. It's crowded. A creaky door leads to my shop. I carry high-end jewelry. The people are well-dressed. There is a fresh loaf of bread on the counter. I have a female assistant who is meek and quiet. She is dressed like a pilgrim, in old clothes.

ML: What happens next?

D: There is an explosion. The window breaks, but it doesn't knock down the building. There are guys, who look like they are in a mob, snickering at me. They are trying to intimidate me. It doesn't work. I walk through the street market, and someone stabs me in my side. I go to the hospital. I see myself in bed laughing. I'm smiling. There is only one person, my assistant, who comes to see me. She rarely speaks, but she is loyal and I count on her.

ML: Do you recognize her as anyone you know in this lifetime?

D: No.

ML: What do you notice next?

D: I see myself dying. It is no big deal. Then I see myself back on the street, and life continues. Except that she now owns the shop and runs it. I'm looking in. I'm dead. Yet, I'm proud. She is doing a good job.

ML: What did you learn from that lifetime?

D: It felt good to leave her the shop. I passed on something valuable. It is the art of giving. It felt good to see that her long years of dedication paid off for her. Eventually she met someone who she married. She had two young boys. Now I can see myself looking down from the ceiling at those same five mob guys. I'm snickering at them, because what they were doing was fruitless.

ML: What do you notice next?

D: I go up the elevator shaft, into the clouds. Now I see a grassy field. I am back with the blond girl from the Roman lifetime. She shows me that she is always there. She is smiling. I look at the field and think "how pretty."

ML: Moving on to the next lifetime, what do you see next?

D: I see alligators. It is a jungle scene. I am a Tarzan-like adventurer. I'm in a canoe, looking at the eyes of the crocodiles. I have hired the help of some natives. I notice monkeys in the background. The mosquitoes whiz by. There are vines, and humidity, and big gorillas. I see a tribe now. They are typical looking. There are ornaments hanging from their noses. I'm not scared. Since being a Roman soldier, nothing can be as rough as what I've faced before. It's not a big deal. We hit the shore. I greet them. I show the leader due respect. I make him laugh and he feels comfortable. He lets us stay there. We have our own tents and nets.

ML: Move ahead to the next significant event that occurs there. What do you notice?

D: I meet a woman. She is beautiful. An English woman. I am in my middle age years, blonde, with receding hair. I believe I am German.

ML: What are you doing there?

D: We are there to observe. We make notes and study. We develop a deep respect for the people and nature. The woman eventually dies of a disease. After that, we leave. I see the same alligators as we leave. I sense a deep sorrow in the entire group concerning the death of that woman. The tribe was affected too.

We followed this session with discussions of his present life adventures. He continues to seek out intense life experiences.

Epilogue

The soul's quest for self-discovery and enlightenment is a driving force underlying all our behaviors, actions, reactions, emotions, and pursuits. It is the most delightful and fascinating journey in which we will ever participate.

Imagine what your subconscious mind will reveal to you in lives to come, when you regress to this present lifetime. Will your memories be exciting? Or will they be depressing or confusing? Will you be proud of your adventures or be filled with remorse or regret?

Remember that your subconscious mind is gathering information continuously throughout the day and night. Every thought, every feeling, and every activity is recorded and saved. What are you doing to ensure that your memories are going to be worthwhile? What are you doing to add depth, growth, expansion, balance, and love of self and life to your soul's experience?

Be the hero of your own saga. Meet the challenge. Plunge to the depths of this physical experience to bring home your own brass ring, your personal holy grail, your true self.

Recommended Reading

"Be still when you have nothing to say; when genuine passion moves you, say what you have to say, and say it hot."
—D. H. Lawrence

The following are only a few of the many reliable and valuable books that provide additional ideas, techniques, and perspectives. Enjoy!

Adams, Douglas, *Hitchhiker's Guide to the Galaxy* (Random House Value Pub., 1996)

Andreas, Connirae with Tamara, *Core Transformations* (Real People Press, 1994)

Bach Richard, *One* (Dell Books, Reissued 1989)

Bach, Richard, *Bridge Across Forever* (Dell Books, Reissued 1986)

Binswanger, Harry, Ed., *Ayn Rand Lexicon* (Penguin Books, 1986)

Bruce, Alexandra, *Beyond the Bleep: The Definitive Unauthorized Guide to What the Bleep Do We Know?* (Disinformation Company, 2005)

Cameron, Julia, *The Artist's Way, A Spiritual Path to Higher Creativity* (Tarcher Putnam, 1992)

Deepak Chopra, M.D., *Quantum Healing, Exploring the Frontiers of Mind/Body Medicine* (Bantam New Age, 1990)

Cunningham, Janet, *A Tribe Returned* (Deep Forest Press, 1994)

Davies, Paul, *God & The New Physics* (Simon & Schuster, 1983)

Davies, Paul, *Mind of God* (Simon & Schuster, 1992)

Fiori, Edith, *The Unquiet Dead* (Ballantine Books, 1991)

Greene, Brian, *The Elegant Universe: Superstrings, Hidden Dimensions, and the Quest for the Ultimate Theory* (Vintage Books, 1999)

Hamer, Dean, *The God Gene: How Faith is Hardwired Into Our Genes* (Anchor Books, 2004)

Ingram, Julia, and Hardin, G.W., *The Messengers: A True Story of Angelic Presence and the Return to the Age of Miracles* (Pocket Star, 1997)

LaBay, Mary Lee, *Hypnotherapy: A Client-Centered Approach* (Pelican Publishing, 2003)

LaBay, Mary Lee, *Past Life Regression: A Guide for Practitioners* (Trafford Publishing, 2004)

LaBay, Mary Lee, and Hogan, Kevin, *Through the Open Door: Secrets of Self-Hypnosis* (Pelican Publishing, 2000)

Levoy, Gregg, *Callings, Finding and Following an Authentic Life* (Three Rivers Press, 1997)

Lipton, Bruce, PhD., *The Biology of Belief, Unleashing the Power of Consciousness, Matter, and Miracles* (Mountain of Love, 2005)

Lucas, Winafred Blake, Ph.D., *Regression Therapy: A Handbook for Professionals Vol. I & II* (Deep Forest Press, Reissued 1999)

Moody, Raymond A., M.D., *Life After Life* (Harper, 2001)

Phillips, Maggie, and Frederick, Claire, *Healing the Divided Self* (W.W. Norton & Co., 1995)

Pike, Diane Kennedy, *Life As A Waking Dream* (Riverhead Books, 1997)

Rucker, Rudy, *The Fourth Dimension, A Guided Tour of the Higher Universes* (Houghton Mifflin Co., 1984)

Swartz, Gary E.R., *The Afterlife Experiments* (Pocket Star, 2002)

Talbot, Michael, *Holographic Universe* (HarperCollins, 1991)

Talbot, Michael, *Mysticism and the New Physics* (Penguin Group, Revised 1993)

Walsch, Neale Donald, *Conversations with God, An Uncommon Dialogue* 1997)

Watson, Lyall, *Beyond Supernature* (Bantam Books, 1989)

Weiss, Brain L., M.D., *Many Lives Many Masters* (Fireside, 1988)

Wolf, Fred Alan, *Mind Into Matter: A New Alchemy of Science and Spirit* (Moment Point Press, 2000)

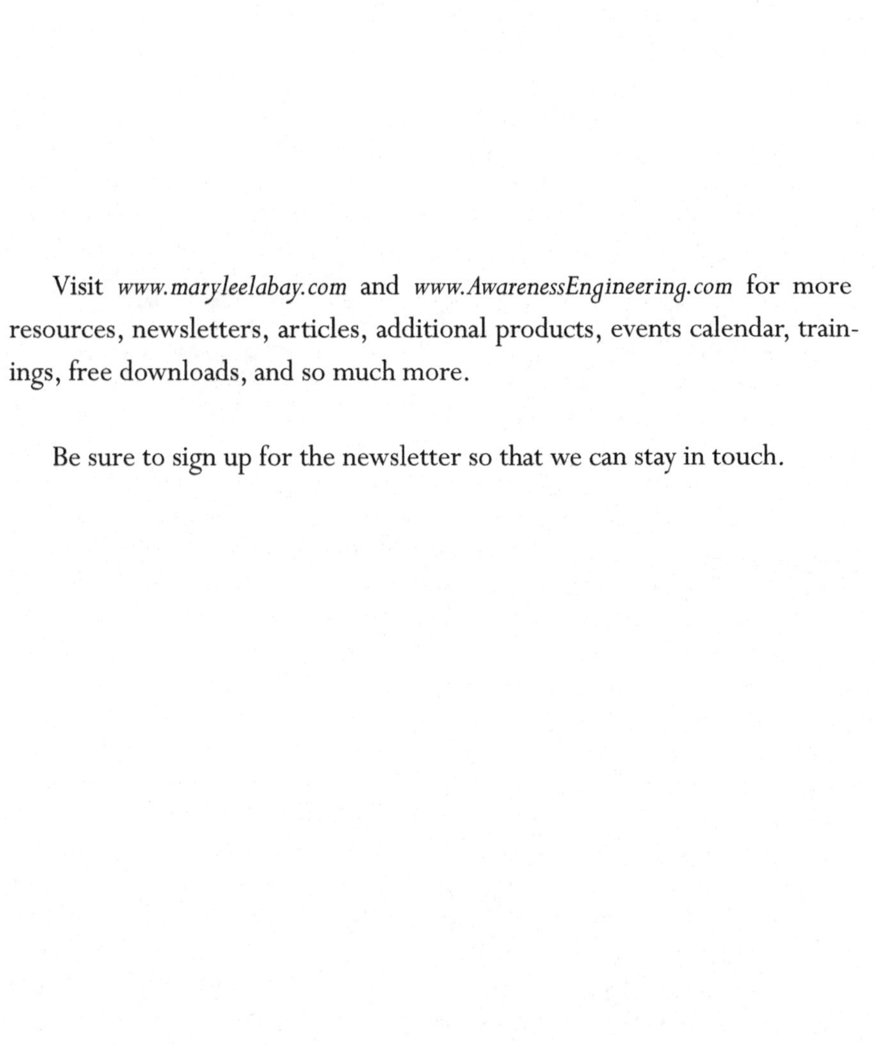

Visit *www.maryleelabay.com* and *www.AwarenessEngineering.com* for more resources, newsletters, articles, additional products, events calendar, trainings, free downloads, and so much more.

Be sure to sign up for the newsletter so that we can stay in touch.